The Trial of Je

Lawyer's Sta

Vol. 1

Walter M. Chandler

Alpha Editions

This edition published in 2024

ISBN : 9789362097279

Design and Setting By
Alpha Editions
www.alphaedis.com
Email - info@alphaedis.com

VOLUME I

PREFACE TO VOLUME ONE

MANY remarkable trials have characterized the judicial history of mankind.

The trial of Socrates before the dicastery of Athens, charged with corrupting Athenian youth, with blaspheming the Olympic gods, and with seeking to destroy the constitution of the Attic Republic, is still a sublime and thrilling chapter in the history of a wonderful people, among the ruins and wrecks of whose genius the modern world still wanders to contemplate, admire, and study the pride of every master and the perfection of every model.

The trial and execution of Charles the First of England sealed with royal blood a new covenant of British freedom, and erected upon the highway of national progress an enduring landmark to civil liberty. The entire civilized world stood aghast at the solemn and awful spectacle of the deliberate beheading of a king. And yet, to-day, the sober, serious judgment of mankind stamps the act with approval, and deems it a legitimate and righteous step in the heroic march of a brave and splendid people toward a complete realization of the inalienable rights of man. The philosopher of history declares these condemnatory and executory proceedings against a Stuart king worthy of all the epoch making movements that have glorified the centuries of English constitutional growth, and have given to mankind the imperishable parchments of Magna Charta, the Bill of Rights, the Petition of Rights, and Habeas Corpus.

The trial of Warren Hastings in the hall of William Rufus has been immortalized by Lord Macaulay. This trial is a virtual reproduction in English history of the ancient Roman trial of Verres. England is substituted for Rome; Sicily becomes India; Hastings takes the place of Verres; and Burke is the orator instead of Cicero. The indictments are identical: Maladministration in the government of a province. In the impeachment of Hastings, England served notice upon her colonial governors and made proclamation to the world that English conquest was not intended to despoil and enslave, but was designed to carry to the inhabitants of distant lands her language, her literature, and her laws. This message to humanity was framed but not inspired by England. It was prompted by the success of the American Revolution, in which Washington and his Continentals had established the immortal principle, that the consent of the governed is the true source of all just powers of government.

The trial of Aaron Burr, omitting Arnold's treason, is the blackest chapter in the annals of our republic. Burr was the most extraordinary man of the first half century of American national history. His powerful and fascinating personality conquered men and enslaved women. He was the finest scholar of the Revolution excepting Thomas Jefferson. He was the greatest orator of the Revolution excepting Patrick Henry. His farewell address to the United States Senate caused his inveterate enemies to weep. His arraignment at the bar of public justice on the charge of high treason—that he had sought to destroy the Country of Washington, the Republic of Jefferson, which is to-day the Union of Lincoln—was the sad and melancholy close of a long and lofty life.

The trial of Alfred Dreyfus is still fresh in the minds and memories of men. Troubled political seas still surge and roll in France because of the hatred, prejudice, and passion that envelope the mysterious *bordereau*. The French Republic is still rent by two contending factions: Dreyfus and anti-Dreyfus. His friends still say that Dreyfus was a Prometheus who was chained to an ocean-girt rock while the vulture of exile preyed upon his heart. His enemies still assert that he was a Judas who betrayed not God or Christ, but France and the Fatherland. His banishment to the Island of the Devil; his wife's deathless devotion; the implacable hatred of his enemies; the undying loyalty of friends; and his own sufferings and woes are the warp and woof of the most splendid and pathetic epoch of a century.

Other trials—of Mary Stuart, the beautiful and brilliant Scottish queen; of Robert Emmet, the grand and gifted Irish patriot martyr—thrilled the world in their day.

But these trials, one and all, were tame and commonplace, compared with the trial and crucifixion of the Galilean peasant, Jesus of Nazareth. These were earthly trials, on earthly issues, before earthly courts. The trial of the Nazarene was before the high tribunals of both Heaven and earth; before the Great Sanhedrin, whose judges were the master-spirits of a divinely commissioned race; before the court of the Roman Empire that controlled the legal and political rights of men throughout the known world, from Scotland to Judea and from Dacia to Abyssinia.

The trial of Jesus was twofold: Hebrew and Roman; or Ecclesiastical and Civil. The Hebrew trial took place before the Great Sanhedrin, consisting of seventy-one members. The Roman trial was held before Pontius Pilate, Roman governor of Judea, and afterwards before Herod, Tetrarch of Galilee. These trials all made one, were links in a chain, and took place within a space of time variously estimated from ten to twenty hours.

The general order of events may be thus briefly described:

(1) About eleven o'clock on the evening of April 6th, A.D. 30, Jesus and eleven of the Apostles left the scene of the Last Supper, which had been celebrated (probably in the home of Mark) on the outskirts of Jerusalem, to go to the Garden of Gethsemane.

(2) Jesus was arrested about midnight in Gethsemane by a band of Temple officers and Roman soldiers guided by Judas.

(3) He was first taken to Annas, and was afterwards sent by Annas to Caiaphas. A private preliminary examination of Jesus was then had before one of these church dignitaries. St. John describes this examination, but does not tell us clearly whether it was Annas or Caiaphas who conducted it.

(4) After His preliminary examination, Jesus was arraigned about two o'clock in the morning before the Sanhedrin, which had convened in the palace of Caiaphas, and was formally tried and condemned to death on the charge of blasphemy against Jehovah.

(5) After a temporary adjournment of the first session, the Sanhedrin reassembled at the break of day to retry Jesus, and to determine how He should be brought before Pilate.

(6) In the early morning of April 7th, Jesus was led before Pontius Pilate, who was then stopping in the palace of Herod on the hill of Zion, his customary residence when he came up from Cæsarea to Jerusalem to attend the Jewish national festivals. A brief trial of Jesus by Pilate, on the charge of high treason against Cæsar, was then had in front of and within the palace of Herod. The result was an acquittal of the prisoner by the Roman procurator, who expressed his verdict in these words: "I find in him no fault at all."

(7) Instead of releasing Jesus after having found Him not guilty, Pilate, being intimidated by the rabble, sent the prisoner away to Herod, Tetrarch of Galilee, who was then in attendance upon the Passover Feast, and was at that moment residing in the ancient palace of the Asmoneans in the immediate neighborhood of the residence of Pilate. A brief, informal hearing was had before Herod, who, having mocked and brutalized the prisoner, sent Him back to the Roman governor.

(8) After the return of Jesus from the Court of Herod, Pilate assembled the priests and elders, announced to them that Herod had found no fault with the prisoner in their midst, reminded them that he himself had acquitted Him, and offered to scourge and then release Him. This compromise and subterfuge were scornfully rejected by the Jews who had demanded the crucifixion of Jesus. Pilate, after much vacillation, finally yielded to the demands of the mob and ordered the prisoner to be crucified.

From this brief outline of the proceedings against Jesus, the reader will readily perceive that there were two distinct trials: a Hebrew and a Roman. He will notice further that each trial was marked by three distinct features or appearances. The Hebrew trial was characterized by:

(1) The appearance before Annas.

(2) The trial at the night session of the Sanhedrin.

(3) The examination at the morning sitting of the same court.

The Roman trial was marked by:

(1) The appearance of Jesus before Pilate.

(2) His arraignment before Herod.

(3) His reappearance before Pilate.

The first volume of this work has been devoted to the Hebrew trial of Jesus, and a distinctively Hebrew impress has been given to all its pages. The second volume has been devoted to the Roman trial, and a distinctively Roman impress has been given it. Each exhibits a distinct view of the subject. Taken together, they comprehend the most important and famous judicial transaction in history.

It is not the purpose of the author of these volumes to usurp the functions or the privileges of the ecclesiastic. To priests and preachers have been left the discussion and solution of theological problems: the divinity of Jesus, the immortality of the soul and kindred religious dogmas. "The Trial of Jesus from a *Lawyer's* Standpoint" is the expanded title of this work. A strict adherence to a secular discussion of the theme proclaimed has been studiously observed in the preparation of these pages. The legal rights of the *man* Jesus at the bar of *human* justice under Jewish and Roman laws have marked the limitations of the argument. Any digression from this plan has been temporary and necessary.

A thorough understanding of any case, judicially considered, involves a complete analysis of the cardinal legal elements of the case: the element called Fact and the element called Law. Whether in ancient or modern times, in a Jewish or Gentile court, of civil or criminal jurisdiction, these elements have always entered into the legal conception of a case. Whether the advocate is preparing a pleading at his desk, is summing up before the jury, or addressing himself to the court, these elements are working forever in his brain. He is constantly asking himself these questions: What are the facts of this case? What is the law applicable to the facts? Do the facts and law meet and harmonize judicially? Do they blend in legal unison according to the latest decision of the court of last resort? If so, a case is made; otherwise, not.

Now many sermons might be differently preached; many books might be differently written. But an intelligent discussion of the trial and crucifixion of Jesus from a lawyer's point of view must be had upon the basis of an analytical review of the agreement or nonagreement of law and fact in the case sought to be made against the Christ.

The first question that naturally suggests itself to the inquiring mind, in investigating this theme, is this: Upon what facts was the complaint against Jesus based? A second question then logically follows: What were the rules and regulations of Hebrew and Roman law directly applicable to those facts in the trials of Jesus before the Sanhedrin and before Pilate? It is respectfully submitted that no clear and comprehensive treatment of the subject can be had without proper answers to these questions.

Having learned the facts of any case, and having determined what rules of law are applicable to them in regard to the controversy in hand, a third step in the proceedings, in all matters of review on appeal, is this: To analyze the record from the viewpoint of the juristic agreement or nonagreement of law and fact; and to determine by a process of judicial dissection and reformation the presence or absence of essential legal elements in the proceedings, with a view to affirmance in case of absence, or reversal of the verdict in the event of the discovery of the presence of error.

In obedience to this natural intellectual tendency and to the usual mode of legal procedure in reviewing and revising matters on appeal, the contents of Volume I have been divided into three parts, corresponding, in a general way, to the successive steps heretofore mentioned.

In Part I, the Record of Fact in the trial of Jesus has been authenticated; not, indeed, according to the strict provisions of modern statutes which regulate the authentication of legal documents, but in the popular sense of the word "authentication." Nevertheless, the authenticity of the Gospel narratives, which form the record of fact in the trial of Jesus, and the credibility of the Evangelists who wrote and published these narratives, have been subjected to the rigorous tests of rules of evidence laid down by Greenleaf and by Starkie. Such an authentication has been deemed necessary in a treatise of this kind.

Two main methods may be employed in investigating and proving the alleged occurrences of Sacred History: (1) The method which is based upon the evidence of spiritual consciousness and experience, derived from religious conversion and from communion with God; (2) the method that rests upon the application of historic facts and legal rules to the testimony of those who have asserted the existence of such occurrences.

It has been contended by many that the first of these methods is the supreme test, and the only proper one, in solving religious problems and in reaching full and final assurance of the existence of spiritual truths. It is confidently asserted by such persons that the true Christian who has accepted Jesus as his personal Redeemer and has thereby found peace with God, needs no assurance from Matthew that the Christ was the Heaven-begotten and Virgin-born. Such a Christian, it is said, has positive proof from within that Jesus was divine. It is further contended that all forms of religious truth are susceptible of the same kind of proof. It is argued that from despairing hope, born of the longing and the tears of a mother who, grief-stricken and broken-hearted, kneels in prayer beside the coffin of her firstborn, springs stronger evidence of a future life and of an everlasting reunion with loved ones, than comes from all the assurances of immortality handed down by saints and sages. The advocates of this theory contend that the fact of the Resurrection of Jesus should be proved mainly by the method of spiritual consciousness and experience, and only incidentally by the historical testimony of the sacred writers. They boldly maintain that the Resurrection was a spiritual fact born of a spiritual truth; and that within the soul of each true believer is the image of the risen Jesus, reflected from Heaven in as perfect form as that seen by Paul while journeying to Damascus.

It would be decidedly ungenerous and unjust to deny the force of the contention that spiritual consciousness and religious experience are convincing forms of proof. To do so would be to offer gratuitous insult to the intelligence and sincerity of millions of consecrated men and women who have repeatedly proclaimed and are still proclaiming that the Spirit of God and Christ within them attests the reality of religion.

But on the other hand the doctrine of religions consciousness, as a mode of proof, certainly has its limitations. Spiritual proofs are obviously the very best means of establishing purely spiritual truths. But not many truths of religion are purely spiritual. The most of them are encased within historic facts which may themselves be separately considered as historic truths. In a sense, all spiritual truth is born of historic truth; that is, historic truths, in the order of our acquisition of a knowledge of them, antedate and create spiritual truths. The religious consciousness of the Resurrection of Jesus would never have been born in our hearts if we had never read the historical records of the physical Resurrection. Nor could we have ever had a religious experience of the divinity of Jesus if we had never read the historical accounts of His miracles, of His Virgin birth, His fulfillment of prophecy, and His Resurrection from the dead, unless Jesus had personally communicated to us evidences of His divinity. These separate and historic facts, of which spiritual truths are born, cannot be proved by religious consciousness and experience.

The distinctions herein suggested are very aptly and beautifully expressed by Professor Inge in his Bampton Lectures on Christian Mysticism, in which he says: "The inner light can only testify to spiritual truths. It always speaks in the present tense; it cannot guarantee any historical event, past or future. It cannot guarantee either the Gospel history or a future judgment. It can tell us that Christ is risen, and He is alive for evermore, but not that He rose again the third day."

From the foregoing, then, it is clear that in dealing with the historical facts and circumstances of the trial and crucifixion of Jesus, we cannot remotely employ the method of proof which is based upon religious consciousness and experience, since these events are matters of the past and not of the present. We have been compelled, therefore, to resort to the legal and historical method of proof; since we could not assume the correctness of the record, as such an assumption would have been lacking in legal requirement and judicial fitness.

It has also been thought not to be within the scope of this treatise, or consistent with the purpose of the author of these volumes, to enter into a discussion of the question of inspiration in the matter of the origin of the New Testament Gospels, as the record of fact in the trial of Jesus. As secular historians, rather than as inspired writers, must the Evangelists be regarded in this connection; since the title of this work suggests and demands a strictly legal treatment of the theme proclaimed. The author would respectfully suggest, however, that the day is past for complete reliance upon the theory of inspiration and a total rejection of all analysis and investigation. That the Scriptures are sacred and inspired, and neither need nor permit questions involving doubt and speculation as to origin and authenticity will no longer meet the challenge or dissipate the fears of the intellectual leaders of the human race. The Christianity of the future must be a religion of reason as well as of faith, else it cannot and will not endure the shocks of time, or survive the onward march of the soul. If the teachings of the Nazarene are a faithful portrayal and a truthful expression of all the verities of Heaven and earth, then Christianity has nothing to fear from the discoveries of Science, from Roman catacombs, Arabian hieroglyphics, the sands of Egypt, or the ruins of Nineveh and Babylon. Science is the High Priestess of Nature and Nature's oracles, and no single revelation of Science can disprove or contradict the simplest truth of Nature's God.

If, on the other hand, Christianity be fundamentally and essentially false, ignorance and bigotry will not preserve and perpetuate it; all the prayers of the faithful, all the martyrdom of the centuries, will not suffice to save it from death and annihilation.

But the Christian need have no fear of the results of scientific investigation or historic revelation. Assyriology, archæology, and paleontology, interpreted and applied by the finest scholarship and the most superb intellects of earth, have spent all their stupendous and concentrated forces in the direction of the discovery of natural and historic facts that would confirm or destroy the Christian theory of things. And yet not one natural or historic fact has been discovered that seriously disturbs the testimony of the Evangelists or impairs the evidence of Christianity. A few unlettered fisherman, casting nets for a livelihood in the waters of Gennesaret, framed a message to humanity based upon the life and martyrdom of a Galilean peasant, their spiritual Lord and Master, and proclaimed it to the world; and all the succeeding centuries of scientific research and skeptical criticism have not shaken mankind's confidence in its truthfulness and its potency. If eighteen hundred years of scientific investigation have resulted only in proof and vindication of the historic asseverations of the Sacred Scriptures, and further investigation gives promise of still further proof and vindication, tending to remove all doubts and destroy all fears, nothing but rank stupidity and crass ignorance will place obstacles in the way of ultimate analysis and complete revelation.

In Part II of this volume, following the plan heretofore suggested, the element of Law has been considered. Hebrew criminal jurisprudence, based upon the Mosaic Code and upon the Talmud, has been outlined and discussed. A more exhaustive treatment has been given than the subject would seem to justify, but the writer is convinced that the Criminal Code of the Jews must be of surpassing interest to the general reader, regardless of whether certain peculiar rules therein contained have reference to the trial of Jesus or not. The bulk of this Code has been inserted in this work because it is felt that a comprehensive view of any system enables the student of a particular trial under that system to grasp more fully and to appreciate more keenly the merits of the proceedings.

In Part III the legal aspects of the trial of Jesus have been reviewed. The elements of Law and Fact have been combined in the form of a "Brief," in which "Points" have been made and errors have been discussed.

During the past decade, the author of this work has delivered occasionally, in the United States and in the Dominion of Canada, a lecture upon the subject, "The Trial of Jesus from a Lawyer's Standpoint." Numerous requests have been made, from time to time, for the lecture in printed form. To supply this demand is the purpose of the publication of these volumes. The voluminous treatment given has been in response to the demands of those who have asked for a topical treatment of the subject. Many auditors in his lecture audiences have asked for special treatment, from a lawyer's standpoint, of the New Testament Gospels. Many have requested an exhaustive handling of Hebrew criminal law. Others have asked for the insertion in this work of the Apocryphal Acts of Pilate. And still others have expressed a desire to have Græco-Roman Paganism dealt with in its relationship to the trial of Jesus. In obedience to these various demands, certain chapters have been incorporated in the general work that may not seem to the average reader to have any direct bearing upon the subject treated. It is felt, however, that in every case at least a partial relevancy exists, and that in a large majority of cases the relevancy is perfect.

The writer wishes, at this time and place, to acknowledge his indebtedness and to express his thanks, for valuable assistance rendered, to all those authors mentioned under the title "Bibliography" at the end of Volume II.

WALTER M. CHANDLER.

NEW YORK CITY, July 1, 1908.

THE GOSPEL NARRATIVES

MATTHEW	MARK
xxvi. 47-68; xxvii. 1-26	xiv. 43-65; xv. 1-15.

MATTHEW	MARK
And while he yet spake, lo, Judas, one of the twelve, came, and with him a great multitude with swords and staves, from the chief priests and elders of the people.... Then came they, and laid hands on Jesus, and took him.... And they that had laid hold on Jesus led him away to Caiaphas the high priest, where the scribes and the elders were assembled.... Now the chief priests, and elders, and all the council, sought false witness against Jesus, to put him to death; But found none: yea, though many false witnesses came, yet found they none. At the last came two false witnesses, And said, This fellow said, I am able to destroy the temple of God, and to build it in three days. And the high priest arose, and said unto him, Answerest thou nothing? what is it which these witness against thee? But Jesus held his peace. And the high priest answered and said unto him, I adjure thee by the living God, that thou tell us whether thou be the Christ, the Son of God. Jesus saith unto him, Thou has said: nevertheless I say unto you, Hereafter shall ye see the Son of man sitting on the right hand of power, and coming in the clouds of heaven. Then the high priest rent his clothes, saying, He hath spoken	And immediately, while he yet spake, cometh Judas, one of the twelve, and with him a great multitude with swords and staves, from the chief priests and the scribes and the elders. And he that betrayed him had given them a token, saying, Whomsoever I shall kiss, that same is he; take him, and lead him away safely. And as soon as he was come, he goeth straightway to him, and saith, Master, Master; and kissed him. And they laid hands on him, and took him. And one of them that stood by drew a sword, and smote a servant of the high priest, and cut off his ear. And Jesus answered and said unto them, Are ye come out, as against a thief, with swords and staves to take me? I was daily with you in the temple teaching, and ye took me not; but the scriptures must be fulfilled. And they all forsook him, and fled. And there followed him a certain young man, having a linen cloth cast about his naked body; and the young man laid hold on him: And he left the linen cloth, and fled from them naked. And they led Jesus away to the high priest: and with him were assembled all the chief priests and the elders and the scribes.... And the chief priests and all the council sought for witness against Jesus to put him to

blasphemy; what further need have we of witnesses? behold, now ye have heard his blasphemy. What think ye? They answered and said, He is guilty of death. Then did they spit in his face, and buffeted him; and others smote him with the palms of their hands, Saying, Prophesy unto us, thou Christ, Who is he that smote thee?

When the morning was come, all the chief priests and elders of the people took counsel against Jesus to put him to death: And when they had bound him, they led him away, and delivered him to Pontius Pilate the governor.... And Jesus stood before the governor: and the governor asked him, saying, Art thou the King of the Jews? And Jesus said unto him, Thou sayest. And when he was accused of the chief priests and elders, he answered nothing. Then said Pilate unto him, Hearest thou not how many things they witness against thee? And he answered him to never a word; insomuch that the governor marvelled greatly. Now at the feast the governor was wont to release unto the people a prisoner, whom they would. And they had then a notable prisoner, called Barabbas. Therefore when they were gathered together, Pilate said unto them, Whom will ye that I release unto you? Barabbas, or Jesus which is called Christ? For he knew that for envy they had delivered him. When he was set down on the judgement seat, his wife sent unto him, saying, Have thou nothing to do with that just death; and found none. For many bare false witness against him, but their witness agreed not together. And there arose certain, and bare false witness against him, saying, We heard him say, I will destroy this temple that is made with hands, and within three days I will build another made without hands. But neither so did their witness agree together. And the high priest stood up in the midst, and asked Jesus, saying, Answerest thou nothing? what is it which these witness against thee? But he held his peace, and answered nothing. Again the high priest asked him, and said unto him, Art thou the Christ, the Son of the Blessed? And Jesus said, I am: and ye shall see the Son of man sitting on the right hand of power, and coming in the clouds of heaven. Then the high priest rent his clothes, and saith, What need we any further witnesses? Ye have heard the blasphemy: what think ye? And they all condemned him to be guilty of death. And some began to spit on him, and to cover his face, and to buffet him, and to say unto him, Prophesy: and the servants did strike him with the palms of their hands.

And straightway in the morning the chief priests held a consultation with the elders and scribes and the whole council, and bound Jesus, and carried him away, and delivered him to Pilate. And Pilate asked him, Art thou the King of the Jews? And he answering said unto him, Thou sayest it. And the chief priests accused him of many things: but he man: for I have suffered many things this day in a dream because of him. But the chief priests and elders persuaded the multitude that they should ask Barabbas, and destroy Jesus. The governor answered and said unto them, Whether of the twain will ye that I release unto you? They said, Barabbas. Pilate saith unto them, What shall I do then with Jesus which is called Christ? They all say unto him, Let him be crucified. And the governor said, Why, what evil hath he done? But they cried out the more, saying, Let him be crucified. When Pilate saw that he could prevail nothing, but that rather a tumult was made, he took water, and washed his hands before the multitude, saying, I am innocent of the blood of this just person: see ye to it. Then answered all the people, and said, His blood be on us, and on our children. Then released he Barabbas unto them: and when he had scourged Jesus, he delivered him to be crucified.

answered nothing. And Pilate asked him again, saying, Answerest thou nothing? behold how many things they witness against thee. But Jesus yet answered nothing; so that Pilate marvelled. Now at that feast he released unto them one prisoner, whomsoever they desired. And there was one named Barabbas, which lay bound with them that had made insurrection with him, who had committed murder in the insurrection. And the multitude crying aloud began to desire him to do as he had ever done unto them. But Pilate answered them, saying, Will ye that I release unto you the King of the Jews? For he knew that the chief priests had delivered him for envy. But the chief priests moved the people, that he should rather release Barabbas unto them. And Pilate answered and said again unto them, What will ye then that I shall do unto him whom ye call the King of the Jews? And they cried out again, Crucify him. Then Pilate said unto them, Why, what evil hath he done? And they cried out the more exceedingly, Crucify him. And so Pilate, willing to content the people, released Barabbas unto them, and delivered Jesus, when he had scourged him, to be crucified.

LUKE	JOHN
xxii. 47-71; xxiii. 1-24.	xviii. 3-38; xix. 1-16.
And while he yet spake, behold a multitude, and he that was called Judas, one of the twelve, went before them, and drew near unto Jesus to kiss him. But Jesus said	Judas then, having received a band of men and officers from the chief priests and Pharisees, cometh thither with lanterns and torches and weapons.... Then the band and

unto him, Judas, betrayest thou the Son of man with a kiss? When they which were about him saw what would follow, they said unto him, Lord, shall we smite with the sword? And one of them smote the servant of the high priest, and cut off his right ear. And Jesus answered and said, Suffer ye thus far. And he touched his ear, and healed him. Then Jesus said unto the chief priests, and captains of the temple, and the elders, which were come to him, Be ye come out, as against a thief, with swords and staves? When I was daily with you in the temple, ye stretched forth no hands against me; but this is your hour, and the power of darkness. Then took they him, and led him, and brought him into the high priest's house. And Peter followed afar off.... And as soon as it was day, the elders of the people and the chief priests and the scribes came together, and led him into their council, saying, Art thou the Christ? tell us. And he said unto them, If I tell you, ye will not believe: And if I also ask you, ye will not answer me, nor let me go. Hereafter shall the Son of man sit on the right hand of the power of God. Then said they all, Art thou then the Son of God? And he said unto them, Ye say that I am. And they said, What need we any further witness? for we ourselves have heard of his own mouth.

And the whole multitude of them arose, and led him unto Pilate. And they began to accuse him, saying, We found this fellow perverting the the captain and officers of the Jews took Jesus, and bound him, And led him away to Annas first; for he was father in law to Caiaphas, which was the high priest that same year.... The high priest then asked Jesus of his disciples, and of his doctrine. Jesus answered him, I spake openly to the world; I ever taught in the synagogue, and in the temple, whither the Jews always resort; and in secret have I said nothing. Why askest thou me? ask them which heard me, what I have said unto them: behold, they know what I said. And when he had thus spoken, one of the officers which stood by struck Jesus with the palm of his hand, saying, Answerest thou the high priest so? Jesus answered him, If I have spoken evil, bear witness of the evil: but if well, why smitest thou me? Now Annas had sent him bound unto Caiaphas the high priest.... Then led they Jesus from Caiaphas unto the hall of judgment: and it was early; and they themselves went not into the judgment hall, lest they should be defiled; but that they might eat the passover. Pilate then went out unto them, and said, What accusation bring ye against this man? They answered and said unto him, If he were not a malefactor, we would not have delivered him up unto thee. xxxiiiThen said Pilate unto them, Take ye him, and judge him according to your law. The Jews therefore said unto him, It is not lawful for us to put any man to death.... Then Pilate entered into the judgment hall again, and called nation, and forbidding to give tribute to Cæsar, saying that he himself is Christ a King. And Pilate asked him, saying, Art thou the King of the Jews? And he answered him and said, Thou sayest it. Then said Pilate to the chief priests and to the people, I find no fault in this man. And they were the more fierce, saying, He stirreth up the people, teaching throughout all Jewry, beginning from Galilee to this place. When Pilate heard of Galilee, he asked whether the man were a Galilæan. And as soon as he knew that he belonged unto Herod's jurisdiction, he sent him to Herod, who himself also was at Jerusalem at that time. And when Herod saw Jesus, he was exceeding glad: for he was desirous to see him of a long season, because he had heard many things of him; and he hoped to have seen some miracle done by him. Then he questioned with him in many words; but he answered him nothing. And the chief priests and scribes stood and vehemently accused him. And Herod with his men of war set him at nought, and mocked him, and arrayed him in a gorgeous robe, and sent him again to Pilate. And the same day Pilate and Herod were made friends together: for before they were at enmity between themselves. And Pilate, when he had called together the chief priests and the rulers and the people, Said unto them, Ye have brought this man unto me, as one that perverteth the people: and, behold, I, having examined him before you,

Jesus, and said unto him, Art thou the King of the Jews? Jesus answered him, Sayest thou this thing of thyself, or did others tell it thee of me? Pilate answered, Am I a Jew? Thine own nation and the chief priests have delivered thee unto me: what hast thou done? Jesus answered, My kingdom is not of this world: if my kingdom were of this world, then would my servants fight, that I should not be delivered to the Jews: but now is my kingdom not from hence. Pilate therefore said unto him, Art thou a king then? Jesus answered, Thou sayest that I am a king. To this end was I born, and for this cause came I into the world, that I should bear witness unto the truth. Everyone that is of the truth heareth my voice. Pilate saith unto him, What is truth? And when he had said this, he went out again unto the Jews, and saith unto them, I find in him no fault at all.

Then Pilate therefore took Jesus, and scourged him. And the soldiers platted a crown of thorns, and put it on his head, and they put on him a purple robe, And said, Hail, King of the Jews! and they smote him with their hands. Pilate therefore went forth again, and saith unto them, Behold, I bring him forth to you, that ye may know that I find no fault in him.... The Jews answered him, We have a law, and by our law he ought to die, because he made himself the Son of God. When Pilate therefore heard that saying, he was the more afraid; And went again into the judgment hall, and have found no fault in this man touching those things whereof ye accuse him: No, nor yet Herod: for I sent you to him; and, lo, nothing worthy of death is done unto him. I will therefore chastise him, and release him.... And they cried out all at once, saying, Away with this man, and release unto us Barabbas.... Pilate therefore, willing to release Jesus, spake again to them. But they cried, saying, Crucify him, crucify him. And he said unto them the third time, Why, what evil hath he done? I have found no cause of death in him: I will therefore chastise him, and let him go. And they were instant with loud voices, requiring that he might be crucified. And the voices of them and of the chief priests prevailed. And Pilate gave sentence that it should be as they required.

saith unto Jesus, Whence art thou? But Jesus gave him no answer.... And from thenceforth Pilate sought to release him: but the Jews cried out, saying, If thou let this man go, thou art nct Cæsar's friend: whosoever maketh himself a king speaketh against Cæsar. When Pilate therefore heard that saying, he brought Jesus forth, and sat down in the judgment seat in a place that is called the Pavement, but in the Hebrew, Gabbatha. And it was the preparation of the passover, and about the sixth hour: and he saith unto the Jews, Behold your King! But they cried out, Away with him, away with him, crucify him. Pilate saith unto them, Shall I crucify your King? The chief priests answered, We have no king but Cæsar. Then delivered he him therefore unto them to be crucified. And they took Jesus, and led him away.

PART I
THE RECORD OF FACT

ST. MATTHEW (REMBRANDT)

CHAPTER I

THE RECORD OF FACT

THE Gospels of the New Testament form the record of fact in the trial of Jesus. There is not a line of authentic history in the literature of the world, sacred or profane, dealing originally and authoritatively with the facts and circumstances of the trial and crucifixion of the Christ, excepting these Gospels. A line from Philo—a dubious passage from Josephus—a mere mention by Tacitus—a few scattering fragments from the Talmud—all else is darkness, save the light that streams down through the centuries from Calvary and the Cross through the books of the Evangelists.

In dealing with the record of fact contained in the Gospels, in the trial of Jesus two questions naturally suggest themselves: (1) Are the Gospel narratives, such as we have them to-day, identical with those that were given to the world by the Evangelists in Apostolic times? That is, have these biographies of the Christ by the Evangelical writers been handed down to us through all the ages substantially uncorrupted and unimpaired?

(2) Are the Gospel writers—Matthew, Mark, Luke, and John—credible witnesses of the facts and circumstances recorded by them in the Gospel histories? That is, did they tell the truth when they wrote and published these narratives to the world? Satisfactory affirmative answers to these questions will establish and authenticate a perfect record of fact. The pages of Part I of this volume will be devoted to giving affirmative and satisfactory answers to these questions. And, in accomplishing this purpose, academic reasoning and metaphysical speculation will be rejected. Well-established rules of evidence, as employed in modern courts of law, will be rigorously applied. So-called "Higher Criticism" has no place in a treatise of this kind, since the critical niceties and dialectic quibbles of men like Strauss, Renan, and Baur would not be seriously considered in a modern judicial proceeding. Reasonable probability, and not mathematical certainty, is the legal test of adequacy in weighing human testimony with a view to a judicial determination.

The reader may ask: Why should not a Christian writer, in a Christian country, assume, without argument, that the testimony of Christian sacred writers is true? The answer is that such conduct would convert a purely legal treatise into a religious one, and substitute faith for logic. The writer of these volumes, as a Christian, believes that the Gospels relate the truth. As a lawyer, he is compelled to respect the opinions of a large proportion of mankind who differ with him, and to employ judicial methods in treating a legal theme.

The two questions above mentioned involve two distinct principles or features in the Law of Evidence: (1) Admissibility or relevancy of evidence; (2) Credibility of witnesses who have rendered testimony. All the pages of Part I will be devoted to a consideration of these features in their relationship to the testimony of the Evangelists.

The first question that naturally arises is this: Is there a well-established rule of the modern Law of Evidence under which the Gospels could be introduced as evidence in a modern judicial proceeding? Suppose that the question of the Resurrection of Jesus—that is, the fact of the truthfulness or falsity of the Resurrection—should become a material fact in issue in a suit in a modern court of law; could the testimony of the Evangelists relating to the Resurrection be introduced in evidence? It would probably be objected that their testimony was hearsay; that they had not been properly subjected to the cardinal tests of truth: an oath, a cross-examination, and personal demeanor while testifying. These objections might prevail if another rule of law could not be successfully invoked. Such a rule exists, and with it we have now to deal.

The author can conceive of no more satisfactory way of establishing the principle of the admissibility of the Gospels in evidence under modern law than by quoting at length from the celebrated treatise on the "Testimony of the Evangelists," by Mr. Simon Greenleaf, the greatest of all writers on the Law of Evidence. The opinion of Greenleaf on a subject of this kind is somewhat in the nature of a decision of a court of last resort, and his authority in matters of this import is unquestioned in every land where English law is practiced. *The London Law Magazine*, a few years ago, paid him the following splendid tribute: "It is no mean honor to America that her schools of jurisprudence have produced two of the first writers and best esteemed legal authorities of this century—the great and good man, Judge Story, and his worthy and eminent associate, Professor Greenleaf. Upon the existing Law of Evidence (by Greenleaf) more light has shone from the New World than from all the lawyers who adorn the courts of Europe."

Concerning the authenticity of the Sacred Scriptures and their admissibility in evidence, Greenleaf has thus written:

That the books of the Old Testament, as we now have them, are genuine; that they existed in the time of our Saviour, and were commonly received and referred to among the Jews as the sacred books of their religion; and that the text of the Four Evangelists has been handed down to us in the state in which it was originally written, that is, without having been materially corrupted or falsified, either by heretics or Christians, are facts which we are entitled to assume as true, until the contrary is shown.

The genuineness of these writings really admits of as little doubt, and is susceptible of as ready proof, as that of any ancient writings whatever. The rule of municipal law on this subject is familiar, and applies with equal force to all ancient writings, whether documentary or otherwise; and as it comes first in order, in the prosecution of these inquiries, it may, for the sake of mere convenience, be designated as our first rule.

Every document, apparently ancient, coming from the proper repository or custody, and bearing on its face no evident marks of forgery, the law presumes to be genuine, and devolves on the opposing party the burden of proving it to be otherwise.

An ancient document, offered in evidence in our courts, is said to come from the proper repository, when it is found in the place where, and under the care of persons with whom, such writings might naturally and reasonably be expected to be found; for it is this custody which gives authenticity to documents found within it. If they come from such a place, and bear no evident marks of forgery, the law presumes that they are genuine, and they are permitted to be read in evidence, unless the opposing party is able successfully to impeach them. The burden of showing them to be false and unworthy of credit is devolved on the party who makes that objection. The presumption of law is the judgment of charity. It presumes that every man is innocent until he is proved guilty; that everything has been done fairly and legally until it is proved to have been otherwise; and that every document found in its proper repository, and not bearing marks of forgery, is genuine. Now this is precisely the case with the Sacred Writings. They have been used in the church from time immemorial, and are thus found in the place where alone they ought to be looked for. They come to us, and challenge our reception of them as genuine writings, precisely as Domesday Book, the Ancient Statutes of Wales, or any other of the ancient documents which have recently been published under the British Record Commission are received. They are found in familiar use in all the churches of Christendom, as the sacred books to which all denominations of Christians refer, as the standard of their faith. There is no pretense that they were engraven on plates of gold and discovered in a cave, nor that they were brought from heaven by angels; but they are received as the plain narratives and writings of the men whose names they respectively bear, made public at the time they were written; and though there are some slight discrepancies among the copies subsequently made, there is no pretense that the originals were anywhere corrupted. If it be objected that the originals are lost, and that copies alone are now produced, the principles of the municipal law here also afford a satisfactory answer. For the multiplication of copies was a public fact, in the faithfulness of which all the Christian community had an interest; and it is a rule of law that

In matters of public and general interest, all persons must be presumed to be conversant, on the principle that individuals are presumed to be conversant with their own affairs.

Therefore it is that, in such matters, the prevailing current of assertion is resorted to as evidence, for it is to this that every member of the community is supposed to be privy. The persons, moreover, who multiplied these copies may be regarded, in some manner, as the agents of the Christian public, for whose use and benefit the copies were made; and on the ground of the credit due to such agents, and of the public nature of the facts themselves, the copies thus made are entitled to an extraordinary degree of confidence, and, as in the case of official registers and other public books, it is not necessary that they should be confirmed and sanctioned by the ordinary tests of truth. If any ancient document concerning our public rights were lost, copies which had been as universally received and acted upon as the Four Gospels have been, would have been received in evidence in any of our courts of justice, without the slightest hesitation. The entire text of the Corpus Juris Civilis is received as authority in all the courts of continental Europe, upon much weaker evidence of its genuineness; for the integrity of the Sacred Text has been preserved by the jealousy of opposing sects, beyond any moral possibility of corruption; while that of the Roman Civil Law has been preserved by tacit consent, without the interest of any opposing school, to watch over and preserve it from alteration.

These copies of the Holy Scriptures having thus been in familiar use in the churches from the time when the text was committed to writing; having been watched with vigilance by so many sects, opposed to each other in doctrine, yet all appealing to these Scriptures for the correctness of their faith; and having in all ages, down to this day, been respected as the authoritative source of all ecclesiastical power and government, and submitted to, and acted under in regard to so many claims of right, on the one hand, and so many obligations of duty, on the other; it is quite erroneous to suppose that the Christian is bound to offer any further proof of their genuineness or authenticity. It is for the objector to show them spurious; for on him, by the plainest rules of law, lies the burden of proof. If it were the case of a claim to a franchise, and a copy of an ancient deed or charter were produced in support of the title, under parallel circumstances on which to presume its genuineness, no lawyer, it is believed, would venture to deny either its admissibility in evidence or the satisfactory character of the proof. In a recent case in the House of Lords, precisely such a document, being an old manuscript copy, purporting to have been extracted from ancient Journals of the House, which were lost, and to have been made by an officer whose duty it was to prepare lists of the peers, was held admissible in a claim of peerage.[1]

Having secured the Gospel writings to be admitted in evidence under the rule laid down by Mr. Greenleaf, we are now ready to consider more at length the question of the credibility of the witnesses. The reader should bear in mind that there is a very important difference between the admission of testimony in evidence and belief in its truthfulness by the court or jury. Evidence is frequently deemed relevant and admissible, and goes to the jury for what it is worth. They may or may not believe it.

We are now ready to consider the credit that should be accorded the testimony of Matthew, Mark, Luke, and John concerning the trial and crucifixion of Jesus. And at the outset it should be borne in mind that there is a legal presumption that they told the truth. This presumption operates in their favor from the very moment that their testimony is admitted in evidence. Here, again, the opinion of Greenleaf—with all the weight and authority that such an opinion carries—is directly in point. In the "Testimony of the Evangelists" he says:

Proceeding further, to inquire whether the facts related by the Four Evangelists are proved by competent and satisfactory evidence, we are led, first, to consider on which side lies the burden of establishing the credibility of the witnesses. On this point the municipal law furnishes a rule which is of constant application in all trials by jury, and is indeed the dictate of that charity which thinketh no evil.

In the absence of circumstances which generate suspicion, every witness is to be presumed credible, until the contrary is shown, the burden of impeaching his credibility lying on the objector.

This rule serves to show the injustice with which the writers of the Gospels have ever been treated by infidels; an injustice silently acquiesced in even by Christians; in requiring the Christian affirmatively, and by positive evidence, *aliunde* to establish the credibility of his witnesses above all others, before their testimony is entitled to be considered, and in permitting the testimony of a single profane writer, alone and uncorroborated, to outweigh that of any single Christian. This is not the course in courts of chancery, where the testimony of a single witness is never permitted to outweigh the oath even of the defendant himself, interested as he is in the case, but, on the contrary, if the plaintiff, after having required the oath of his adversary, cannot overthrow it by something more than the oath of one witness, however credible, it must stand as evidence against him. But the Christian writer seems, by the usual course of the argument, to have been deprived of the common presumption of charity in his favor; and reversing the ordinary rule of administering justice in human tribunals, his testimony is unjustly presumed to be false, until it is proved to be true. This treatment, moreover, has been applied to them all in a body; and without due regard to the fact, that, being independent historians, writing at different periods, they are entitled to the support of each other; they have been treated, in the argument, almost as if the New Testament were the entire production, at once, of a body of men, conspiring by a joint fabrication, to impose a false religion upon the world. It is time that this injustice should cease; that the testimony of the evangelists should be admitted to be true, until it can be disproved by those who would impugn it; that the silence of one sacred writer on any point should no more detract from his own veracity or that of other historians, that the like circumstance is permitted to do among profane writers; and that the Four Evangelists should be admitted in corroboration of each other, as readily as Josephus and Tacitus, or Polybius and Livy.[2]

The reader will notice from the last extract that the eminent writer quoted has sought to establish the credibility of the Evangelists by a legal presumption in favor of their veracity. But it should be borne in mind that this presumption is a disputable one, and may be overturned by opposing evidence; that objections may be raised which will destroy the force of the presumption and shift the burden again to him who asserts the credibility of the witnesses. Now, let us suppose that such objections have been made, and that sufficient opposing evidence has been offered to accomplish this result; what has the Christian then to say in support of the credibility of the first historians of his faith? What proofs has he to offer, independent of legal presumption, that the first biographers of the Master were truthful men? Can he show that the application of legal tests to their credibility will save them in the eyes of a critical and unbelieving world? The writer believes that the Christian can do it, and will at once assume the task.

In "Starkie on Evidence" we find elaborated a rule of municipal law, at once concise and comprehensive, which furnishes a complete test of the credibility of witnesses. The various elements of this rule are constantly operating in the mind of the successful cross-examiner in the course of any extensive cross-examination.

The credit due to the testimony of witnesses depends upon, firstly, their honesty; secondly, their ability; thirdly, their number and the consistency of their testimony; fourthly, the conformity of their testimony with experience; and fifthly, the coincidence of their testimony with collateral circumstances.[3]

Let us apply these successive tests, in the order above enumerated, to the Evangelists.

(1) In the first place, let us consider the question of their *honesty*.

The meaning of the word "honesty," used in this connection, is peculiar. It relates rather to personal sincerity than to personal integrity, and suggests the idea of perjury rather than theft in criminal law. Were the witnesses honest? That is, were they sincere? Did they intend to tell the truth? That is, did they themselves believe what they testified? If so, they were honest witnesses, though their testimony was false, as a result of error in judgment or mistake of fact.

In the sense, then, of *sincerity* is the test of honesty to be applied to the Evangelists as witnesses of the facts which they relate in the New Testament narratives. And in making this test let us bear in mind the nature and scope of this work; that it is not a religious treatise, and that the question of inspiration must not be allowed to confuse a purely legal and historical discussion. As secular historians, and not as inspired writers, must the Evangelists be considered. And in testing their credibility, the customary standards employed in analyzing the motives and conduct of ordinary men in the usual experiences and everyday affairs of life must be applied. To regard them as strange or supernatural beings, subject to some awful influence, and acting under the guidance and protection of some god or hero, is decidedly foreign to the present purpose.

It is felt that only two considerations are needed in applying the test of sincerity to the Evangelists: (1) Character; (2) Motive. And this for the reason that honest character and righteous motive are the legitimate parentage of perfect sincerity. Then, as a primary consideration, in discussing their sincerity, it may be reasonably contended that the Gospel writers were either good men or bad. A middle ground is not possible in their case, since the issues joined and the results attained were too terrible and stupendous to have been produced by negative or indifferent forces. Were they good men, then they believed what they taught and wrote, and were sincere, else they deliberately palmed off an imposture on the world, which is inconsistent with the hypothesis that they were good. Were they bad men, then their lives and teachings furnish a contradiction in principle and an inversion in the nature and order of cause and effect which history has not elsewhere recorded, either before or since; for, in their discourses and their writings, they portrayed the divinest character and proclaimed the sublimest truths known to the children of men. Every serious, thoughtful mind at once inquires: Could bad men, conspirators and hypocrites, have painted such a character—one whose perfect purity and sinless beauty mock and shame the mental and spiritual attributes of every false prophet and of all heathen gods? The Olympian Zeus, the sovereign creation of the superb Greek intellect, was a fierce and vindictive deity—at times a faithless spouse and a drunken debauchee. Mahomet, whom two hundred millions of the human race worship as the Inspired of Allah, was cruel and treacherous in warfare, and base and sensual in private life. The Great Spirit of the Indian granted immortality to dogs, but denied it to women. Other hideous and monstrous attributes deformed the images and blurred the characters of pagan prophets and heathen divinities. But Jesus of Nazareth was a pure and perfect being who claimed to be sinless,[4] and whose claims have been admitted by all the world, believers and unbelievers alike. The great truths taught by the gentle Nazarene and transmitted by the Evangelists have brought balm and healing to the nations, have proclaimed and established universal brotherhood among men. Is it probable that such a character was painted and such truths proclaimed by dishonest and insincere men? Can Vice be the mother of Virtue? "Do men gather grapes of thorns or figs of thistles?" If Jesus was not really the pure and holy being portrayed by the Gospels, then the Evangelists have created a sublime character in a superb fiction which surpasses anything to be found in profane literature, and that evil-minded men could neither have conceived nor executed. It is impossible to derive from these reflections any other conclusion than the absolute honesty and perfect sincerity of the Evangelists. Besides, the mere perusal of their writings leaves a deep impression that they were pure and pious men.

Again, a second and more serious consideration than that of character, as affecting the sincerity of the Gospel writers, is the question of motive. If the Evangelists were insincere and did not believe their own story, what motive prompted them to tell it, to preach it and to die for it? It is not believed that all men are now or have ever been wholly selfish, but it is contended that desire for compensation is the main inducement to human action, mental and manual. Reward is the great golden key that opens the door of the Temple of Labor, and some form of recompense, here or hereafter, explains all the bustling activity of men. The Apostles themselves acted in obedience to this law, for we find them quarreling among themselves as to place and precedence in the New Kingdom. They even demanded of the Master the exact nature of their reward for labors performed and sacrifices endured. To which reply was made that they should sit on twelve thrones and judge the Twelve Tribes of Israel.

Now let us apply this principle of expectation of reward to the conduct of the Evangelists in preaching and publishing the Gospel of the Nazarene, and let us note particularly the result as it affects the question of motive in human conduct. But first let us review, for a moment, the political and religious situation at the beginning of the Apostolic ministry. The Master and Savior of the first Christians had just perished as a malefactor on the cross. The religion which the Apostles began to preach was founded in the doctrine of repentance from sins, faith in the Crucified One, and belief in His resurrection from the dead. Christianity, of which these elements were the essentials, sought to destroy and supplant all other religions. No compromises were proposed, no treaties were concluded. The followers of the Nazarene raised a black flag against paganism and every heathen god. No quarter was asked and none was given. This strange faith not only defied all other religions, but mocked all earthly government not built upon it. The small, but devoted, band, thus arrayed against themselves in the very beginning all the opposing religious and secular forces of the earth. Judaism branded the new creed as a disobedient and rebellious daughter. Paganism denounced it as a sham and a fraud, because its doctrines were unknown to the Portico and the Academy, and because its teachings were ridiculed by both Stoics and Epicureans. The Roman State cast a jealous and watchful eye upon the haughty pretensions of a religious system that taught the impotence of kings and sought to degrade earthly royalty.

In seeking, then, to establish the new faith and to inculcate its doctrines, what could and did the Evangelists expect but the bitter opposition which they met? Did they seriously hope to see the proud and haughty Sadducee, who despised the common people, or the kingly aristocracy of Rome, that vaunted a superhuman excellence, complacently accept a religion that taught the absolute equality and the universal brotherhood of men? Did they not expect what they actually received—bitter persecution, horrible torture, and cruel death? Then we are led to ask: Was this the recompense which they sought? Again, we pose the question: What was the motive of these men in thus acting, if they were dishonest and insincere? If they knew that they were preaching a falsehood, what reward did they expect? Was it of an earthly or a heavenly kind? It is unreasonable to suppose that they looked forward to earthly recompense when their teachings arrayed against them every spiritual and temporal potentate who had honors to grant or favors to confer. Were they looking for heavenly reward? It is ridiculous to imagine that they hoped to gain this by preaching a falsehood in this world. Nothing could be, therefore, more absurd than the proposition that a number of men banded themselves together, repudiated the ancient faith of their fathers, changed completely their mode of life, became austere in professing and practicing principles of virtue, spent their entire lives proclaiming certain truths to mankind, and then suffered the deaths of martyrs—all for the sake of a religion which they knew to be false. If they did not believe it to be false, they were sincere, and one element of their credibility is established. It is not a question at this time as to the absolute correctness of their statements. These statements might have been false, though their authors believed them to be true—it is a question of sincerity at this point; and the test of sincerity, as an element of credibility, rests upon the simple basis that men are more disposed to believe the statement of a witness if it is thought that the witness himself believes it.

(2) In the second place, let us consider the *ability* of the Evangelists as a test of their credibility as witnesses.

The text writers on the Law of Evidence are generally agreed that the ability of a witness to speak truthfully and accurately depends upon two considerations: (1) His natural powers of observation, which enable him to clearly perceive, and his strength of memory, which enables him to fully retain the matters of fact to which his testimony relates; (2) his opportunities for observing the things about which he testifies.

To what extent the Gospel writers possessed the first of these qualifications—that is, power of observation and strength of memory—we are not informed by either history or tradition. But we are certainly justified in assuming to be true what the law actually presumes: that they were at least men of sound mind and average intelligence. This presumption, it may be remarked, continues to exist in favor of the witness until an objector appears who proves the contrary by competent and satisfactory evidence. It is not believed that this proof has ever been or can ever be successfully established in the case of the Evangelists.

Aside from this legal presumption in their favor, there are certain considerations which lead us to believe that they were well qualified to speak truthfully and authoritatively about the matters relating to Gospel history. In the first place, the writings themselves indicate extraordinary mental vigor, as well as cultivated intelligence. The Gospels of Luke and John, moreover, reveal that the elegance of style and lofty imagery which are the invariable characteristics of intellectual depth and culture. The "ignorant fishermen" idea is certainly not applicable to the Gospel writers. If they were ever very ignorant, at the time of the composition of the Evangelical writings they had outgrown the affliction. The fact that the Gospels were written in Greek by Hebrews indicates that they were not entirely illiterate.

Again, the occupations of two of them are very suggestive. Matthew was a collector at the seat of customs,[5] and Luke was a physician.[6] Both these callings required more than ordinary knowledge of men, as well as accurate powers of observation, discrimination, and analysis.

But it has been frequently urged that, regardless of their natural endowments, the Evangelists were biased in favor of Jesus and His teachings, and bitterly prejudiced against all opposing faiths. In other words, they were at the same moment both enthusiasts and fanatics. For this reason, it is contended, their testimony is unreliable. This is without doubt the weakest assault ever made upon the trustworthiness of the Gospel narratives. That the Gospel writers were neither fanatics nor enthusiasts is evident from the very tone and style of the Sacred Writings themselves. The language of fanaticism and enthusiasm is the language of rant and rage, of vituperation and of censure, on the one hand, and of eulogy and adulation on the other. The enthusiast knows no limit to the praise of those whose cause he advocates. The fanatic places no bounds to his denunciation of those whom he opposes. Now, the most remarkable characteristic of the New Testament histories is the spirit of quiet dignity and simple candor which everywhere pervades them. There is nowhere the slightest trace of bitterness or resentment. There is enthusiasm everywhere in the sense of religious fervor, but nowhere in the sense of unbecoming heat or impatient caviling. The three eventful years of the ministry of Jesus afforded many opportunities for the display of temper and for the use of invective in the Evangelical writings. The murder of the Baptist by Herod; his cunning designs against Jesus; the constant dogging of the footsteps of the Master by the spies of the Sanhedrin; and His crucifixion by the order of Pontius Pilate—what more could be desired to make the heart rage and the blood boil? But nowhere is there the slightest exhibition of violent feeling or extravagant emotion. A gentle forbearance, a mild equanimity, a becoming dignity, mark every thought and utterance. The character of Pilate, as portrayed in the New Testament, is a supreme illustration of the fairness and magnanimity of the Gospel writers. Philo and Josephus describe the Roman procurator as stubborn, cruel, and vindictive. The only kindly suggestion touching the character of Pilate that has come down from the ancient world, is that contained in the writings of men who, above all others, would have been justified in describing him as cowardly and craven. Instead of painting him as a monster, they have linked conscience to his character and stored mercy in his heart, by their accounts of his repeated attempts to release Jesus. Fanatics and enthusiasts would not have done this.

Again, the absence of both bias and prejudice in the minds and hearts of the Evangelists is shown by the fact that they did not hesitate to record their own ludicrous foibles and blunders, and to proclaim them to the world. A disposition to do this is one of the surest indications of a truthful mind. It is in the nature of "a declaration against interest," in the phraseology of the law; and such declarations are believed because it has been universally observed that "men are not likely to invent anecdotes to their own discredit." "When we find them in any author," says Professor Fisher in his "Grounds of Theistic and Christian Belief," "a strong presumption is raised in favor of his general truthfulness." Many passages of New Testament Scriptures place Jesus and the Apostles in a most unfavorable light before the world. The denial of the Master by Peter[7] and His betrayal by Judas;[8] the flight of the Eleven from the Garden at the time of the arrest;[9] the ridiculous attempt of Peter to walk upon the sea and his failure because of lack of faith;[10] the frequent childish contentions among the disciples for place and precedence in the affections of Jesus and in the New Kingdom;[11] the embassy from John the Baptist to Jesus asking if He, Jesus, was the Messiah, after the latter had already visited the former, and had been baptized by him;[12] the belief of the family of Jesus that He was mad;[13] and the fact that His neighbors at Nazareth threatened to kill Him by hurling Him from a cliff[14]—these various recitals have furnished a handle to skeptical criticism in every age. They might as well have been omitted from the Gospel histories; and they would have been omitted by designing and untruthful men.

Again, touching the question of bias and prejudice, it is worthy of observation that skeptics fail to apply the same rules of criticism to sacred that they employ in profane literature. It is contended by them that the Evangelists are unworthy of belief because their writings record the words and deeds of their own Lord and Master. It is asserted that this sacred and tender relationship warped and blinded their Judgment, and disqualified them to write truthfully the facts and circumstances connected with the life and ministry of the founder of their faith. But these same critics do not apply the same tests of credibility to secular writers sustaining similar relationships. The Commentaries of Cæsar and the Anabasis of Xenophon record the mighty deeds and brilliant achievements of their authors; but this fact does not destroy their reliability as historical records in the estimation of those who insist that the Gospel writers shall be rejected on grounds of bias and partiality. The Memorabilia of Xenophon, "Recollections of Socrates," is the tribute of an affectionate and admiring disciple; and yet, all the colleges and universities of the world employ this work as a text-book in teaching the life and style of conversation of the great Athenian philosopher. It is never argued that the intimate relationship existing between Xenophon and Socrates should affect the credibility of the author of the Memorabilia. The best biography in the English language is Boswell's "Life of Johnson." Boswell's admiration for Dr. Johnson was idolatrous. At times, his servile flattery of the great Englishman amounted to disgusting sycophancy. In spite of this, his work is a monumental contribution to historical literature. The "Encyclopedia Britannica" says that "Boswell has produced the best biography the world has yet seen"; but why not reject this book because of its author's spaniel-like devotion to the man whose life he has written? If Matthew, Mark, Luke, and John are to be repudiated on the ground of bias, why not repudiate Cæsar, Xenophon, and Boswell? It is respectfully submitted that there is no real difference in logic between the tests of credibility applicable to sacred, and those required in the case of profane writers. A just and exact criticism will apply the same rules to both.

As to the second qualification above mentioned, under the second legal test of credibility laid down by Starkie, that is, the opportunity of observing facts and circumstances about which testimony is given, it may safely be said that the majority of the Evangelists possessed it in the highest degree. The most convincing testimony that can possibly be offered in a court of law is that of an eyewitness who has seen or heard what he testifies. Now, it is reasonably certain that all of the Gospel writers were eyewitnesses of most of the events recorded by them in the Gospel histories. Both Matthew and John were numbered among the Twelve who constantly attended the Master in all His wanderings, heard His discourses, witnessed the performance of His miracles, and proclaimed His faith after He was gone. It is very probable that Mark was another eyewitness of the events in the life and ministry of the Savior. It is now very generally agreed that the author of the Second Gospel was the young man who threw away his garment and fled at the time of the arrest in the Garden.[15] If Mark was actually present at midnight in Gethsemane peering through the shadows to see what would be done to the Nazarene by the mob, it is more than probable that he was also a witness of many other events in the life and ministry of the great Teacher. But, whether this be true or not, it is very well settled that the Second Gospel was dictated to Mark by Peter, who was as familiar with all the acts and words of Jesus as was Matthew or John. The Christian writers of antiquity unanimously testify that Mark wrote the Gospel ascribed to him, at the dictation of Peter. If their testimony is true, Peter is the real author of the Second Gospel. That the Gospel of Mark was written by an eyewitness is the opinion of Renan, the skeptic, who says: "In Mark, the facts are related with a clearness for which we seek in vain amongst the other Evangelists. He likes to report certain words of Jesus in Syro-Chaldean. He is full of minute observations, coming doubtless from an eye-witness. There is nothing to prevent our agreeing with Papias in regarding this eye-witness, who evidently had followed Jesus, who had loved Him and observed Him very closely, and who had preserved a lively image of Him, as the Apostle Peter himself."[16] The same writer declares Matthew to have been an eyewitness of the events described by him. He says: "On the whole, I admit as authentic the four canonical Gospels. All, in my opinion, date from the first century, and the authors are, generally speaking, those to whom they are attributed; but their historic value is diverse. Matthew evidently merits an unlimited confidence as to the discourses; they are the Logia, the identical notes taken from a clear and lively remembrance of the teachings of Jesus."[16]

That Luke was an eyewitness of many of the things recorded by him, and that the others were related to him by eyewitnesses, is perfectly clear from the introductory verses of his Gospel. In addressing his royal patron, Theophilus, he assures him that those who communicated the information contained in the Gospel to him were eyewitnesses; and follows by saying that he himself had had "perfect understanding of all things from the very first."[17] The evident meaning of this is that, desiring full information for Theophilus, he had supplemented his own personal knowledge by additional facts secured from eyewitnesses to those things which, not being of the Twelve, he himself had not seen.

St. John was peculiarly well qualified to record the sayings and doings of the Christ. He was called "the disciple whom Jesus loved.' He was admitted into the presence of the Savior, at all times, on terms of the utmost intimacy and friendship. At the Last Supper, his head reposed confidingly and lovingly upon the bosom of the Master. Together with Peter and James, he witnessed the resurrection of Jairus' daughter; was present at the Transfiguration on the Mount, and at the agony of the Savior in the Garden. From the cross, Jesus placed upon him the tender and pathetic burden of caring for His mother; and, running ahead of Peter, he was the first among the Twelve to arrive at the open sepulcher. By means of a favorable acquaintanceship with the High Priest, he was enabled to gain access to the palace and to be present at the trial of Jesus, as well as to introduce Peter, his friend.

It is thus clearly evident that the Evangelists were amply able, from any point of view, to truthfully and accurately record the events narrated in the Gospel histories. As eyewitnesses, being on the ground and having the situation well in hand, they were certainly better qualified to write truthful history of the events then occurring than historians and critics who lived centuries afterwards.

But it is frequently contended that, if the Evangelists were eyewitnesses of the leading events which they recorded, they committed them to writing so long afterwards that they had forgotten them, or had confused them with various traditions that had in the meantime grown up. There may be some little truth in this contention, but not enough to destroy the credibility of the witnesses as to events such as the Crucifixion and Resurrection of Jesus. These are not matters to be easily forgotten or confused with other things. The date of the composition and publication of the different Gospels is not known. But Professor Holtzmann, of Heidelberg (a man who cannot be said to be favorable to Christianity, since he was for several years the leader of the freethinkers in the Grand Duchy of Baden), after many years of careful study of the subject, declared that the Synoptic Gospels, the first three, were committed to writing between the years 60 and 80 of our era.[18] This was only from thirty to fifty years after the death of Jesus. Could men of average memory and intelligence who had been almost daily preaching the life and deeds of Jesus during these thirty or fifty years have forgotten them? The testimony of Principal Drummond, of Oxford, is very pertinent at this point. He says: "If we suppose that the Synoptic Gospels were written from forty to sixty years after the time of Christ, still they were based on earlier material, and even after forty years the memory of characteristic sayings may be perfectly clear.... I have not a particularly good memory, but I can recall many sayings that were uttered forty, or even fifty, years ago, and in some cases can vividly recollect the scene."[19]

If the Evangelists were eyewitnesses, which the records seem clearly to indicate, they possessed one of the strongest tests of credibility.

(3) In the third place, as to their *number* and the *consistency* of their testimony.

The credibility of a witness is greatly strengthened if his testimony is corroborated by other witnesses who testify to substantially the same thing. The greater the number of supporting witnesses, fraud and collusion being barred, the greater the credibility of the witness corroborated. But corroboration implies the presence in evidence of due and reasonable consistency between the testimony of the witness testifying and that of those corroborating. A radical discrepancy on a material point not only fails to strengthen, but tends to destroy the credibility of one or both the witnesses.

Now, the fierce fire of skeptical criticism during all the ages has been centered upon the so-called discrepancies of the Gospel narratives. It is asserted by many critics that these inconsistencies are so numerous and so palpable, that the Gospel records are worthless, even as secular histories. The authors of these writings, according to the skeptics, mutually destroy each other.

ST. MARK AND ST. PAUL (DÜRER)

In considering this phase of the credibility of the Gospel writers, it must again be remembered that the question of inspiration has no place in this discussion; and that Matthew, Mark, Luke, and John must be regarded simply as secular historians. The reader is urged to consider the biographers of the Christ as he would consider ordinary witnesses in a court of law; to apply to them the same tests of credibility; to sift and weigh their testimony in the same manner; and to subject them to the same rules of cross-examination. If this is done, it is felt that the result will be entirely favorable to the veracity and integrity of the sacred writers.

In considering the subject of discrepancies it should be constantly kept in mind that contradictions in testimony do not necessarily mean that there has been falsehood or bad faith on the part of the witnesses. Every lawyer of experience and every adult citizen of average intelligence knows that this is true. Men of unquestioned veracity and incorruptible integrity are frequently arrayed against each other in both civil and criminal trials, and the record reveals irreconcilable contradictions in their testimony. Not only do prosecutions for perjury not follow, but, in many instances, the witnesses are not even suspected of bad faith or an intention to falsify. Defects in sight, hearing, or memory; superior advantage in the matter of observation; or a sudden change in the position of one or both the parties, causing distraction of attention, at the time of the occurrence of the events involved in litigation—all or any of these conditions, as well as many others, may create discrepancies and contradictions where there is a total absence of any intention to misrepresent. A thorough appreciation of this fact will greatly aid in a clear understanding of this phase of the discussion.

Again, an investigation of the charge of discrepancy against the Gospel writers shows that the critics and skeptics have classified mere *omissions* as contradictions. Nothing could be more absurd than to consider an omission a contradiction, unless the requirements of the case show that the facts and circumstances omitted were essential to be stated, or that the omission was evidently intended to mislead or deceive. Any other contention would turn historical literature topsy-turvy and load it down with contradictions. Dion Cassius, Tacitus, and Suetonius have all written elaborately of the reign of Tiberius. Many things are mentioned by each that are not recorded by the other two. Are we to reject all three as unreliable historians because of this fact? Abbott, Hazlitt, Bourrienne, and Walter Scott have written biographies of Napoleon Bonaparte. No one of them has recited all the facts recorded by the others. Are these omissions to destroy the merits of all these writers and cause them to be suspected and rejected? Grafton's Chronicles rank high in English historical literature. They comprise the reign of King John; and yet make no mention of the granting of Magna Charta. This is as if the life of Jefferson had been written without mention of the Declaration of Independence; or a biography of Lincoln without calling attention to the Emancipation Proclamation. Notwithstanding this strange omission, Englishmen still preserve Grafton's Chronicles as valuable records among their archives. And the same spirit of generous criticism is everywhere displayed in matters of profane literature. The opponents of Christianity are never embarrassed in excusing or explaining away omissions or contradictions, provided the writer is a layman and his subject secular. But let the theme be a sacred one, and the author an ecclesiastic—preacher, priest, or prophet—and immediately incredulity rises to high tide, engulfs the reason, and destroys all dispassionate criticism. Could it be forgotten for a moment that Matthew, Mark, Luke, and John were biographers of the Christ, a sacred person, no difficulties would arise in the matter of inconsistencies, no objections would be made to their credibility. The slight discrepancies that undoubtedly exist would pass unnoticed, or be forever buried under the weight of an overwhelming conviction that they are, in the main, accurate and truthful.

But the Evangelists were guided by inspiration, the skeptics say; and discrepancies are inconsistent with the theory of inspiration. God would not have inspired them to write contradictory stories. But the assumption is false that they claimed to be guided by inspiration; for, as Marcus Dods truthfully says, "none of our Gospels pretends to be infallible or even *inspired*. Only one of them tells us how its writer obtained his information, and that was by careful inquiry at the proper sources."[20]

But whether the Gospel writers were inspired or not is immaterial so far as the purpose of this chapter is concerned. The rules of evidence testing their credibility would be the same in either case.

A more pertinent observation upon the Gospel discrepancies has not been made than that by Paley in his "Evidences of Christianity," where he says:

I know not a more rash or more unphilosophical conduct of the understanding than to reject the substance of a story by reason of some diversity in the circumstances with which it is related. The usual character of human testimony is substantial truth under circumstantial variety. This is what the daily experience of courts of justice teaches. When accounts of a transaction come from the mouths of different witnesses it is seldom that it is not possible to pick out apparent or real inconsistencies between them. These inconsistencies are studiously displayed by an adverse pleader, but oftentimes with little impression upon the minds of the judges. On the contrary, a close and minute agreement induces the suspicion of confederacy and fraud. When written histories touch upon the same scenes of action, the comparison almost always affords ground for a like reflection. Numerous, and sometimes important, variations present themselves; not seldom, also, absolute and final contradictions; yet neither one nor the other are deemed sufficient to shake the credibility of the main fact. The embassy of the Jews to deprecate the execution of Claudian's order to place his statue in their temple, Philo places in the harvest, Josephus in seed-time; both contemporary writers. No reader is led by this inconsistency to doubt whether such an embassy was sent, or whether such an order was given. Our own history supplies examples of the same kind. In the account of the Marquis of Argyll's death, in the reign of Charles II, we have very remarkable contradiction. Lord Clarendon relates that he was condemned to be hanged, which was performed the same day; on the contrary, Burnet, Woodrow, Heath, Echard, concur in stating that he was condemned upon the Saturday and executed upon a Monday. Was any reader of English history ever skeptic enough to raise from hence a question, whether the Marquis of Argyll was executed or not? Yet this ought to be left in uncertainty, according to the principles upon which the Christian history has sometimes been attacked.[21]

The reader should most carefully consider the useful as well as the damaging effect of Gospel inconsistencies in the matter of the credibility of the Evangelists. A certain class of persons have imagined the Gospel writers to be common conspirators who met together at the same time and place to devise ways and means of publishing a false report to the world. This is a silly supposition, since it is positively known that the authors of the Evangelical narratives wrote and published them at different times and places. Moreover, the style and contents of the books themselves negative the idea of a concerted purpose to deceive. And, besides, the very inconsistencies themselves show that there was no "confederacy and fraud"; since intelligent conspirators would have fabricated exactly the same story in substantially the same language.

Furthermore, a just and impartial criticism will consider not only the discrepant but also the corroborative elements in the New Testament histories. It should not be forgotten that the authors of the Gospels were independent historians who wrote at different times and places. Then, in all matters of fact in which there is a common agreement, they may be said to fully corroborate each other. And it may be contended without fear of successful contradiction that, when so considered, there will be found numerous cases of corroboration where there is one of discord or inconsistency.

The corroborative elements or features in the Evangelical narratives may be classified under three headings: (1) Instances in which certain historical events related by one of the Gospel writers are also told by one or more of the others. These are cases of ordinary corroboration. (2) Instances in which the recital of a certain fact by one of the Evangelists would be obscure or meaningless unless explained or supplemented by another. These may be regarded as examples of internal confirmation. (3) Instances in which the fact related by one Evangelist must be true from the nature of the case, regardless of what the others have said. This is the simple confirmation of logic or reason.

A few illustrations will serve to make clear this classification.

Under the first heading of "ordinary corroboration" may be mentioned the accounts of the miracle of feeding the five thousand. All the Evangelists tell us of this event, and each records the fact that the fragments taken up were *twelve baskets full.*[22]

Under the second heading of "internal confirmation" the following instances may be cited:

Matt. xxvi. 67, 68: "And others smote him with the palms of their hands, saying, Prophesy unto us, thou Christ, Who is he that smote thee?"

A caviling criticism would demand: Why ask of the Christ to *prophesy* to those in His presence? And the obscurity would be damaging, were it not for an additional sentence in Luke, who records the same circumstance. "*And when they had blindfolded him,* they struck him on the face, and asked him, saying, Prophesy, Who is it that smote thee?"[23] The fact that Jesus was blindfolded, which is told by Luke, explains the use of the word "prophesy" by Matthew, which would otherwise be absurd.

Again, Matt. xiii. 2: "And great multitudes were gathered together with him, so that he went into the ship, and sat." Here, the definite article points to a particular ship which Matthew fails to mention. But Mark comes to his aid and clearly explains the statement: "And he spake to his disciples, that a small vessel should wait upon him because of the multitude, lest they should throng him." These two passages taken together identify the ship.

Again, John vi. 5: "When Jesus lifted up his eyes, and saw a great company come to him, he saith unto Philip, Whence shall we buy bread that these may eat?" This is one of the only two places in the Gospel where Jesus addressed this Apostle. But why ask Philip instead of one of the others? Two other passages, one from John and one from Luke, furnish an explanation. In John i. 44 we read that "Philip was of Bethsaida." In Luke ix. 10 we learn that the scene of the event, the miracle of feeding the five thousand, was "a desert place belonging to the city called Bethsaida." The reason, then, for addressing Philip, instead of one of the other Apostles, is clear. Bethsaida was the home of Philip; and he would naturally, therefore, be more familiar with the location of the bread shops than the others. In John vi., where the question is asked, neither the place of the feeding nor the apostle questioned is even remotely connected with the city of Bethsaida; and in Luke the account of the miracle says nothing of Philip or the question put to him. But when the passages are connected the striking coincidence appears, and the explanation is complete.

Again, John xviii. 10: "Then Simon Peter, having a sword, drew it and smote the high priest's servant, and cut off his right ear. The servant's name was Malchus." It has been objected that there is nowhere an account of the arrest or punishment of Peter for this assault and resistance to armed authority; and that, therefore, there was no such occurrence. A passage from Luke explains the failure to arrest. "And Jesus answered and said, Suffer ye thus far, and he touched his ear and healed him."[24] The healing of the ear explains why no arrest followed; for, if charges had been made, there would have been no evidence of the gravity of the offense. Indeed, witnesses against Peter would have been completely confounded and humiliated by the result of the miracle; and might have been driven from court as malicious accusers. Then, the failure to arrest is a silent corroboration of the statement that the event occurred and that the miracle was performed.

Under the third heading, of the "confirmation of logic or reason," a single instance will suffice.

John xx. 4: "And the other disciple did outrun Peter and came first to the sepulchre." The "other disciple" was St. John, who is generally conceded to have been the youngest of the Apostles. And St. Peter, we may judge from John xxi. 18, was already past the meridian of life. What could be more natural than that the younger man should outrun the older and arrive first at the sepulcher? What better proof could be expected of the fact of the existence of that sweetness and modesty in youth which respects old age, and that endeared John to Jesus above all others, than we have here, where the younger man awaits the arrival of the older before beginning to explore the deserted tomb?

Examples similar to these might be multiplied at length, since the Gospel histories are filled with them; but those above mentioned are deemed sufficient to illustrate the theory of corroboration. The instances of internal confirmation in the New Testament narratives are especially convincing. They are arguments and proofs in the nature of undesigned coincidences which, from the very nature of the case, shut out all possibility of collusion or fraud. In most cases they are expressed in a single phrase and represent an isolated thought corroborative of some other elsewhere expressed. Though small, detached, and fragmentary, like particles of dynamite, they operate with resistless force when collected and combined.

Once more attention is called to the fact that these discrepancies negative completely the idea that the Gospel writers were conspirators, bent upon the common purpose of deceiving mankind by publishing a false history to the world. Nothing could be more absurd than to suppose that men conspiring to perpetrate a fraud, would neglect a fundamental principle underlying all successful conspiracy; that is, the creation and maintenance of a due and reasonable consistency between the words and deeds of the conspirators in formulating plans for carrying out the common purpose. Then, if there was no previous concert, the fact that four men, writing at different times and places, concurred in framing substantially the same history, is one of the strongest proofs of the credibility of the writers and the truthfulness of their narratives. And on this point the testimony of a very great writer may be quoted: that "in a number of concurrent testimonies, where there has been no previous concert, there is a probability distinct from that which may be termed the sum of the probabilities resulting from the testimonies of the witnesses; a probability which would remain, even though the witnesses were of such a character as to merit no faith at all. This probability arises from the concurrence itself. That such a concurrence should spring from chance is as one to infinite; that is, in other words, morally impossible. If, therefore, concert be excluded, there remains no cause but the reality of the fact."[25]

Apply the theory of probability, arising from concurrent testimonies, where there has been no previous concert, to the case of the Evangelists, and we are at once convinced that they were truthful and that their histories are true.

(4) Let us now consider the *conformity of the testimony of the Evangelists with human experience*. This is the fourth legal test of the credibility of witnesses prescribed by Starkie.

The conformity of testimony with experience is one of the most potent and universally applied tests of the credibility of witnesses. And it may be remarked that its application is not confined to judicial proceedings or to courts of law. It requires no professional attainments to make it effective. The blacksmith and carpenter, as well as the judge and jury, employ it in every mental operation where the statements of others are submitted to analysis and investigation. A new theory being proposed, the correctness of which is questioned, the test of experience is at once applied. If it is not in harmony with what we have seen and heard and felt, we usually reject it; or, at least, doubt it. If an explorer should return from the Arctic regions and tell us that he had seen oranges, such as we import from Florida, growing on trees near the North Pole, we would not believe him. Neither would we credit the statement of a traveler from South America that he had seen Polar bears browsing on the banks of the Amazon. These representations would be utterly inconsistent with what we know to be the essential conditions of orange culture, and with the well-known habits and climatic nature of the Polar bear. An ancient document, purporting to date from the time of Washington and the Revolution, and containing recitals about railways, telegraphs, telephones, and electric lights, would be recognized at once as spurious, because our own experience as well as facts of history would tell us that there were no such things in the days of Washington and the American Revolution. These are simple illustrations of the application of the test of experience in the mental processes of weighing and sifting the testimony of others.

Now, no serious objection to the credibility of the Gospel writers has been made under the test of the conformity of their statements with experience, except in the matter of miracles. It is generally admitted, even by skeptics, that the facts stated in the New Testament narratives might have happened in the due course of nature and in harmony with human experience, except where miracles are related.

A few skeptics have declared that a miracle is an impossibility and that the Evangelists were either deceivers or deceived when they wrote their accounts of the miraculous performances of the Christ; and that, whether deceivers or deceived, they are unworthy of belief. The great antagonist of the theory of miracles among those who assert their impossibility is Spinoza, who has thus written: "A miracle, whether contrary to or above nature, is a sheer absurdity. Nothing happens in nature which does not follow from its laws; these laws extend to all which enters the Divine mind; and, lastly, nature proceeds in a fixed and changeless course—whence it follows that the word 'miracle' can only be understood in relation to the opinions of mankind, and signifies nothing more than an event, a phenomenon, the cause of which cannot be explained by another familiar instance.... I might say, indeed, that a miracle was *that*, the cause of which cannot be explained by our *natural understanding from the known principles of natural things*."

The radical antagonism of Spinoza to the doctrine of miracles, as taught in the New Testament scriptures, was the legitimate offspring of his peculiar philosophy. He was a pantheist and identified God with nature. He did not believe in a personal God, separate from and superior to nature. He repudiated the theory of a spiritual kingdom having a spiritual sovereign to whom earth and nature are subject and obedient. Therefore, every manifestation of power which he could not identify with a natural force he believed was unreal, if not actually deceptive and fraudulent; since he could not imagine anything superior to nature that could have created the phenomenon. His denial of miracles was, then, really nothing less than a denial of the existence of a personal God who spoke the earth into being in the very beginning; and has since, with a watchful paternal eye, followed its movements and controlled its destiny.

The question of miracles is really a matter of faith and not a problem of science. It is impossible to either prove or disprove the nature of a miracle by physical demonstration. In other words, it is impossible to analyze a miracle from the standpoint of chemistry or physics. The performance of a miracle, nevertheless, may be proved by ordinary human testimony, as any other event may be proved. We may testify to the fact without being able to understand or to demonstrate the cause.

Those who believe that there are distinct spiritual as well as physical forces in the universe; that there is somewhere an omniscient and omnipotent Spiritual Being who has but to will the creation of a planet or the destruction of matter in order to accomplish the result desired, can easily believe in the exercise of miraculous power. Those who believe the Bible account of the creation, that God said in the beginning, "Let there be light: and there was light"—such persons find no difficulty in believing that Jesus converted water into wine or caused the lame to walk, if they believe that He was this same God "manifest in the flesh." A divinity who, in the morning of creation, spoke something out of nothing, would certainly not be impotent to restore life to Lazarus or sight to the blind Bartimeus.

The trouble with the philosophy of Spinoza is that his own high priestess—Nature—seems to be constantly working miracles under his own definition; and miracles, too, that very closely resemble the wonders said to have been wrought by the Christ. Milk is taken into the stomach, subjected to various processes of digestion, is then thrown into the blood and finally becomes flesh and bone. The ultimate step in this process of transformation is unknown and, perhaps, unknowable to scientists. No deeper mystery is suggested by the New Testament scriptures. The conversion of water into wine is no stranger, no more incomprehensible than the transformation of milk into flesh and bone. It may be admitted that the chemical elements are the same throughout in one process and different in the other. Nevertheless, the results of both are perfectly described by Spinoza's definition, "that a miracle was *that*, the cause of which cannot be explained by our *natural understanding from the known principles of natural things.*"

It may be truthfully remarked that nature is everywhere and at all times working wonders in harmony with and parallel to the miracles wrought by the spiritual forces of the universe. God's sovereign miracle may be described as the changing of a man, with all his sins and imperfections, into a winged spirit, thus fitting him to leave the coarse and vulgar earth for life among the stars. Nature, in her feeble way, tries to imitate the wonder by transforming the caterpillar into a butterfly, thus fitting it to leave the dunghill for life among the flowers.

Spinoza insists that miracles are impossible because "nature proceeds in a fixed and changeless course." But is this really true? Are the laws of nature invariably uniform? Does not nature seem at times tired of uniformity and resolved to rise to liberty by the creation of what we call a miracle, or more vulgarly, a "freak"? Moving in what Spinoza is pleased to call a "fixed and changeless course," nature ordinarily provides a chicken with two legs and a snake with one head. But what about chickens with three legs and snakes with two heads, such as are frequently seen? Was nature moving in a fixed and changeless course when these things were created? Could Spinoza have explained such phenomena by his "natural understanding from the known principles of natural things"? Would he have contented himself with calling them natural "accidents" or "freaks"? Nevertheless, they are miracles under his definition; and the entire subject must be discussed and debated with reference to some standard or definition of a miracle. If nature occasionally, in moments of sportiveness or digression, upsets her own laws and creates what we call "freaks," why is it unreasonable to suppose that the great God who created nature should not, at times, temporarily suspend the laws which He has made for the government of the universe, or even devote them to strange and novel purposes in the creation of those noble phenomena which we call miracles?

Other skeptics, like Renan, do not deny the possibility of miracles, but simply content themselves with asserting that there is no sufficient proof that such things ever happened. They thus repudiate the testimony of the Evangelists in this regard. "It is not," says Renan, "then, in the name of this or that philosophy, but in the name of universal experience, that we banish miracle from history. We do not say that miracles are impossible. We do say that up to this time a miracle has never been proved." Then the Breton biographer and philosopher gives us his idea of the tests that should be made in order to furnish adequate proof that a miracle has been performed. "If to-morrow," he says, "a thaumaturgus presents himself with credentials sufficiently important to be discussed and announces himself as able, say, to raise the dead, what would be done? A commission composed of physiologists, physicists, chemists, persons accustomed to historical criticism would be named. This commission would choose a corpse, would assure itself that the death was real, would select a room in which the experiment should be made, would arrange the whole system of precautions, so as to leave no chance of doubt. If, under such conditions, the resurrection were effected, a probability almost equal to certainty would be established. As, however, it ought to be possible always to repeat an experiment—to do over again that which has been done once; and as, in the order of miracle, there can be no question of ease or difficulty, the thaumaturgus would be invited to reproduce his marvelous act under other circumstances, upon other corpses, in another place. If the miracle should succeed each time, two things would be proved: first, that supernatural events happen in the world; second, that the power of producing them belongs or is delegated in certain persons. But who does not see that no miracle ever took place under these conditions? But that always hitherto the thaumaturgus has chosen the subject of the experiment, chosen the spot, chosen the public?"[26]

This is an extract from the celebrated "Life of Jesus" by Renan, and is intended to demolish the Gospel account of the miracles of the Christ. It is not too much to say that the great skeptic has failed to exhibit his usual fairness in argument. He has indirectly compared Jesus to a thaumaturgus, and has inferentially stated that in the performance of His miracles He "chose the subject of his experiment, chose the spot, chose the public." Every student of New Testament history knows that this is not true of the facts and circumstances surrounding the performance of miracles by Christ. It is true that vulgar curiosity and caviling incredulity were not gratified by the presence of specially summoned "physiologists, physicists, and chemists." But it is equally true that such persons were not prevented from being present; that there was no attempt at secrecy or concealment; and that no subject of experiment, particular spot, or special audience was ever chosen. The New Testament miracles were wrought, as a general thing, under the open sky, in the street, by the wayside, on the mountain slope, and in the presence of many people, both friends and enemies of Jesus. There was no searching or advertising for subjects for experiment. Far from choosing the subject, the spot, and the public, Jesus exercised His miraculous powers upon those who came voluntarily to Him suffering with some dreadful malady and asking to be cured. In some instances, the case of affliction was of long standing and well known to the community. The healing was done publicly and witnessed by many people.

Renan suggests that the thaumaturgus mentioned in his illustration would be required to repeat his performance in the matter of raising the dead before he would be fully believed. This reminds us that Jesus wrought many miracles. More than forty are recorded in the Gospel narratives; and in the closing verse of St. John, there is a strong intimation that He performed many that were never recorded. These, it is respectfully submitted, were amply sufficient to demonstrate His miraculous powers.

Whatever form infidelity may assume in its antagonism to the doctrine of miracles, it will be found that the central idea is that such things are not founded in experience; and that this test of credibility fails in the case of the Gospel writers, because they knowingly recorded impossible events. It would be idle to attempt to depreciate the value of this particular test; but it must be observed that nothing is more fallacious, unless properly defined and limited. It must be remembered that the experience of one man, nation, or generation is not necessarily that of another man, nation, or generation. The exact mechanical processes employed by the Egyptians in raising the pyramids are as much a mystery to modern scientists as a Marconigram would be to a savage of New Guinea. The Orient and the Occident present to each other almost miraculous forms of diversity in manners, habits, and customs, in modes of thought and life. "The Frenchman says, 'I am the best dyer in Europe: nobody can equal me, and nobody can surpass Lyons.' Yet in Cashmere, where the girls make shawls worth $30,000, they will show him three hundred distinct colors, which he not only cannot make, but cannot even distinguish." Sir Walter Scott, in his "Tales of the Crusaders," thrillingly describes a meeting between the Turkish Saladin and the English Richard Cœur-de-Lion. Saladin asked Richard to give him an exhibition of his marvelous strength. The Norman monarch picked up an iron bar from the floor of the tent and severed it. The Mahometan crusader was amazed. Richard then asked him what he could do. Saladin replied that he could not pull iron apart like that, but that he could do something equally as wonderful. Thereupon, he took an eider-down pillow from the sofa, and drew his keen, Damascus-tempered blade across it, which caused it to fall into two pieces. Richard cried in astonishment: "This is the black art; it is magic; it is the devil: you cannot cut that which has no resistance!" Here Occidental strength and Oriental magic met and wrought seeming miracles in the presence of each other. In his great lecture on "The Lost Arts," Wendell Phillips says that one George Thompson told him that he saw a man in Calcutta throw a handful of floss silk into the air, and that a Hindoo severed it into pieces with his saber. A Western swordsman could not do this.

Objectors to miracles frequently ask why they are not performed to-day, why we never see them. To which reply may be made that, under Spinoza's definition, miracles are being wrought every day not only by nature, but by man. Why call Edison "the magician" and "the wizard," unless the public believes this? But is it any argument against the miracles of Jesus that similar ones are not seen to-day? Have things not 49been done in the past that will never be repeated? We have referred to the pyramids of Egypt and to the lost art involved in their construction. A further illustration may be found in the origin of man. One of two theories is undoubtedly true: that the first man and woman came into the world without being born; or that man and woman are the products of evolution from lower orders of animals. No other theories have ever been advanced as to the origin of the human race. Now, it is certain that modern generations have never experienced either of these things, for all the human beings of to-day were undoubtedly born of other human beings, and it is certain that the process of evolution stopped long ago, since men and women were as perfect physically and mentally four thousand years ago as they are to-day. In other words, the processes which originated man are things of the past, since we have no Garden of Eden experiences to-day, nor is there any universal metamorphosis of monkeys going on. Therefore, to argue that the miracles of Jesus did not happen, because we do not see such things to-day, is to deny the undoubted occurrences of history and developments of human life, because such occurrences and developments are no longer familiar to us and our generation.

To denounce everything as false that we have not individually seen, heard, and felt, would be to limit most painfully the range of the mental vision. The intellectual horizon would not be greatly extended should we join with our own the experience of others that we have seen and known. Much information is reported by telegraphic despatch and many things are told us by travelers that we should accept as true; although such matters may have no relation to what we have ever seen or heard. Else, we should be as foolish as the king of Siam who rejected the story of the Dutch ambassador, that in Holland water was frequently frozen into a solid mass. In the warm climate of the East Indian tropics the king had never seen water so congealed and, therefore, he refused to believe that such a thing had ever happened anywhere.

Experience is a most logical and reasonable test if it is sufficiently extended to touch all the material phases of the subject under investigation. It is a most dangerous one if we insist upon judging the material and spiritual universe, with its infinite variety of forms and changes, by the limited experience of a simple and isolated life, or by the particular standards of any one age or race. A progressive civilization, under such an application of the test, would be impossible, since each generation of men would have to begin *de novo*, and be restricted to the results of its own experience. The enforcement of such a doctrine would prevent, furthermore, the acceptance of the truths of nature discovered by inventive genius or developed by physical or chemical research, until such truths had become matters of universal experience. Every man would then be in the position of the incredulous citizen who, having been told that a message had been sent by wire from Baltimore to Washington announcing the nomination of James K. Polk for the presidency, refused to believe in telegraphic messages until he could be at both ends of the line at once. The art of telegraphy was a reality, nevertheless, in spite of his incredulity and inexperience. The American savages who first beheld the ships of Columbus are said to have regarded them as huge birds from heaven and to have refused to believe that they were boats, because, in their experience, they had never seen such immense canoes with wings. Herodotus tells us of some daring sailors who crept along the coast of Africa beyond the limits usually visited at that time. They came back home with a wonderful account of their trip and told the story that they had actually reached a country where their shadows fell toward the south at midday. They were not believed, and their report was rejected with scorn and incredulity by the inhabitants of the Mediterranean coasts, because their only experience was that a man's shadow always pointed toward the north; and they did not believe it possible that shadows could be cast otherwise. But the report of the sailors was true, nevertheless.[27]

These simple illustrations teach us that beings other than ourselves have had experiences which are not only different from any that we have ever had, but are also either temporarily or permanently beyond our comprehension. And the moral of this truth, when applied to the statements of the Evangelists regarding miracles, is that the fortunate subjects and witnesses of the miraculous powers of Jesus might have had experiences which we have never had and that we cannot now clearly comprehend.

(5) In the fifth and last place, as to the *coincidence of their testimony with collateral circumstances.*

This is the chief test of credibility in all those cases where the witness, whose testimony has been reduced to writing, is dead, absent, or insane. Under such circumstances it is impossible to apply what may be termed personal tests on cross-examination; that is, to develop the impeaching or corroborating features of bias, prejudice, and personal demeanor to the same extent as when the witness is still living and testifies orally. When a written narrative is all that we have, its reliability can only be ascertained by a close inspection of its parts, comparing them with each other, and then with collateral and contemporaneous facts and circumstances. The value of this test cannot be over-estimated, and Greenleaf has stated very fully and concisely the basis upon which it rests. "Every event," he says, "which actually transpires, has its appropriate relation and place in the vast complication of circumstances of which the affairs of men consist; it owes its origin to the events which have preceded it, is intimately connected with all others which occur at the same time and place, and often with those of remote regions, and in its turn gives birth to numberless others which succeed. In all this almost inconceivable contexture and seeming discord, there is perfect harmony; and while the fact which really happened tallies exactly with every other contemporaneous incident related to it in the remotest degree, it is not possible for the wit of man to invent a story, which, if closely compared with the actual occurrences of the same time and place, may not be shown to be false."[28]

ST. JOHN AND ST. PETER (DÜRER)

This principle offers a wide field to the skill of the cross-examiner, and enables him frequently to elicit truth or establish falsehood when all other tests have failed. It is a principle also perfectly well known to the perjurer and to the suborner of witnesses. Multiplicity of details is studiously avoided by the false witness, who dreads particularity and feels that safety lies in confining his testimony as nearly as possible to a single fact, whose attendant facts and circumstances are few and simple. When the witness is too ignorant to understand the principle and appreciate the danger, his attorney, if he consents to dishonor his profession and pollute the waters of justice with corrupt testimony, may be depended upon to administer proper warning. The witness will be told to know as few things and to remember as little as possible concerning matters about which he has not been previously instructed. The result will be that his testimony, especially in matters in which he is compelled by the court to testify, will be hesitating, restrained, unequal, and unnatural. He will be served at every turn by a most convenient memory which will enable him to forget many important and to remember many unimportant facts and circumstances. He will betray a painful hesitancy in the matter of committing himself upon any particular point upon which he has not been already drilled. The truthful witness, on the other hand, is usually candid, ingenuous, and copious in his statements. He shows a willingness to answer all questions, even those involving the minutest details, and seems totally indifferent to the question of verification or contradiction. The texture of his testimony is, therefore, equal, natural, and unrestrained.

Now these latter characteristics mark every page of the New Testament histories. The Gospel writers wrote with the utmost freedom, and recorded in detail and with the utmost particularity, the manners, customs, habits, and historic facts contemporaneous with their lives. The naturalness and ingenuousness of their writings are simply marvelous. There is nowhere any evidence of an attempt to conceal, patch up, or reconcile. No introductory exclamations or subsequent explanations which usually characterize false testimony appear anywhere in their writings. They were seemingly absolutely indifferent to whether they were believed or not. Their narratives seem to say: These are records of truth; and if the world rejects them it rejects the facts of history. Such candor and assurance are always overwhelmingly impressive; and in every forum of debate are regarded as unmistakable signs of truth.

The Evangelists, it must be assumed, were fully aware of the danger of too great particularity in the matter of false testimony, and would have hesitated to commit themselves on so many points if their statements had been untrue. We have already noted the opinion of Professor Holtzmann, of Heidelberg, that the Synoptic Gospels were committed to writing between the years 60 and 80 of our era. At that time it is certain that there were still living many persons who were familiar with the events in the life and teachings of the Savior, as well as with the numerous other facts and circumstances related by the sacred writers. St. Paul, in I Cor. xv. 6, speaks of five hundred brethren to whom the risen Jesus appeared at one time; and he adds, "*of whom the greater part remain unto this present, but some are fallen asleep.*" And it must be remembered that this particular group of two hundred and fifty or more were certainly not the only persons then living who had a distinct remembrance of the Master, His teachings, and His miracles. Many who had been healed by Him, children who had sat upon His knee and been blessed by Him, and many members of the Pharisaic party and of the Sadducean aristocracy who had persecuted Him and had then slain Him, were doubtless still living and had a lively recollection of the events of the ministry of the Nazarene. Such persons were in a position to disprove from their personal knowledge false statements made by the Evangelists. A consciousness of this fact would have been, within itself, a strong inducement to tell the truth.

But not only are the Gospels not contradicted by contemporaneous writers; they are also not impeached or disproved by later scientific research and historical investigation. And at this point we come to make a direct application of the test of the coincidence of their testimony with collateral and contemporaneous history. For this purpose, as a matter of illustration, only facts in profane history corroborative of the circumstances attending the trial and crucifixion of the Master will be cited.

In the first place, the Evangelists tell us that Pontius Pilate sat in judgment on the Christ. Both Josephus and Tacitus tell us that Pilate was governor of Judea at that time.[29]

In John xviii. 31 we read: "Then said Pilate unto them, Take ye him, and judge him according to your law. The Jews therefore said unto him, *It is not lawful for us to put any man to death.*" From many profane historians, ancient and modern, we learn that the power of life and death had been taken from the Jews and vested in the Roman governor.[30]

In John xix. 16, 17 occurs this passage: "And they took Jesus, and led him away; and he, *bearing his cross,* went forth." This corroborative sentence is found in Plutarch: "Every kind of wickedness produces its own particular torment; just as every malefactor, when he is brought forth to execution, *carries his own cross.*"[31]

In Matthew xxvii. 26 we read: "When he had scourged Jesus, he delivered him to be crucified." That scourging was a preliminary to crucifixion among the Romans is attested by many ancient writers, among whom may be mentioned Josephus and Livy. The following passages are taken from Josephus:

Whom, having *first scourged with whips,* he crucified.[32]

Being *beaten,* they were crucified opposite to the citadel.[33]

He was burned alive, *having been first beaten.*[34]

From Livy, a single sentence will suffice:

All were led out, *beaten with rods,* and beheaded.[35]

In John xix. 19, 20 we read: "And Pilate wrote a title and put it on the cross; and it was written in Hebrew, and Greek, and Latin." That it was a custom among the Romans to affix the accusation against the criminal to the instrument of his punishment appears from several ancient writers, among them Suetonius and Dion Cassius. In Suetonius occurs this sentence: "He exposed the father of the family to the dogs, with this *title,* 'A gladiator, impious in speech.'"[36] And in Dion Cassius occurs the following: "Having led him through the midst of the court or assembly, *with a writing signifying the cause of his death, and afterwards crucifying him.*"[37]

And finally, we read in John xix. 32: "Then came the soldiers and *brake the legs* of the first, and of the other which was crucified with him." By an edict of Constantine, the punishment of crucifixion was abolished. Speaking in commendation of this edict, a celebrated heathen writer mentions the circumstances of *breaking the legs*. "He was pious to such a degree," says this writer, "that he was the first to set aside that very ancient punishment, the cross, with the *breaking of legs*."[38]

If we leave the narrow circle of facts attendant upon the trial and crucifixion of Jesus with its corroborative features of contemporary history, and consider the Gospel narratives as a whole, we shall find that they are confirmed and corroborated by the facts and teachings of universal history and experience. An examination of these narratives will also reveal a divine element in them which furnishes conclusive proof of their truthfulness and reliability. A discussion of the divine or spiritual element in the Gospel histories would be foreign to the purpose of this treatise. The closing pages of Part I will be devoted to a consideration of the human element in the New Testament narratives. This will be nothing more than an elaboration of the fifth legal test of credibility mentioned by Starkie.

By the human or historical element of credibility in the Gospel histories is meant that likeness or resemblance in matters of representation of fact to other matters of representation of fact which we find recorded in secular histories of standard authority whose statements we are accustomed to accept as true. The relations of historic facts to each other, and the connections and coincidences of things known or believed to be true with still others sought to be proved, form a fundamental ground of belief, and are, therefore, reliable modes of proof. The most casual perusal of the New Testament narratives suggests certain striking resemblances between the events therein narrated and well-known historical occurrences related by secular historians whose statements are implicitly believed. Let us draw a few parallels and call attention to a few of these resemblances.

Describing the anguish of the Savior in the Garden, St. Luke says: "And being in an agony, He prayed more earnestly: And his sweat was as it were great drops of blood falling down to the ground."[39]

This strange phenomenon of the "bloody sweat" has been of such rare occurrence in the history of the world that its happening in Gethsemane has been frequently denied. The account of it has been ascribed to the overwrought imagination of the third Evangelist in recording the errors of tradition. And yet similar cases are well authenticated in the works of secular writers. Tissot reports a case of "a sailor who was so alarmed by a storm, that through fear he fell down, and his face sweated blood which, during the whole continuance of the storm, returned like ordinary sweat, as fast as it was wiped away."[40] Schenck cites the case of "a nun who fell into the hands of soldiers; and, on seeing herself encompassed with swords and daggers threatening instant death, was so terrified and agitated that she discharged blood from every part of her body, and died of hemorrhage in the sight of her assailants."[41] Writing of the death of Charles IX of France, Voltaire says: "The disease which carried him off is very uncommon; his blood flowed from all his pores. This malady, of which there are some examples, is the result either of excessive fear, furious passion, or of a violent and melancholic temperament."[42] The same event is thus graphically described by the old French historian, De Mezeray: "After the vigor of his youth and the energy of his courage had long struggled against his disease, he was at length reduced by it to his bed at the castle of Vincennes, about the 8th of May, 1574. During the last two weeks of his life his constitution made strange efforts. He was affected with spasms and convulsions of extreme violence. He tossed and agitated himself continually and his blood gushed from all the outlets of his body, even from the pores of his skin, so that on one occasion he was found bathed in a bloody sweat."[43]

If the sailor, the nun, and the king of France were afflicted with the "bloody sweat," why should it seem incredible that the man Jesus, the carpenter of Nazareth, should have been similarly afflicted? If Tissot, Schenck, and Voltaire are to be believed, why should we refuse to believe St. Luke? If St. Luke told the truth in this regard, why should we doubt his statements concerning other matters relating to the life, death, and resurrection of the Son of God? Does not Voltaire, the most brilliant and powerful skeptic that ever lived, corroborate in this particular the biographer of the Christ?

Let us pass to another instance of resemblance and corroboration. While describing the crucifixion, St. John wrote the following: "But one of the soldiers with a spear pierced his side, and forthwith came there out *blood and water*."[44] Early skeptical criticism denied the account of the flowing of blood and water from the side of the Savior because, in the first place, the other Evangelists did not mention the circumstance; and, in the second place, it was an unscientific fact stated. But modern medical science has very cleverly demonstrated that Jesus, according to the Gospel accounts, died of rupture of the heart. About the middle of the last century, a celebrated English physician and surgeon, Dr. Stroud, wrote a treatise entitled, "Physical Cause of the Death of Christ." In this book, he proved very clearly that cardiac rupture was the immediate cause of the death of Jesus on the cross. Many arguments were adduced to establish this fact. Among others, it was urged that the shortness of time during which the sufferer remained upon the cross and His loud cry just before "He gave up the ghost," tended to prove that a broken heart was the cause of the death of the Man of Sorrows. But the strongest proof, according to the author of this work, was the fact that blood and water flowed from the dead man when a spear was thrust into His side. This, says Dr. Stroud, has happened frequently when the heart was suddenly and violently perforated after death from cardiac rupture. Within a few hours after death from this cause, he says, the blood frequently separates into its constituent parts or essential elements: *crassamentum*, a soft clotted substance of deep-red color, and *serum*, a pale, watery liquid—popularly called blood and water, which will flow out separately, if the pericardium and heart be violently torn or punctured. In this treatise numerous medical authorities are cited and the finished work is indorsed by several of the most famous physicians and surgeons of England.

It is very probable that St. John did not know the physical cause of the strange flow of blood and water from the side of Jesus. It seems that he was afraid that he would not be believed; for, in the following verse, he was careful to tell the world that he himself had personally seen it. "And he that *saw it* bare record, and his record is true: And he knoweth that he saith true that ye might believe."[45]

Here again modern medical science has corroborated, in the matter of the flowing of blood and water from the side of Jesus, the simple narrative of the gentle and loving Evangelist.

Still another illustration of resemblance, coincidence, and corroboration is furnished by the incident of the arrest of Jesus in the Garden. St. John says: "As soon, then, as he had said unto them, I am he, they went backward and fell to the ground."[46]

This is only one of several cases mentioned in history where ordinary men have been dazed and paralyzed in the presence of illustrious men against whom they were designing evil. When a Gallic trooper was sent by Sulla to Minturnæ to put Marius to death, the old Roman lion, his great eyes flashing fire, arose and advanced toward the slave, who fled in utter terror from the place, exclaiming, "I cannot kill Caius Marius!"[47]

Again, we learn from St. Matthew that at the moment of the arrest in the Garden, "all the disciples forsook him and fled."

This is no isolated case of cowardice and desertion. It is merely an illustration of a universal truth: that the multitude will follow blindly and adore insanely the hero or prophet in his hour of triumph and coronation, but will desert and destroy him at the moment of his humiliation and crucifixion.

Note the burning of Savonarola. The patriot-priest of the Florentine Republic believed himself inspired of God; his heroic life and martyr death seemed to justify his claim. From the pulpit of St. Mark's he became the herald and evangel of the Reformation, and his devoted followers hung upon his words as if inspiration clothed them with messages from the skies. And yet when a wicked Inquisition had nailed him to the cross and fagots were flaming about him, this same multitude who adored him, now reviled him and jeered and mocked his martyrdom.

Note the career of Napoleon. When the sun of Austerlitz rose upon the world the whole French nation grew delirious with love and homage for their emperor, who was once a subaltern of Corsica. But when the Allies entered Paris after the battle of Leipsic, this same French nation repudiated their imperial idol, cast down his images, canceled his decrees, and united with all Europe in demanding his eternal banishment from France. The voyage to Elba followed. But the historic melodrama of popular fidelity and fickleness was not yet completely played. When this same Napoleon, a few months later, escaped from his islet prison in the Mediterranean and landed on the shores of France, this same French nation again grew delirious, welcomed the royal exile with open arms, showered him with his eagles, and almost smothered him with kisses. A hundred days passed. On the frightful field of Waterloo, "Chance and Fate combined to wreck the fortunes of their former king." Again the fickle French multitude heaped execrations upon their fallen monarch, declared the Napoleonic dynasty at an end and welcomed with acclamations of joy the return of the exiled Bourbon Louis XVIII.

And when the Evangelist wrote these words: "All the disciples forsook him and fled," he simply gave expression to a form of truth which all history reflects and corroborates.

Again, the parallels and resemblances of sacred and profane history do not seem to stop with mere narratives of facts. Secular history seems to have produced at times characters in the exact likeness of those in sacred history. The resemblance is often so striking as to create astonishment. For instance, who was St. Peter but Marshal Ney by anticipation? Peter was the leader of the Apostolic Twelve; Ney was the chief of the Twelve Marshals of Napoleon. Peter was impulsive and impetuous; so was Ney. Peter was the first to speak and act in all the emergencies of the Apostolic ministry; Ney, so Dumas tells us, was always impatient to open the battle and lead the first charge. Peter was probably the last to leave the garden in which the great tragedy of his Master had begun; Ney was the last to leave the horrors of a Russian winter in which the beginning of the end of the career of his monarch was plainly seen. Peter denied Jesus; Ney repudiated Napoleon, and even offered to bring him, at the time of his escape from Elba, in a cage to Louis XVIII. Peter was afterwards crucified for his devotion to Jesus whom he had denied; Ney was afterwards shot for loyalty to Napoleon whom he had once repudiated.

The examples heretofore given involve the idea of comparison and are based upon resemblance. These illustrations could be greatly extended, but it is believed that enough has been said in this connection. However, in closing this brief discussion of the human element in the sacred writings as evidenced by the coincidences and resemblances of their narratives to those of profane history, slight mention may be made of another test of truth which may be applied to the histories of the Evangelists. This test is not derived from a comparison which is focused upon any particular group of historic facts. It springs from an instantaneously recognized and inseparable connection between the statements made by the Gospel writers and the experience of the human race. A single illustration will suffice to elucidate this point. When Jesus was nailed upon the cross, the sad and pathetic spectacle was presented of the absence of the Apostolic band, with the exception of St. John, who was the only Apostle present at the crucifixion. The male members of the following of the Nazarene did not sustain and soothe their Master in the supreme moment of His anguish. But the women of His company were with Him to the end. Mary, his mother, Mary Magdalene, Mary, the wife of Cleophas, Salome, the mother of St. John the Evangelist, and others, doubtless among "the women that followed him from Galilee," ministered to His sufferings and consoled Him with their presence. They were the last to cling to His cross and the first to greet Him on the morning of the third day; for when the resurrection morn dawned upon the world, these same women were seen hastening toward the sepulcher bearing spices—fragrant offerings of deathless love. What a contrast between the loyalty and devotion of the women and the fickle, faltering adherence of the men who attended the footsteps of the Man of Sorrows in His last days! One of His Apostles denied Him, another betrayed Him, and all, excepting one, deserted Him in His death struggle. His countrymen crucified Him ignominiously. But "not one woman mentioned in the New Testament ever lifted her voice against the Son of God."

This revelation from the sacred pages of the devotion of woman is reflected in universal history and experience. It is needless to give examples. Suffice it to say that when Matthew, Mark, Luke, and John tell us of this devotion, we simply answer: yes, this has been ever true in all countries and in every age. We have learned it not only from history but from our own experience in all the affairs of life, extending from the cradle to the grave. The night of sorrow never grows so dark that a mother's love will not irradiate the gloom. The criminal guilt of a wayward son can never become so black that her arms will not be found about him. If we pass from loving loyalty to the individual, to patriotic devotion to the causes of the nations, woman's fidelity is still undying. The women of France are said to have paid the German war debt. The message of the Spartan mother to her soldier son is too well known to be repeated. When the legions of Scipio engirdled the walls of Carthage and desperation seized the inhabitants of the Punic city, Carthaginian women cut their long black hair to furnish bowstrings to the Carthaginian archers. Illustrations might be multiplied; but these will suffice to show that Mary and Martha and Salome, the women of the Gospels, are simply types of the consecrated women of the world.

When we come to summarize, we are led to declare that if the Gospel historians be not worthy of belief we are without foundation for rational faith in the secular annals of the human race. No other literature bears historic scrutiny so well as the New Testament biographies. Not by a single chain, but by three great chains can we link our Bible of to-day with the Apostolic Bible. The great manuscripts: the Vatican, the Alexandrian, and the Sinaitic, dating from the middle of the fourth and fifth centuries, must have been copies of originals, or at least of first copies. The Bible is complete in these manuscripts to-day.

The Versions, translations of the original Scriptures from the language in which they were first written into other languages, form a perfect connection between the days of the Apostles and our own. The Vulgate, the celebrated Latin version of St. Jerome, was completed A.D. 385. In making this translation the great scholar has himself said that he used "ancient (Greek) copies." Manuscripts that were ancient, A.D. 385, must have been the original writings, or, at least, first copies. The Vulgate, then, is alone a perfect historic connection between the Bible that we read to-day and that studied by the first Christians.

Again, the Writings of the Church Fathers furnish a chain, without a single missing link, between the Bible of this generation and that of the first generation of the followers of the Christ. It has been truthfully said that if all the Bibles in the world were destroyed an almost perfect Bible could be reconstructed from quotations from these writings, so numerous and so exact are they. Beginning with Barnabas and Clement, companions of St. Paul, and coming down through the ages, there is not a single generation in which some prince or potentate of the Church has not left convincing evidence in writing that the Books of the Old and New Testament which we read to-day are identical with those read by the first propagators of our faith. The chain of proof forged from the Writings of the early Fathers is made up of a hundred links, each perfect within itself and yet relinked and welded with a hundred others that make each and all doubly strong. If these various testimonies, the Manuscripts, the Versions, and the Writings of the Church Fathers, be taken, not singly, but collectively, in support and corroboration of each other, we have, then, not merely a chain but rather a huge spiritual cable of many wires, stretching across the great sea of time and linking our Bible of to-day inseparably with that of the Apostolic Age.

If it be objected that these various writings might have been and probably were corrupted in coming down to us through the centuries, reply may be made that the facts of history repel such suggestions. As Mr. Greenleaf has suggested, the jealousy of opposing sects preserved them from forgery and mutilation. Besides these sects, it may be added, there were, even in the earliest times, open and avowed infidels who assaulted the cardinal tenets of the Christian faith and made the Gospel histories the targets for their attacks. They, too, would have detected and denounced any attempt from any source to corrupt these writings.

Another and final, and probably the most cogent reason for the remarkable preservation of the books of the Bible, is the reverential care bestowed upon them by their custodians in every age. It is difficult for the modern world to fully appreciate the meaning and extent of this reverence and care. Before the age of printing, it must be remembered, the masses of the people could not and did not possess Bibles. In the Middle Ages it required a small fortune to own a single copy. The extreme scarcity enhanced not only the commercial value but added to the awful sanctity that attached to the precious volume; on the principle that the person of a king becomes more sacred and mysterious when least seen in public. Synagogues and monasteries were, for many centuries, the sole repositories of the Holy Books, and the deliberate mutilation of any portion of the Bible would have been regarded like the blaspheming of the Deity or the desecration of a shrine. These considerations alone are sufficient reason why the Holy Scriptures have come down to us uncorrupted and unimpaired.

These various considerations are the logical basis of that rule of law laid down by Mr. Greenleaf, under which the Gospel histories would be admitted into a modern court of law in a modern judicial proceeding.

Under legal tests laid down by Starkie, we have seen that the Evangelists should be believed, because: (1) They were honest and sincere, that is, they believed that they were telling the truth; (2) they were undoubtedly men of good intelligence and were eyewitnesses of the facts narrated by them in the New Testament histories; (3) they were independent historians, who wrote at different times and places and, in all essential details, fully corroborate each other; (4) excepting in the matter of miracles, which skepticism has never been able to fully disprove, their testimony is in full conformity with human experience; (5) their testimony coincides fully and accurately with all the collateral, social, historical, and religious circumstances of their time, as well as with the teachings and experience of universal history in every age.

Having received from antiquity an uncorrupted message, born of truth, we have, it is believed, a perfect record of fact with which to discuss the trial of Jesus.

PART II
HEBREW CRIMINAL LAW

MOSES AND THE LAW (MICHAEL ANGELO)

CHAPTER I

HEBREW CRIMINAL LAW—MOSAIC AND TALMUDIC

THE Pentateuch and the Talmud form the double basis of Hebrew jurisprudence. "The wisdom of the lawgiver," says Bacon, "consists not only in a platform of justice, but in the application thereof." The Mosaic Code, embodied in the Pentateuch, furnished to the children of Israel the necessary platform of justice; ancient tradition and Rabbinic interpretation contained in the Talmud, supplied needed rules of practical application. Employing classic terminology, it may be said that the ordinances of Moses were the substantive and the provisions of the Talmud were the adjective laws of the ancient Hebrews. These terms are not strictly accurate, however, since many absolute rights are declared and defined in the Talmud as well as in the Pentateuch. Another definition, following the classification of Roman legists, describes Mosaic injunction as the *lex scripta* and Talmudic provision as the *lex non scripta* of the Commonwealth of Israel. In other words, the Pentateuch was the foundation, the cornerstone; the Talmud was the superstructure, the gilded dome of the great temple of Hebrew justice.

Bible students throughout the world are familiar with the provisions of the Mosaic Code; but the contents of the Talmud are known to few, even among scholars and literary men. The most appalling ignorance has existed in every age among the Gentile uninitiated as to the nature and identity of this gigantic literary compilation. Henricus Segnensis, a pious monk of the Middle Ages, having heard and read many things about the despised heretical Talmud, conceived it to be a person and, in a transport of religious frenzy, declared that he would sooner or later have *him, the Talmud,* put to death by the hangman![48]

For the benefit of the average reader as well as to illuminate the general subject, a short description of the Talmud will be given.

Definition.—Many attempts have been made to define the Talmud, but all definition of this monumental literary production is necessarily inaccurate and incomplete because of the vastness and peculiarity of the matter treated. To describe it as an encyclopedia of the life and literature, law and religion, art and science of the Hebrew people during a thousand years would convey only an approximately correct idea of its true meaning, for it is even more than the foregoing descriptive terms would indicate. Emanuel Deutsch in his brilliant essay on the Talmud defines it as "a Corpus Juris, an encyclopedia of law, civil and penal, ecclesiastical and international, human and divine. It is a microcosm, embracing, even as does the Bible, heaven and earth. It is as if all the prose and poetry, the science, the faith and speculation of the Old World were, though only in faint reflections, bound up in it *in nuce.*"

Benny describes it as "the Talmud—that much maligned and even more misunderstood compilation of the rabbins; that digest of what Carlyle would term *allerlei-wissenschaften*; which is at once the compendium of their literature, the storehouse of their tradition, the exponent of their faith, the record of their acquirements, the handbook of their ceremonials and the summary of their legal code, civil and penal."

To speak of the Talmud as a book would be inaccurate. It is a small library, or collection of books. "Modern editions of the Talmud, including the most important commentaries, consist of about 3,000 folio sheets, or 12,000 folio pages of closely printed matter, generally divided into twelve or twenty volumes. One page of Talmudic Hebrew intelligibly translated into English would cover three pages; the translation of the whole Talmud with its commentaries would accordingly make a library of 400 volumes, each numbering 360 octavo pages."[49]

It would be well to bear in mind that the contents of the Talmud were not proclaimed to the world by any executive, legislative, or judicial body; that they were not the result of any resolution or mandate of any congregation, college, or Sanhedrin; that they were not, in any case, formal or statutory. They were simply a great mass of traditionary matter and commentary transmitted orally through many centuries before being finally reduced to writing. Rabbinism claims for these traditions a remote antiquity, declaring them to be coeval with the proclamation of the Decalogue. Many learned doctors among the Jews ascribe this antiquity to the whole mass of traditional laws. Others maintain that only the principles upon which Rabbinic interpretation and discussion are based, can be traced back so far. But it is certain that distinct traditions are to be found at a very early period in the history of the children of Israel, and that on their return from Babylonian captivity these traditions were delivered to them by Ezra and his coadjutors of the Great Assembly.

This development of Hebrew jurisprudence along lines of written and oral law, Pentateuch and Talmud, Mosaic ordinance and time-honored tradition, seems to have followed in obedience to a general principle of juristic growth. *Lex scripta* and *lex non scripta* are classical Roman terms of universal application in systems of enlightened jurisprudence. A charter, a parchment, a marble column, a table of stone, a sacred book, containing written maxims defining legal rights and wrongs are the beginnings of all civilized schemes of justice. Around these written, fundamental laws grow and cluster the race traditions of a people which attach themselves to and become inseparable from the prime organic structure. These oral traditions are the natural and necessary products of a nation's growth and progress. The laws of the Medes and Persians, at once unalterable and irrevocable, represent a strange and painful anomaly in the jurisprudence of mankind. No written constitution, incapable of amendment and subject to strict construction, can long survive the growth and expansion of a great and progressive people. The ever-changing, perpetually evolving forms of social, commercial, political, and religious life of a restless, marching, ambitious race, necessitate corresponding changes and evolutions in laws and constitutions. These necessary legal supplements are as varied in origin as are the nations that produce them. Magna Charta, wrung from John at Runnymede, became the written basis of English law and freedom, and around it grew up those customs and traditions that—born on the shores of the German Ocean, transplanted to the Isles of Britain, nurtured and developed through a thousand years of judicial interpretation and application—became the great basic structure of the Common Law of England.

What the Mosaic Code was to the ancient Hebrews, what Magna Charta is to Englishmen, the Koran is to Mahometans: the written charter of their faith and law. Surrounding the Koran are many volumes of tradition, made up of the sayings of Mahomet, which are regarded as equally sacred and authoritative as the Koran itself. These volumes of Mahometan tradition are called the Sonna and correspond to the Talmud of the Hebrews. An analysis of any great system of jurisprudence will reveal the same natural arrangement of written and oral law as that represented by the Pentateuch and the Talmud of the Jews.

The word "Talmud" has various meanings, as it appears in Hebrew traditional literature. It is an old scholastic term, and "is a noun formed from the verb 'limmed'='to teach.' It therefore means, primarily, 'teaching,' although it denotes also 'learning'; it is employed in this latter sense with special reference to the Torah, the terms 'Talmud' and 'Torah' being usually combined to indicate the study of the Law, both in its wider and its more restricted sense."[50] It is thus frequently used in the sense of the word "exegesis," meaning Biblical exposition or interpretation. But with the etymological and restricted, we are not so much interested as with the popular and general signification of the term "Talmud." Popularly used, it means simply a small collection of books represented by two distinct editions handed down to posterity by the Palestinian and Babylonian schools during the early centuries of the Christian era.

Divisions of the Talmud.—The Talmud is divided into two component parts: the Mishna, which may be described as the *text*; and the Gemara, which may be termed the *commentary*.[51] The Mishna, meaning tradition, is almost wholly law. It was, indeed, of old, translated as the Second or Oral Law— the δευτέρωσις—to distinguish it from the Written Law delivered by God to

Moses. The relationship between the Mishna, meaning oral law, and the Gemara, meaning commentary, may be illustrated by a bill introduced into Congress and the debates which follow. In a general way, the bill corresponds to the Mishna, and the debates to the Gemara. The distinction, however, is that the law resulting from the passage of the bill is the effect and culmination of the debate; while the Mishna was already law when the Gemara or commentary was made.

As we have seen above, Hebrew jurisprudence in its principles and in the manner of their interpretation was chiefly transmitted by the living voice of tradition. These laws were easily and safely handed down from father to son through successive generations as long as Jewish nationality continued and the Temple at Jerusalem still stood. But, with the destruction of the Temple and the banishment of the Jews from Palestine (A.D. 70), the danger became imminent that in the loss of their nationality would also be buried the remembrance of their laws. Moved with pity and compassion for the sad condition of his people, Judah the Holy, called Rabbi for preëminence, resolved to collect and perpetuate for them in writing their time-honored traditions. His work received the name Mishna, the same which we have discussed above. But it must not be imagined that this work was the sudden or exclusive effort of Rabbi Judah. His achievement was merely the sum total and culmination of the labors of a long line of celebrated Hebrew sages. "The Oral Law had been recognized by Ezra; had become important in the days of the Maccabees; had been supported by Pharisaism; narrowed by the school of Shammai, codified by the school of Hillel, systematized by R. Akiba, placed on a logical basis by R. Ishmael, exegetically amplified by R. Eliezer, and constantly enriched by successive rabbis and their schools. Rabbi Judah put the coping-stone to the immense structure."[52]

Emanuel Deutsch gives the following subdivisions of the Mishna:

The Mishna is divided into six sections. These are subdivided again into 11, 12, 7, 9 (or 10), 11, and 12 chapters, respectively, which are further broken up into 524 paragraphs. We shall briefly describe their contents:

Section I. Seeds: of Agrarian Laws, commencing with a chapter on Prayers. In this section, the various tithes and donations due to the Priests, the Levites, and the poor, from the products of the lands, and further the Sabbatical year and the prohibited mixtures in plants, animals, garments, are treated of.

Section II. Feasts: of Sabbaths, Feast, and Fast days, the work prohibited, the ceremonies ordained, the sacrifices to be offered, on them. Special chapters are devoted to the Feast of the Exodus from Egypt, to the New Year's Day, to the Day of Atonement (one of the most impressive portions of the whole book), to the Feast of Tabernacles and to that of Haman.

Section III. Women: of betrothal, marriage, divorce, etc., also of vows.

Section IV. Damages: including a great part of the civil and criminal law. It treats of the law of trover, of buying and selling, and the ordinary monetary transactions. Further, of the greatest crime known to the law, viz., idolatry. Next of witnesses, of oaths, of legal punishments, and of the Sanhedrin itself. This section concludes with the so-called "Sentences of the Fathers," containing some of the sublimest ethical dicta known in the history of religious philosophy.

Section V. Sacred Things: of sacrifices, the first-born, etc.; also of the measurements of the Temple (Middoth).

Section VI. Purifications: of the various levitical and other hygienic laws, of impure things and persons, their purification, etc.[53]

Recensions.—The Talmud exists in two recensions: the Jerusalem and the Babylonian. These two editions represent a double Gemara; the first (Jerusalem) being an expression of the schools in Palestine and redacted at Tiberias about 390 A.D.; the second (Babylonian) being an expression of the schools in Babylonia and redacted about 365-427 A.D.

The Mishna, having been formed into a code, became in its turn what the Pentateuch had been before it, a basis of discussion and development. The Gemara of the Jerusalem Talmud embodies the critical discussions and disquisitions on the Mishna by hundreds of learned doctors who lived in Palestine, chiefly in Galilee, from the end of the second till about the middle of the fifth century of the Christian era. The Gemara of the Babylonian Talmud embodies the criticisms and dissertations on the same Mishna of numerous learned doctors living in various places in Babylonia, but chiefly those of the two great schools of Sura and Pumbaditha.[54] The Babylonian Talmud is written in "West Aramæan," is the product of six or seven generations of constant development, and is about four times as large as that of the Jerusalem Talmud, which is written in "East Aramæan."[55] It should be kept clearly before the mind that the only difference between these two recensions is in the matter of commentary. The two sets of doctors whose different commentaries distinguish the two Talmuds dealt with the same Mishna as a basis of criticism. But decided differences are noticeable in the subject matter and style of the two Gemaras represented by the two recensions of the Talmud. The discussions and commentaries in the Jerusalem Talmud are simple, brief, and pointed, while those of the Babylonian Talmud are generally subtle, abstruse, and prolix. The dissertations in the Jerusalem Talmud are filled to overflowing with archæology, geography, and history, while the Babylonian Talmud is more marked by legal and religious development.

But the reader should not form a wrong impression of the contents of the Talmud. They are a blending of the oral law of the Mishna and the notes and comments of the sages. The characteristics of both the editions are legal and religious, but a multitude of references are made in each to things that have no connection with either religion or law. "The Talmud does, indeed, offer us a perfect picture of the cosmopolitanism and luxury of those final days of Rome, such as but few classical or postclassical writings contain. We find mention made of Spanish fish, of Cretan apples, Bithynian cheese, Egyptian lentils and beans, Greek and Egyptian pumpkins, Italian wine, Median beer, Egyptian Zyphus; garments imported from Pelusium and India, shirts from Cilicia, and veils from Arabia. To the Arabic, Persian, and Indian materials contained, in addition to these, in the Gemara, a bare allusion may suffice. So much we venture to predict, that when once archæological and linguistic science shall turn to this field, they will not leave it again soon."

Relation of Talmud to Mishna.—The relation of the Talmud, used in the popular sense, to the Mishna, raises the question of the relation of the whole to one of its parts. The varying meanings of Mishna, Gemara, and Talmud very easily confuse the ordinary reader. If these terms are considered separately in the order in which they appear in the preceding sentence, simple mathematical addition will greatly aid in elucidating matters. The Mishna is a vast mass of tradition or oral law which was finally reduced to writing about the close of the second century of the Christian era. The Gemara is the Rabbinical exposition of the meaning of the Mishna. The Talmud is the sum of the Mishna plus the Gemara. In other words, the Talmud is the elaboration or amplification of the Mishna by manifold commentaries, designated as the Gemara. It frequently happens that the Talmud and the Mishna appear in the same sentence as terms designating entirely different things. This association in a different sense inevitably breeds confusion, unless we pause to consider that the Mishna has a separate existence from the Talmud and a distinct recension of its own. In this state it is simply a naked code of laws. But when the Gemara has been added to it the Talmud is the result, which, in its turn, becomes a distinct entity and may be referred to as such in the same sentence with the Mishna.

Relation of Talmud to Pentateuch.—As before suggested, the Pentateuch, or Mosaic Code, was the Written Law and the very foundation of ancient Hebrew jurisprudence. The Talmud, composed of the Mishna, i.e., Tradition, and the Gemara, i.e., Commentary, was the Oral Law, connected with, derived from, and built upon the Written Law. It must be remembered that the commonwealth of the Jews was a pure theocracy and that all law as well as all religion emanated directly or indirectly from Jehovah. This was as true of Talmudic tradition as of Mosaic ordinance. Hillel, who interpreted tradition, was as much inspired of God as was Moses when he received the

Written Law on Sinai. Emanuel Deutsch is of the opinion that from the very beginning of the Mosaic law there must have existed a number of corollary laws which were used to interpret and explain the written rules; that, besides, there were certain enactments of the primitive Council of the Desert, and certain verdicts issued by the later "judges within the gates"—all of which entered into the general body of the Oral Law and were transmitted side by side with the Written Law through the ages.[56] The fourth book of Ezra, as well as other Apocryphal writings, together with Philo and certain of the Church Fathers, tells us of great numbers of books that were given to Moses at the same time that he received the Pentateuch. These writings are doubtless the source of the popular belief among the Jews that the traditional laws of the Mishna had existed from time immemorial and were of divine origin. "Jewish tradition traces the bulk of the oral injunctions, through a chain of distinctly named authorities, to 'Sinai itself.' It mentions in detail how Moses communicated those minutiæ of his legislation, in which he had been instructed during the mysterious forty days and nights on the Mount, to the chosen guides of the people, in such a manner that they should forever remain engraven on the tablets of their hearts."[57] This direct descent of the Oral Law from the Sacred Mount itself would indicate an independent character and authority. Nevertheless, Talmudic interpretation of tradition professed to remain always subject to the Mosaic Code; to be built upon, and to derive its highest inspiration from it. But, as a matter of fact, while claiming theoretically to be subordinate to it, the Talmud finally superseded and virtually displaced the Pentateuch as a legal and administrative code. This was the inevitable consequence and effect of the laws of growth and progress in national existence. Altered conditions of life, at home and in exile, necessitated new rules of action in the government of the Jewish commonwealth. The Mosaic Code was found inadequate to the ever-changing exigencies of Hebrew life. As a matter of fact, Moses laid down only general principles for the guidance of Hebrew judges. He furnished the body of the law, but a system of legal procedure was wholly wanting. The Talmud supplied the deficiency and completed a perfect whole. While yet in the Wilderness, Moses commanded the Israelites to establish courts and appoint judges for the administration of justice as soon as they were settled in Palestine.[58] This clearly indicates that the great lawgiver did not intend his ordinances and injunctions to be final and exclusive. Having furnished a foundation for the scheme, he anticipated that the piety, judgment, and learning of subsequent ages would do the rest. His expectations were fulfilled in the development of the traditions afterwards embodied in the Mishna, which is the principal component part of the Talmud.

As before suggested, with the growth in population and the ever-increasing complications in social, political, and religious life, and with the general advance in Hebrew civilization, Mosaic injunction began to prove entirely inadequate to the national wants. In the time intervening between the destruction of the first and second Temples, a number of Mosaic laws had become utter anachronisms; others were perfectly impracticable, and several were no longer even understood. The exigencies of an altered mode of life and the changed conditions and circumstances of the people rendered imperative the enactment of new laws unknown to the Pentateuch. But the divine origin of the Hebrew system of law was never for a moment forgotten, whatever the change and wherever made. The Rabbins never formally repealed or abolished any Mosaic enactment. They simply declared that it had fallen into desuetude. And, in devising new laws rendered necessary by changed conditions of life they invariably invoked some principle or interpretation of the Written Law.

In the declining years of Jewish nationality, many characteristic laws of the Pentateuch had become obsolete. The ordinance which determined the punishment of a stubborn and rebellious son; the enactment which commanded the destruction of a city given to idolatry; and, above all, the *lex talionis* had become purely matters of legend. On the other hand, many new laws appear in the Talmud of which no trace whatever can be discovered in the Pentateuch. "The Pharisees," says Josephus, "have imposed upon the people many laws taken from the tradition of the Fathers, which are not written in the law of Moses."[59] The most significant of these is the one providing for Antecedent Warning in criminal prosecutions, the meaning and purpose of which will be fully discussed in another chapter.

Vicissitudes of the Talmud.—An old Latin adage runs: "Habent sua fata libelli."[60] (Even books are victims of fate). This saying is peculiarly applicable to the Talmud, which has had, in a general way, the same fateful history as the race that created it. Proscription, exile, imprisonment, confiscation, and burning was its lot throughout the Middle Ages. During a thousand years, popes and kings vied with each other in pronouncing edicts and hurling anathemas against it. During the latter half of the sixteenth century it was burned not fewer than six different times by royal or papal decree. Whole wagonloads were consigned to the flames at a single burning. In 1286, in a letter to the Archbishop of Canterbury, Honorius IV described the Talmud as a "damnable book" (liber damnabilis), and vehemently urged that nobody in England be permitted to read it, since "all other evils flow out of it."[61] On New Year's day, 1553, numerous copies of the Talmud were burned at Rome in compliance with a decree of the Inquisition. And, as late as 1757, in Poland, Bishop Dembowski, at the instigation of the Frankists, convened a public assembly at Kamenetz-Podolsk, which decreed that all copies of the Talmud found in the bishopric should be confiscated and burned by the hangman.[62]

Of the two recensions, the Babylonian Talmud bore the brunt of persecution during all the ages. This resulted from the fact that the Jerusalem Talmud was little read after the closing of the Jewish academies in Palestine, while the Babylonian Talmud was the popular edition of eminent Jewish scholars throughout the world.

It is needless to say that the treatment accorded the venerable literary compilation was due to bitter prejudice and crass ignorance. This is well illustrated by the circumstance that when, in 1307, Clement V was asked to issue a bull against the Talmud, he declined to do so, until he had learned something about it. To his amazement and chagrin, he could find no one who could throw any light upon the subject. Those who wished it condemned and burned were totally ignorant of its meaning and contents. The surprise and disgust of Clement were so great that he resolved to found three chairs in Hebrew, Arabic, and Chaldee, the three tongues nearest the idiom of the Talmud. He designated the Universities of Paris, Salamanca, Bologna, and Oxford as places where these languages should be taught, and expressed the hope that, in time, one of these universities might be able to produce a translation of "this mysterious book."[63] It may be added that these plans of the Pope were never consummated.

The Message and Mission of the Talmud.—To appreciate the message and mission of the Talmud, its contents must be viewed and contemplated in the light of both literature and history. As a literary production it is a masterpiece—strange, weird, and unique—but a masterpiece, nevertheless. It is a sort of spiritual and intellectual cosmos in which the brain growth and soul burst of a great race found expression during a thousand years. As an encyclopedia of faith and scholarship it reveals the noblest thoughts and highest aspirations of a divinely commissioned race. Whatever the master spirits of Judaism in Palestine and Babylon esteemed worthy of thought and devotion was devoted to its pages. It thus became a great twin messenger, with the Bible, of Hebrew civilization to all the races of mankind and to all the centuries yet to come. To Hebrews it is still the great storehouse of information touching the legal, political, and religious traditions of their fathers in many lands and ages. To the Biblical critic of any faith it is an invaluable help to Bible exegesis. And to all the world who care for the sacred and the solemn it is a priceless literary treasure.

As an historical factor the Talmud has only remotely affected the great currents of Gentile history. But to Judaism it has been the cementing bond in every time of persecution and threatened dissolution. It was carried from Babylon to Egypt, northern Africa, Spain, Italy, France, Germany, and Poland. And when threatened with national and race destruction, the children of Abraham in every land bowed themselves above its sacred pages and caught therefrom inspiration to renewed life and higher effort. The

Hebrews of every age have held the Talmud in extravagant reverence as the greatest sacred heirloom of their race. Their supreme affection for it has placed it above even the Bible. It is an adage with them that, "The Bible is salt, the Mischna pepper, the Gemara balmy spice," and Rabbi Solomon ben Joseph sings:

"The Kabbala and Talmud hoar
Than all the Prophets prize I more;
For water is all Bible lore,
But Mischna is pure wine."

More than any other human agency has the Talmud been instrumental in creating that strangest of all political phenomena—a nation without a country, a race without a fatherland.

CHAPTER II

HEBREW CRIMINAL LAW—CRIMES AND PUNISHMENTS

Capital crimes, under Hebrew law, were classified by Maimonides according to their respective penalties. His arrangement will be followed in this chapter.[64]

Hebrew jurisprudence provided four methods of capital punishment: (1) Beheading; (2) Strangling; (3) Burning; (4) Stoning.

Crucifixion was unknown to Hebrew law. This cruel and loathsome form of punishment will be fully discussed in the second volume of this work.

Thirty-six capital crimes are mentioned by the Pentateuch and the Talmud.

Beheading was the punishment for only two crimes:

- (1) Murder.
- (2) Communal apostasy from Judaism to idolatry.

Strangling was prescribed for six offenses:

- (1) Adultery.
- (2) Kidnaping.
- (3) False prophecy.
- (4) Bruising a parent.
- (5) Prophesying in the name of heathen deities.
- (6) Maladministration (the "Rebellious Elder").

Burning was the death penalty for ten forms of incest—criminal commerce:

- (1) With one's own daughter.
- (2) With one's own son's daughter.
- (3) With one's own daughter's daughter.
- (4) With one's own stepdaughter.
- (5) With one's own stepson's daughter.
- (6) With one's own stepdaughter's daughter.
- (7) With one's own mother-in-law.
- (8) With one's own mother-in-law's mother.

- (9) With one's own father-in-law's mother.

- (10) With a priest's daughter.[65]

Stoning was the penalty for eighteen capital offenses:

- (1) Magic.

- (2) Idolatry.

- (3) Blasphemy.

- (4) Pythonism.

- (5) Pederasty.

- (6) Necromancy.

- (7) Cursing a parent.

- (8) Violating the Sabbath.

- (9) Bestiality, practiced by a man.

- (10) Bestiality, practiced by a woman.

- (11) Sacrificing one's own children to Moloch.

- (12) Instigating individuals to embrace idolatry.

- (13) Instigating communities to embrace idolatry.

- (14) Criminal conversation with one's own mother.

- (15) Criminal conversation with a betrothed virgin.

- (16) Criminal conversation with one's own stepmother.

- (17) Criminal conversation with one's own daughter-in-law.

- (18) Violation of filial duty (making the "Prodigal Son").[66]

The crime of *false swearing* requires special notice. This offense could not be classified under any of the above subdivisions because of its peculiar nature. The Mosaic Code ordains in Deut. xix. 16-21: "If a false witness rise up against any man to testify against him that which is wrong ... and, behold, if the witness be a false witness, and hath testified falsely against his brother; then shall ye do unto him, as he had thought to have done unto his brother ... and thine eye shall not pity, but life shall go for life, eye for eye, tooth for tooth, hand for hand, foot for foot." Talmudic construction of this law awarded the same kind of death to him who had sworn falsely against his brother that would have been meted out to the alleged criminal, if the testimony of the false swearer had been true.

Imprisonment, as a method of punishment, was unknown to the Mosaic Code. Leviticus xxiv. 12 and Numbers xv. 34 seem to indicate the contrary; but the imprisonment therein mentioned undoubtedly refers to the mere detention of the prisoner until sentence could be pronounced against him. Imprisonment as a form of punishment was a creation of the Talmudists who legalized its application among the Hebrews. According to Mendelsohn, five different classes of offenders were punished by *imprisonment*:

(1) Homicides; whose crime could not be legally punished with death, because some condition or other, necessary to produce a legal conviction, had not been complied with.

(2) Instigators to or procurers of murder; such, for instance, as had the deed committed by the hands of a hireling.

(3) Accessories to loss of life, as, for instance, when several persons had clubbed one to death, and the court could not determine the one who gave the death blow.

(4) Persons who having been twice duly condemned to and punished with flagellation for as many transgressions of one and the same negative precept, committed it a third time.

(5) Incorrigible offenders, who, on each of three occasions, had failed to acknowledge as many warnings antecedent to the commission of one and the same crime, the original penalty for which was excision.[67]

Flagellation is the only corporal punishment mentioned by the Pentateuch. The number of stripes administered were not to exceed forty and were to be imposed in the presence of the judges.[68] Wherever the Mosaic Code forbade an act, or, in the language of the sages, said "Thou shalt not," and prescribed no other punishment or alternative, a Court of Three might impose stripes as the penalty for wrongdoing. Mendelsohn gives the following classification:

Flagellation is the penalty of three classes of offenses:

(1) The violation of a negative precept, deadly in the sight of heaven.

(2) The violation of any negative precept, when accomplished by means of a positive act.

(3) The violation of any one of the prohibitive ordinances punishable, according to the Mosaic law with *excision*, to which, however, no capital punishment at the instance of a human tribunal is attached.[69]

The Mishna enumerates fifty offenses punishable by stripes, but this enumeration is evidently incomplete. Maimonides gives a full classification of all the offenses punishable by flagellation, the number of which he estimates to be two hundred and seven. The last three in his list are cases in which the king takes too many wives, accumulates too much silver or gold, or collects too many horses.[70]

Slavery was the penalty for *theft* under ancient Hebrew law. This is the only case where the Mosaic law imposed slavery upon the culprit as a punishment for his crime; and a loss of liberty followed only where the thief was unable to make the prescribed restitution. Exodus xxii. 1-3 says:

If a man shall steal an ox, or a sheep, and kill it, or sell it, he shall restore five oxen for an ox, and four sheep for a sheep ... if he have nothing, then he shall be sold for his theft.

Penal servitude, or slavery, was imposed only on men, never on women. Slavery, as a penalty for theft, was limited to a period of six years in obedience to the Mosaic ordinance laid down in Exodus xxi. 2.

If thou buy a Hebrew servant, six years he shall serve: and in the seventh, he shall go free for nothing.

It should be remarked, in this connection, that slavery, as a punishment for crime, carried with it none of the odium and hardship usually borne by the slave. The humanity of Hebrew law provided that the culprit, thief though he was, should not be degraded or humiliated. He could be compelled to do work for his master, such as he had been accustomed to do while free, but was relieved by the law from all degrading employment, such as "attending the master to the bath, fastening or unfastening his sandals, washing his feet, or any other labor usually performed by the regular slave." Hebrew law required such kindly treatment of the convict thief by his master that this maxim was the result: "He who buys a Hebrew slave, buys himself a master."

Internment in a city of refuge was the punishment for accidental homicide. Mischance or misadventure, resulting in the slaying of a fellow-man, was not, properly speaking, a crime; nor was exile in a city of refuge considered by the Talmudists a form of punishment. But they are so classified by most writers on Hebrew criminal law. Among nearly all ancient nations there was a place of refuge for the unfortunate and downtrodden of the earth; debtors, slaves, criminals, and political offenders; some sacred spot—an altar, a grave, or a sanctuary dedicated and devoted to some divinity who threw about the hallowed place divine protection and inviolability. Such was at Athens the Temple of Theseus, the sanctuary of slaves. It will be remembered that the orator Demosthenes took refuge in the Temple of Poseidon as a sanctuary, when pursued by emissaries of Antipater and the Macedonians.[71] Among the ancient Hebrews, there were six cities of refuge; three on either side of the Jordan. They were so located as to be nearly opposite each other. Bezer in Reuben was opposite Hebron in Judah; Schechem in Ephraim was opposite to Ramoth in Gad; and Golan in Manasseh was opposite to Kedesh in Naphtali.[72] Highways in excellent condition led from one to the other. Signposts were placed at regular intervals to indicate the way to the nearest city of refuge. These cities were designated by the law as asylums or sanctuaries for the protection of innocent slayers of their fellow-men from the "avenger of blood." Among nearly all primitive peoples of crude political development, such as the early Germans, the ancient Greeks and Slavs, certain North American savage tribes and the modern Arabs, Corsicans and Sicilians, the right of private vengeance was and is taught and tolerated. Upon the "next of kin," the "avenger of blood," devolved the duty of hunting down and slaying the guilty man. Cities of refuge were provided by Mosaic law for such an emergency among the Hebrews. This provision of the Mosaic Code doubtless sprang from a personal experience of its founder. Bible students will remember that Moses slew an Egyptian and was compelled to flee in consequence.[73] Remembering his dire distress on this occasion, the great lawgiver was naturally disposed to provide sanctuaries for others similarly distressed. But the popular notion of the rights of sanctuary under the Mosaic law is far from right. That a common murderer could, by precipitate flight, reach one of the designated places and be safe from his pursuers and the vengeance of the law, is thought by many. The observation of Benny on this point is apt and lucid:

Internment in one of the cities of refuge was not the scampering process depicted in the popular engraving: a man in the last stage of exhaustion at the gate of an Eastern town; his pursuers close upon him, arrows fixed and bows drawn; his arms stretched imploringly towards a fair Jewish damsel, with a pitcher gracefully poised upon her head. This may be extremely picturesque, but it is miserably unlike the custom in vogue among the later Hebrews. Internment in a city of refuge was a sober and judicial proceeding. He who claimed the privilege was tried before the Sanhedrin like any ordinary criminal. He was required to undergo examination; to confront witnesses, to produce evidence, precisely as in the case of other offenders. He had to prove that the homicide was purely accidental; that he had borne no malice against his neighbor; that he had not lain in wait for him to slay him. Only when the judges were convinced that the crime was homicide by misadventure was the culprit adjudged to be interned in one of the sheltering cities. There was no scurrying in the matter; no abrupt flight; no hot pursuit, and no appeal for shelter. As soon as judgment was pronounced the criminal was conducted to one of the appointed places. He was accompanied the whole distance by two talmide-chachamin-disciples of the Rabbins. The avengers of the blood dared not interfere with the offender on the way. To slay him would have been murder, punishable with death.

Execution of Capital Sentences. (1) *Beheading.*—The Hebrews considered beheading the most awful and ignominious of all forms of punishment. It was the penalty for deliberate murder and for communal apostasy from Judaism to idolatry, the most heinous offenses against the Hebrew theocracy. Beheading was accomplished by fastening the culprit securely to a post and then severing his head from his body by a stroke with a sword.[74]

(2) *Strangling.*—The capital punishment of strangling was effected by burying the culprit to his waist in soft mud, and then tightening a cord *wrapped in a soft cloth* around his neck, until suffocation ensued.[75]

(3) *Burning.*—The execution of criminals by burning was not done by consuming the living person with fire, as was practiced in the case of heretics by prelates in the Middle Ages and in the case of white captives by savages in colonial days in America. Indeed, the term "burning" seems to be a misnomer in this connection, for the culprit was not really burned to death. He was simply suffocated by strangling. As in the case of strangling, the condemned man was placed in a pit dug in the ground. Soft dirt was then thrown in and battered down, until nothing but his head and chest protruded. A cord, wrapped in a soft cloth, was then passed once around his neck. Two strong men came forward, grasped each an end, and drew the cord so hard that suffocation immediately followed. As the lower jaw dropped from insensibility and relaxation, a lighted wick was quickly thrown into his mouth. This constituted the burning.[76] There is authority for the statement that instead of a lighted wick, molten lead was poured down the culprit's throat.[77]

(4) *Stoning.*—Death by stoning was accomplished in the following manner: The culprit was taken to some lofty hill or eminence, made to undress completely, if a man, and was then precipitated violently to the ground beneath. The fall usually broke the neck or dislocated the spinal cord. If death did not follow instantaneously the witnesses hurled upon his prostrate body heavy stones until he was dead. If the first stone, so heavy as to require two persons to carry it, did not produce death, then bystanders threw stones upon him until death ensued. Here, again, "stoning" to death is not strictly accurate. Death usually resulted from the fall of the man from the platform, scaffold, hill, or other elevation from which he was hurled. It was really a process of neck-breaking, instead of stoning, as burning was a process of suffocation, instead of consuming with fire.

These four methods of execution—beheading, strangling, burning, and stoning—were the only forms of capital punishment known to the ancient Hebrews. Crucifixion was never practiced by them; but a posthumous indignity, resembling crucifixion, was employed as an insult to the criminal, in the crimes of idolatry and blasphemy. In addition to being stoned to death, as a punishment for either of these crimes, the dead body of the culprit was then hanged in public view as a means of rendering the offense more hideous and the death more ignominious. This *hanging* to a tree was in obedience to a Mosaic ordinance contained in Deut. xxi. 22. The corpse was not permitted, however, to remain hanging during the night.

The burial of the dead body of the criminal immediately followed execution, but interment could not take place in the family burial ground. Near each town in ancient Palestine were two cemeteries; in one of them were buried those criminals who had been executed by beheading or strangling; in the other were interred those who had been put to death by stoning or burning. The bodies were required to remain, thus buried, until the flesh had completely decayed and fallen from the bone. The relatives were then permitted to dig up the skeletons and place them in the family sepulchers.

CHAPTER III

HEBREW CRIMINAL LAW—COURTS AND JUDGES

THE Hebrew tribunals were three in kind: the Great Sanhedrin; the Minor Sanhedrin; and the Lower Tribunal, or the Court of Three.

The Great Sanhedrin, or Grand Council, was the high court of justice and the supreme tribunal of the Jews. It sat at Jerusalem. It numbered seventy-one members. Its powers were legislative, executive, and judicial. It exercised all the functions of education, of government, and of religion. It was the national parliament of the Hebrew Theocracy, the human administrator of the divine will. It was the most august tribunal that ever interpreted or administered religion to man.

The Name.—The word "Sanhedrin" is derived from the Greek (συνέδριον) and denotes a legislative assembly or an ecclesiastical council deliberating in a sitting posture. It suggests also the gravity and solemnity of an Oriental synod, transacting business of great importance. The etymology of the word indicates that it was first used in the later years of Jewish nationality. Several other names are also found in history to designate the Great Sanhedrin of the Jews. The Council of Ancients is a familiar designation of early Jewish writers. It is called Gerusia, or Senate, in the second book of Maccabees.[78] Concilium, or Grand Council, is the name found in the Vulgate.[79] The Talmud designates it sometimes as the Tribunal of the Maccabees, but usually terms it Sanhedrin, the name most frequently employed in the Greek text of the Gospels, in the writings of the Rabbins, and in the works of Josephus.[80]

Origin of the Great Sanhedrin.—The historians are at loggerheads as to the origin of the Great Sanhedrin. Many contend that it was established in the Wilderness by Moses, who acted under divine commission recorded in Numbers xi. 16, 17: "Gather unto me seventy of the elders of Israel, whom thou knowest to be the elders of the people, and officers of them; and bring them unto the tabernacle of the congregation, that they may stand with thee; and I will take of the Spirit that is upon thee and will put it upon them; and they shall bear the burden of the people with thee, that thou bearest it not alone." Over the seventy elders, Moses is said to have presided, making seventy-one, the historic number of the Great Sanhedrin. Several Christian historians, among them Grotius and Selden, have entertained this view; others equally celebrated have maintained contrary opinions. These latter contend that the council of seventy ordained by Moses existed only a short time, having been established to assist the great lawgiver in the administration of justice; and that, upon the entrance of the children of Israel into the Promised Land, it disappeared altogether. The writers who hold this view contend that if the great assembly organized in the Wilderness was perpetuated side by side with the royal power, throughout the ages, as the Rabbis maintained, some mention of this fact would, in reason, have been made by the Bible, Josephus, or Philo.

The pages of Jewish history disclose the greatest diversity of opinion as to the origin of the Great Sanhedrin. The Maccabean era is thought by some to be the time of its first appearance. Others contend that the reign of John Hyrcanus, and still others that the days of Judas Maccabeus, marked its birth and beginning. Raphall, having studied with care its origin and progress, wrote: "We have thus traced the existence of a council of Zekenim or Elders founded by Moses, existing in the days of Ezekiel, restored under the name of Sabay Yehoudai, or Elders of the Jews, under Persian dominion; Gerusia, under the supremacy of the Greeks; and Sanhedrin under the Asmonean kings and under the Romans."[81]

Brushing aside mere theory and speculation, one historical fact is clear and uncontradicted, that the first Sanhedrin Council clothed with the general judicial and religious attributes of the Great Sanhedrin of the times of Jesus, was established at Jerusalem between 170 and 106 B.C.

Organization of the Great Sanhedrin.—The seventy-one members composing the Great Sanhedrin were divided into three chambers:

- The chamber of priests;

- The chamber of scribes;

- The chamber of elders.

The first of these orders represented the religious or sacerdotal; the second, the literary or legal; the third, the patriarchal, the democratic or popular element of the Hebrew population. Thus the principal Estates of the Commonwealth of Israel were present, by representation, in the great court and parliament of the nation.

Matthew refers to these three orders and identifies the tribunal that passed judgment upon Christ: "From that time forth, began Jesus to shew unto his disciples, how that he must go unto Jerusalem, and suffer many things of the elders and chief priests and scribes, and be killed and raised again the third day."[82]

Theoretically, under the Hebrew constitution, the "seventy-one" of the three chambers were to be equally divided:

- Twenty-three in the chamber of priests,

- Twenty-three in the chamber of scribes,

- Twenty-three in the chamber of elders.

A total of sixty-nine, together with the two presiding officers, would constitute the requisite number, seventy-one. But, practically, this arrangement was rarely ever observed. The theocratic structure of the government of Israel and the pious regard of the people for the guardians of the Temple, gave the priestly element a predominating influence from time to time. The scribes, too, were a most vigorous and aggressive sect and frequently encroached upon the rights and privileges of the other orders. Abarbanel, one of the greatest of the Hebrew writers, has offered this explanation: "The priests and scribes naturally predominated in the Sanhedrin because, not having like the other Israelites received lands to cultivate and improve, they had abundant time to consecrate to the study of law and justice, and thus became better qualified to act as judges."[83]

Qualifications of Members of the Great Sanhedrin.—The following qualifications were requisite to entitle an applicant to membership in the Great Sanhedrin:

(1) *He must have been a Hebrew and a lineal descendant of Hebrew parents.*[84]

(2) *He must have been "learned in the law"; both written and unwritten.*

His legal attainment must have included an intimate acquaintance with all the enactments of the Mosaic Code, with traditional practices, with the precepts and precedents of the colleges, with the adjudications of former courts and the opinions of former judges. He must have been familiar not only with the laws then actively in force, but also with those that had become obsolete.[85]

(3) *He must have had judicial experience; that is, he must have already filled three offices of gradually increasing dignity, beginning with one of the local courts, and passing successively through two magistracies at Jerusalem.*[86]

(4) *He must have been thoroughly proficient in scientific knowledge.*

The ancient Sanhedrists were required to be especially well grounded in astronomy and medicine. They were also expected to be familiar with the arts of the necromancer.[87] We are also led to believe from the revelations of the Talmud that the judges of Israel were well versed in the principles of physiology and chemistry, as far as these sciences were developed and understood in those days. History records that Rabbi Ismael and his disciples once engaged in experimental dissection in order to learn the anatomy of the human frame. On one occasion a deceitful witness tried to impose upon a Hebrew court by representing spermatic fluid to be the albumen of an egg. Baba bar Boutah was enabled, from his knowledge of the elements of chemistry, to demonstrate the fact of fraud in the testimony of the witness.

Eighty disciples of the famous Academy of Hillel are said to have been acquainted with every branch of science known in those days.[88]

(5) *He must have been an accomplished linguist; that is, he must have been thoroughly familiar with the languages of the surrounding nations.*

Interpreters were not allowed in Hebrew courts. A knowledge of several languages was, therefore, indispensable to the candidate who sought membership in the Great Sanhedrin. "In the case of a foreigner being called as a witness before a tribunal, it was absolutely necessary that two members should understand the language in which the stranger's evidence was given; that two others should speak to him; while another was required to be both able to understand and to converse with the witness. A majority of three judges could always be obtained on any doubtful point in the interpretation of the testimony submitted to the court. At Bither there were three Rabbins acquainted with every language then known, while at Jabneh there were said to be four similarly endowed with the gift of 'all the tongues.'"[89]

(6) *He must have been modest, popular, of good appearance, and free from haughtiness.*[90]

The Hebrew mind conceived modesty to be the natural result of that learning, dignity, and piety which every judge was supposed to possess. The qualification of "popularity" did not convey the notion of electioneering, hobnobbing and familiarity. It meant simply that the reputation of the applicant for judicial honors was so far above reproach that his countrymen could and would willingly commit all their interests of life, liberty, and property to his keeping. By "good appearance" was meant that freedom from physical blemishes and defects, and that possession of physical endowments that would inspire respect and reverence in the beholder. The haughty judge was supposed to be lacking in the elements of piety and humility which qualified him for communion with God. Haughtiness, therefore, disqualified for admission to the Great Sanhedrin.

(7) *He must have been pious, strong, and courageous.*[91]

Piety was the preëminent qualification of a judge of Israel. Impiety was the negation of everything Israelitish. Strength and courage are attributes that all judges in all ages and among all races have been supposed to possess in order to be just and righteous in their judgments.

Disqualifications.—Disqualifications of applicants for membership in the Great Sanhedrin are not less interesting than qualifications. They are in the main mere negatives of affirmatives which have already been given, and would seem, therefore, to be superfluous. But they are strongly accentuated in Hebrew law, and are therefore repeated here.

(1) *A man was disqualified to act as judge who had not, or had never had, any regular trade, occupation, or profession by which he gained his livelihood.*

The reason for this disqualification was based upon a stringent maxim of the Rabbins: "He who neglects to teach his son a trade, is as though he taught him to steal!" A man who did not work and had never labored in the sweat of his brow for an honest livelihood, was not qualified, reasoned the Hebrew people, to give proper consideration or extend due sympathy to the cause of litigants whose differences arose out of the struggles of everyday life.

(2) *In trials where the death penalty might be inflicted, an aged man, a person who had never had any children of his own, and a bastard were disqualified to act as judge.*

A person of advanced years was disqualified because according to the Rabbins old age is frequently marked by bad temper; and "because his years and infirmities were likely to render him harsh, perhaps obstinate and unyielding." On the other hand, youth was also a disqualification to sit in the Sanhedrin. According to the Rabbis, twenty-five years was the age which entitled a person to be called a Man;[92] but no one was eligible to a seat in the Sanhedrin until he had reached the age of forty years.[93] The ancient Hebrews regarded that period as the beginning of discretion and understanding.

A person without children was not supposed to possess those tender paternal feelings "which should warm him on behalf of the son of Israel who was in peril of his life."

The stain of birth and the degradation in character of a bastard were wholly inconsistent with the high ideals of the qualifications of a Hebrew judge.

(3) *Gamblers, dice players, bettors on pigeon matches, usurers, and slave dealers were disqualified to act as judges.*

The Hebrews regarded gambling, dice playing, betting on pigeon matches, and other such practices as forms of thievery; and thieves were not eligible to sit as judges in their courts. No man who was in the habit of lending money in an usurious manner could be a judge. It was immaterial whether the money was lent to a countryman or a stranger. Slave dealers were disqualified to act as judges because they were regarded as inhuman and unsympathetic.

(4) *No man was qualified to be a judge who had dealt in the fruits of the seventh year.*

Such a person was deemed lacking in conscience and unfitted to perform judicial functions.

(5) *No man who was concerned or interested in a matter to be adjudicated was qualified to sit in judgment thereon.*

This is a universal disqualification of judges under all enlightened systems of justice. The weakness and selfishness of human nature are such that few men are qualified to judge impartially where their own interests are involved.

(6) *All relatives of the accused man, of whatever degree of consanguinity, were disqualified from sitting in judgment on his case.*

This is only a variation of the disqualification of interest.

(7) *No person who would be benefited, as heir, or otherwise, by the death or condemnation of an accused man, was qualified to be his judge.*

This, too, is a variation of the disqualification of interest.

(8) *The king could not be a member of the Sanhedrin.*

Royalty disqualified from holding the place of judge because of the high station of the king and because his exercising judicial functions might hamper the administration of justice.

And, finally, in closing the enumeration of disqualifications, it may be added that an election to a seat obtained by fraud or any unfair means was null and void. No respect was shown for the piety or learning of such a judge; his judicial mantle was spat upon with scorn, and his fellow judges fled from him as from a plague or pest. Hebrew contempt for such a judge was expressed in the maxim: "The robe of the unfairly elected judge is to be respected not more than the blanket of an ass."

Officers of the Great Sanhedrin.—Two presiding officers directed the proceedings of the Great Sanhedrin. One of these, styled *prince* (nasi), was the chief and the president of the court. The other, known as the *father of the Tribunal* (ab-beth-din), was the vice-president.

There has been much discussion among the historians as to the particular chamber from which the president was chosen. Some have contended that the presidency of the Sanhedrin belonged by right to the high priest. But the facts of history do not sustain this contention. Aaron was high priest at the time when Moses was president of the first Sanhedrin in the Wilderness; and, besides, the list of presidents preserved by the Talmud reveals the names of many who did not belong to the priesthood. Maimonides has made the following very apt observation on the subject: "Whoever surpassed his colleagues in wisdom was made by them chief of the Sanhedrin."[94]

According to most Jewish writers, there were two scribes or secretaries of the Sanhedrin. But several others contend that there were three. Benny says: "Three scribes were present; one was seated on the right, one on the left, the third in the center of the hall. The first recorded the names of the judges who voted for the acquittal of the accused, and the arguments upon which the acquittal was grounded. The second noted the names of such as decided to condemn the prisoner and the reasons upon which the conviction was based. The third kept an account of both the preceding so as to be able at any time to supply omissions or check inaccuracies in the memoranda of his brother reporters."[95]

In addition to these officers, there were still others who executed sentences and attended to all the police work of legal procedure. They were called *shoterim*.[96]

There was no such officer as a public prosecutor or State's attorney known to the laws of the ancient Hebrews. The witnesses to the crime were the only prosecutors recognized by Hebrew criminal jurisprudence; and in capital cases they were the legal executioners as well.

There was also no such body as the modern Grand Jury known to ancient Hebrew criminal law. And no similar body of committee of the Sanhedrin performed the accusatory functions of the modern Grand Jury. The witnesses were the only accusers, and their testimony was both the indictment and the evidence. Until they testified, the man suspected was deemed not only innocent but unaccused.

The profession of the law, in the modern sense of the term, was no part of the judicial system of the ancient Hebrews. There were no advocates as we know them. There were, indeed, men learned in the law—Pharisees and Sadducees—who knew all the law. There were doctors of the law: men whom Jesus confounded when a youth in the Temple at the age of twelve.[97] But there were no lawyers in the modern sense: professional characters who accept fees and prosecute cases. The judges and disciples performed all the duties of the modern attorney and counselor-at-law. The prophets were the sole orators of Hebrew life, but they were never allowed to appear as defendants of accused persons. Indeed, they themselves were at times compelled to play the role of defendants. Jeremiah is an illustrious example.[98] Both Keim[99] and Geikie[100] speak of a Baal Rib, a counsel appointed to see that everything possible was done to secure the rights of an accused person at a Hebrew criminal trial. But these statements are not in accord with standard works on ancient Hebrew jurisprudence. Indeed, Friedlieb emphatically denies that there was any such person as a Baal Rib or Dominus Litis among the ancient Hebrews.[101] It seems that in the closing years of Jewish nationality, specially retained advocates were known, for St. Luke tells us that the Jews employed Tertullus, a certain orator, to prosecute St. Paul.[102] But this was certainly an exceptional case. It is historically certain that in the early ages of the Jewish Commonwealth litigants pleaded their own causes. This we learn from the case of the two women who appeared before King Solomon, and laid before him their respective claims to a child.[103]

Compensation of Officers.—The judges of Israel were originally not paid anything for their services. The honor of the office itself was considered sufficient emolument for labors performed. Indeed, the office of teacher and judge in Israel was so highly prized that the struggles and sacrifices of a lifetime were not considered too great to pay for a place in the Great Sanhedrin. Such high station was regarded as a sacred sphere into which the idea of material gain should not enter. The regular court days were, therefore, spent by the judge on the bench, without any expectation of reward for his services. The other days of the week he spent in earning a livelihood. But in later years of the national life a change seems to have taken place. The ancient rule was so far modified that when the services of the judge were required on days when he was engaged in his private pursuits, custom and the law gave him the right to claim a substitute during the time he was occupied on the bench; or, in default of a substitute, to claim remuneration for the time which he had lost. Another modification was that if his legal duties required his entire time, the judge in Israel was entitled to support from the communal treasury, and was even permitted to accept fees from litigants. This practice was discouraged, however, by the Rabbis, who looked with disfavor upon the appointment of judges who were not entirely able to support themselves.

The secretaries and other officers of subordinate dignity were paid for their services.[104]

Sessions of the Courts.—In the early days of the Hebrew Commonwealth the laws provided for no regular court days. The Sanhedrin convened as occasion required, to transact such business and dispose of such cases as came before it. But this practice was oftentimes found to be expensive and annoying to litigants who came into Jerusalem from the country and found no courts in session. To accommodate the country folk, the farmers, and shepherds, Ezra and his coadjutors of the Great Assembly designated Mondays and Thursdays as regular court days. This enactment was not prohibitive, however. Court might be held on any day of the week that necessity required. The reason assigned by the Rabbins for the selection of Mondays and Thursdays as court days was that on those days people from the country usually congregated in populous places, in their houses of worship, to hear the law read and interpreted. While in attendance upon these sacred services, it was thought that the time was both convenient and propitious for the settlement of their legal difficulties.[105]

The authorities are divided as to the exact official hours of the day for holding court. "The Sanhedrin sat from the close of the morning sacrifice to the time of the evening sacrifice," is the language of the Jerusalem Talmud.[106] Mendelsohn says: "The official hours for holding court were between the morning service and noon; but a suit entered upon during the legal hours could be carried on until evening, and civil cases could be continued even after nightfall."[107] But in no case of a criminal nature could the court continue its session during the night.[108]

The Minor Sanhedrins in the provinces, as well as the local Courts of Three, usually held their sessions in the most public place, that is, at the city gate. The two Minor Sanhedrins of Jerusalem held their sessions at the entrance to the Temple-mound and to the woman's department respectively. The Great Sanhedrin convened in an apartment of the national temple at Jerusalem, known as the *Lishkath haggazith*. This apartment was the celebrated "Hall of Hewn Stones."[109]

Recruitments.—The young Hebrew disciple who possessed the necessary mental, spiritual, and personal qualifications for judicial honors was styled Haber, which means associate, fellow.[110] Such a disciple was first solemnly ordained and received the title of Zaken (elder) or Rabbi. This title rendered him eligible to membership in the different courts. But that he might acquire necessary experience for membership in the Great Sanhedrin and became a sage worthy of Israel, he was required to begin at the lowest rung of the judicial ladder and work gradually to the top. He was first appointed by the Great Sanhedrin to a place in one of the local courts, consisting of three members; he then served as a member of one of the provincial Sanhedrins; was then promoted to the first, and afterwards to the second Minor Sanhedrin at Jerusalem; and was elevated finally to the Great Sanhedrin itself.[111] After this manner, all the courts of the ancient Hebrews were recruited and replenished from time to time; the young aspirant to judicial favors beginning in the local Court of Three and rising by successive steps to the Great Sanhedrin at Jerusalem.

The exact method of filling vacancies and thus replenishing the membership of the Great Sanhedrin is not certainly known.[112] The following extract from the Talmud, however, is thought to be authoritative:

In front of them (the judges of the Great Sanhedrin) sat three rows of learned disciples; each of them had his own special place. Should it be necessary to promote one of them to the office of judge, one of those in the foremost row was selected. His place was then supplied by one in the second row, while one from the third was in turn advanced to the second. This being done, someone was then chosen from the congregation to supply the vacancy thus created in the third row. But the person so appointed did not step directly into the place occupied by the one last promoted from the third row, but into the place that beseemed one who was only newly admitted.[113]

Quorum of the Great Sanhedrin.—Twenty-three members constituted a quorum of the Great Sanhedrin. This was the full number of the membership of a Minor Sanhedrin.

Number of Votes Required to Convict.—"In criminal trials a majority of one vote is sufficient for an acquittal; but for a condemnation a majority of two is necessary," is the language of the Mishna.[114] The full membership of the Great Sanhedrin was seventy-one. A condemnation by thirty-five acquitted the accused; a condemnation by thirty-six also acquitted. At least thirty-seven votes were needed to convict. If a bare quorum was present, at least thirteen votes were necessary to condemn.

A very peculiar rule of Hebrew law provided that "a simultaneous and unanimous verdict of guilty rendered on the day of trial, had the effect of an acquittal."[115] Such a verdict was considered to be lacking in the element of mercy, and was thought to result more from conspiracy and mob violence than from mature judicial deliberation.

Jurisdiction of the Great Sanhedrin.—The jurisdiction of the Great Sanhedrin is briefly and concisely stated in the Mishna:

The judgement of the seventy-one is besought when the affair concerns a whole tribe or is regarding a false prophet or the high-priest; when it is a question whether war shall be declared or not; when it has for its object the enlargement of Jerusalem or its suburbs; whether tribunals of twenty-three shall be instituted in the provinces, or to declare that a town has become defiled, and to place it under ban of excommunication.[116]

Edward Gibbon has also defined the jurisdiction of the same court as follows:

With regard to civil objects, it was the supreme court of appeal; with regard to criminal matters, a tribunal constituted for the trial of all offences that were committed by men in any public station, or that affected the peace and majesty of the people. Its most frequent and serious occupation was the exercise of judicial power. As a council of state and as a court of justice, it possessed many prerogatives. Every power was derived from its authority, every law was ratified by its sanction.

The Great Sanhedrin possessed all the powers and attributes of a national parliament and a supreme court of judicature. It corresponded to the Areopagus of Athens and to the senate of Rome. It took cognizance of the misconduct of priests and kings. Josephus tells us that Herod the Great was arraigned as a criminal before its judges, and that King Hyrcanus himself obeyed its mandates and decrees.

Appeals.—Appeals were allowed from a Minor Sanhedrin to the Great Sanhedrin. But there was no appeal from a mandate, judgment, or decree of the Great Sanhedrin. "Its authority was supreme in all matters; civil and political, social, religious, and criminal."

It is believed that enough has been said touching the character, organization, and jurisdiction of the supreme tribunal of the ancient Hebrews to satisfy the average reader. Indeed, it may be that this limit has been exceeded. The remainder of this chapter will be devoted to a short review of the Minor Sanhedrins and the Courts of Three.

Minor Sanhedrins.—There was no fixed number of Minor Sanhedrins for the administration of Justice in the Hebrew Commonwealth. Wherever and whenever, in any town or city inhabited by at least one hundred and twenty families, the people desired a Sanhedrin of three-and-twenty members, such a tribunal was established. For this purpose, an application was made to the Great Sanhedrin at Jerusalem, which dispatched a mandate to the town ordering the residents to assemble and to nominate from among themselves persons qualified to act as judges. The electors were expected to bear in mind the qualifications that would fit a judge for membership in the Great Sanhedrin, to which all local judges might eventually be elevated. Accordingly, only "good men and true" were chosen at the town mass meeting. Immediately upon receipt of the return to the mandate, an authorization was sent back from Jerusalem to the town or city which confirmed the election and constituted the judges selected a Sanhedrin of three-and-twenty members.[117]

Jurisdiction of the Minor Sanhedrins.—The jurisdiction of the Minor Sanhedrins extended to nearly all criminal cases involving imprisonment or seclusion for life, internment in a city of refuge, and capital punishment. Adultery, seduction, blasphemy, incest, manslaughter, and murder belonged to these different classes. This court condemned an ox to be butchered that had gored a man to death. The condemnation proceedings were something in the nature of a trial of the beast; and the owner was severely fined where the evidence proved that he knew the vicious disposition and habits of the animal. The deliberations at the trial of the bull were most careful and solemn, since the value of a human life was involved in the proceedings and had to be estimated in the judgment.

Besides jurisdiction in criminal matters, the Sanhedrins of three-and-twenty members performed certain civil functions. They were the tax boards of the various provinces. They constituted the regular agencies of government for the distribution of public charity. The management and administration of public elementary schools were under their control. The legal standards of weights and measures were inspected by them and received their seals.

Sanitary regulations, repairing the defenses of walled cities, and maintaining the public highways in good condition, were among the duties of the Minor Sanhedrins.

The qualifications of judges of these courts were the same as those required for membership in the Great Sanhedrin. This was true because the judges of the provincial courts might be promoted to the supreme tribunal at Jerusalem. The Minor Sanhedrins might be very aptly described as the *nisi prius* courts of the Commonwealth of Israel. It was in these courts of three-and-twenty members that the bulk of Hebrew litigation was disposed of. It seems that, though equal in number, they were not all regarded as equal in learning or authority. It is distinctly stated that appeals could be taken from one Minor Sanhedrin to another "deemed of superior authority."[118] The difference was probably due to the fact that in the larger towns were located colleges and schools, some of whose professors were doubtless either advisers or members of the local Sanhedrin. At any rate, when a difficult question, civil or criminal, could not be determined, for want of an authoritative and registered decision, by an ordinary Sanhedrin of three-and-twenty judges, the matter was referred to the nearest neighboring Sanhedrin thought to be of greater repute. If no authentic tradition offering a solution of the litigated question was in the possession of the Sanhedrin to which appeal had been taken, the matter was then referred to the first Minor Sanhedrin in Jerusalem which sat in the Har-habaith. If the judges of this court were themselves without precedent touching upon the litigated proposition, it was still further referred to the second Minor Sanhedrin of Jerusalem, located in the Azarah. If, again, this Court was without the necessary tradition that would enable it to decide the question, the matter was finally brought before the Great Sanhedrin. If this august tribunal was without precedent and tradition that would enable its members to dispose of the question according to adjudicated cases, they then decided, nevertheless, in accordance with the sentiments and principles of natural justice.

It should be remembered that of the Minor Sanhedrins to which every town of one hundred and twenty families was entitled, two sat at Jerusalem. It was left optional with a litigant from the provinces to appeal to the local Sanhedrin or to one of the Minor Sanhedrins in Jerusalem. Local bias or prejudice was thus avoided.

Lower Tribunals.—The lowest order of Hebrew tribunal was the Court of Three, composed of judges selected by the litigants themselves. The plaintiff chose one member, the defendant selected another, and these two chose a third. A majority opinion decided all questions. In the later years of Jewish nationality, it was thought best to have at least one authorized jurist (mumcha) in the Court of Three. This particular judge was probably an appointee of the Great Sanhedrin from among the young disciples (Zaken or Rabbis). This appointment was doubtless intended to give repute to the local court and experience to the legal aspirant, as well as to furnish a possible recruit to the Great Sanhedrin.[119]

These courts corresponded very nearly to the modern courts of Justices of the Peace. Their jurisdiction extended to civil matters of small importance and to petty criminal offenses. They were not permanent, being more in the nature of referees or arbitrators, and sat only when occasion required. Their sessions were public and were held in the open air under trees, or at the city gate.

Thus much for the judicial system of courts and judges among the ancient Hebrews. It was simple in the extreme, democratic to the core, and seems to have been thoroughly reliable and effective. It was founded upon universal suffrage, subject only to the general supervision and occasional appointments of the Great Sanhedrin. The judges were ever in touch with the sympathies and the best interests of the people.

Peculiarities of the Hebrew System.—Certain very striking peculiarities marked the Hebrew system:

(1) There were no lawyers or advocates. These judicial disputants have been known to every other system of enlightened jurisprudence. But there were no Ciceros, Erskines, Choates among the ancient Hebrews. The judges were the defenders as well as the judges of the accused. It may be easily read between the lines that the framers and builders of the Hebrew judicial system regarded paid advocates as an abomination and a nuisance. King Ferdinand, of Spain, seems to have had the Hebrew notion when, more than a thousand years after Jerusalem fell, he sent out colonists to the West Indies, with special instructions "that no lawyers should be carried along, lest lawsuits should become ordinary occurrences in the New World."[120] Ferdinand evidently agreed with Plato that lawyers are the plague of the community.[121]

(2) There was no secret body, with the accusatory functions of the modern Grand Jury, connected with the ancient Hebrew judicial system. The witnesses were the accusers, and their testimony constituted both the indictment and the evidence.

(3) There were no public prosecutors or State's attorneys known to the Hebrew system. Here, again, the witnesses were the informants, prosecutors, and, in capital cases, executioners of the accused.

(4) No court, among the ancient Hebrews, could consist of a single judge. Three was the number of the lowest court; three-and-twenty, of the next highest; and seventy-one, of the Great Sanhedrin at Jerusalem. A single

intelligence acting judicially would have been regarded as a usurpation of divine prerogative. The basis of this peculiar Hebrew notion is a single sentence from the Pirke Aboth, iv. 8: "Be not a sole judge, for there is no sole judge but One."[122]

CHAPTER IV

HEBREW CRIMINAL LAW—WITNESSES AND EVIDENCE

COMPETENCY.—The qualifications of a competent witness, under Hebrew law, were almost identical with those of a qualified judge, mentioned in a previous chapter. Self-evidently, all persons who were not incompetent, were competent.

Incompetency.—The following persons were incompetent to be witnesses: Gentiles, women,[123] minors, slaves,[124] idiots and lunatics, deaf mutes, blind men, gamblers, usurers, illiterate or immodest persons, persons who had been convicted of irreligion or immorality, relatives by affinity or consanguinity, and all persons directly interested in the case.

The witness must have been a Hebrew, though the Talmud mentions cases in which certain facts were allowed to stand proved upon statements "made innocently" by a Gentile; that is, not as a witness in court.

Women were not permitted to be witnesses ordinarily, because of the "levity and boldness of the sex."[125] In capital cases, they were not allowed to testify against the accused, because the law required the witnesses to become the executioners of the condemned man, and it was not deemed proper to impose this solemn and awful duty upon the weaker sex.

Puberty or adolescence marked the age which qualified a person to be a witness in criminal cases; that is, the thirteenth year must have been passed.

Immoral and irreligious persons were incompetent to testify. Such men were termed "wicked" in reference to the law as laid down in Exodus xxiii. 1: "Thou shalt not raise a false report: put not thine hand with the wicked to be an unrighteous witness." Under the stigma of the immoral and irreligious came dicers, usurers, pigeon fliers, and those who traded in the fruits of the Sabbatical year. Maimonides also mentions as incompetent "men who showed lack of self-respect by eating on the street, walking about naked at their work, or living openly on the charity of Gentiles."[126] Publicans—tax-gatherers—were usually classed with heathens and sinners as being among the immoral and irreligious. This class of persons were suspected by the Jews, not only because they were regarded as the official representatives of the Roman oppressors of Judea, but also because extortion and cruelty were frequently practiced by them. Theocritus being asked which was the most cruel of all beasts, replied: "Among the beasts of the wilderness, the bear and the lion are the most cruel, but among the beasts of the city, the Publican and the Parasite."[127]

The doctrine of interest as a disqualification to testify was carried to the limit of declaring a person incompetent to be a witness when he was the citizen of a town where claim of title to the public bath house or the square was made, until he had first divested himself of all share in the title to the litigated property.[128]

Number Required to Convict.—*Under Hebrew law, both Mosaic and Talmudic, at least two witnesses were required to convict an accused person. The prosecuting witness being included, three were necessary.*

Concerning capital punishment, the Mosaic ordinance, referring to this rule, runs thus:

At the mouth of *two* witnesses, or *three* witnesses, shall he that is worthy of death be put to death; but at the mouth of *one* witness he shall not be put to death.[129]

Whoso killeth any person, the murderer shall be put to death by the mouth of witnesses; but *one* witness shall not testify against any person to cause him to die.[130]

From the Talmud we learn that this Mosaic provision was maintained with scrupulous fidelity in the administration of justice throughout all the years of Jewish nationality. It was a requirement of prudence and safety which commends itself to every logician and legist. It is not necessary to be a criminal lawyer of large experience to know that the blackest falsehood can almost always secure at least one champion. Pliny, the historian, knew this when he wrote: "*Nullum tam impudens mendacium est quod teste careat.*"[131]

The requirement of two witnesses was not, however, peculiar to the jurisprudence of the Hebrews. Nearly every ancient code contained a similar enactment. It was especially prominent in Roman law.[132] But it can scarcely be found to-day in any modern legislation. In prosecutions for the crimes of treason and perjury under the Common Law of England, two witnesses were required; in almost all other cases, one positive witness was sufficient.[133]

The American Constitution requires two witnesses to the same overt act, to convict of treason.[134] And the penal laws of the majority of the American States have provisions requiring at least two witnesses, or one witness corroborated by circumstantial evidence, to establish guilt in the prosecution of certain crimes; notably, the sexual crimes of rape and seduction, the crime of perjury, as well as all crimes where it is sought to convict upon the testimony of an accomplice.

More than one hundred years ago, Montesquieu boasted of such a requirement in French law and declared that those laws which condemn a man to death on the testimony of a single witness are fatal to liberty.[135] The reason of the rule proclaimed by the great French writer is the same as that put forth by the ancient Rabbins. It was assumed that the defendant in a criminal case would plead not guilty and deny the facts of the crime. His plea and denial would simply counterbalance and destroy the testimony of a single witness swearing for the commonwealth. The testimony of a third witness was, therefore, indispensable to a decision. It may be objected that this rule was absurd, since a conviction was impossible unless the State could produce more witnesses than the accused. But we shall learn later that the doctrine of sifting testimony and weighing the credibility of witnesses did not obtain so strictly among the ancient Hebrew judges as it does in cases of modern trial by jury under English and American law.

Agreement of Witnesses.—The witnesses were required to agree in all essential details; else, their testimony was invalid and had to be rejected.

The Talmudic provision is: "If one witness contradicts another, the testimony is not accepted."[136]

The illustration of the rule given by Maimonides, in his commentary on this provision, is: "For instance, if one witness were to testify to having seen an Israelite in the act of worshiping the sun, and another to having seen the same man worshiping the moon, yet, although each of the two facts proves clearly that the man had committed the horrible crime of idolatry, the discrepancy in the statements of the witnesses invalidates their testimony and the accused is free."[137]

This rule of strict agreement, it is supposed, extended, at first, only to criminal cases, but it was undoubtedly afterwards applied to civil causes as well. An eminent contributor to the "Jewish Encyclopedia" says:

In civil cases, however, it is not necessary that the two witnesses should agree very closely as to the time and place. Thus, if of two witnesses to a loan one should say, "A lent B a jar of oil," the other, "He lent him a jar of wine"; or, if one should say, "I was present when the money was paid at Jerusalem," the other, "I saw it paid at Hebron"; or, if one should say, "I saw it paid in the month of Nisan," the other, "I saw it paid in Iyyar," their testimony would be void. But if one says he saw it paid in the upper and the other in the lower story; or if he says on the first of the month and the other on the second of the month, such evidence is within the limit of fair mistake and the testimony stands. Even less does a disagreement as to circumstances other than time and place affect the testimony; for instance, if one say the money is black from usage, the other that it was new, this would be regarded as an immaterial circumstance, and the testimony would stand. Where the two witnesses vary only in the matter of quantity, the lesser quantity is sufficiently proved.[138]

One of the strangest provisions of Hebrew law was the requirement that the testimony of each witness to the transaction should cover the entire case.

This was a Talmudic rule resulting from Rabbinic construction of the Mosaic ordinance, requiring at least two witnesses to establish a crime. The doctors of the law construed the rule to mean that the testimony of each witness was to be complete within itself and to extend to the whole case. Hebrew law did not permit the use of circumstantial evidence in criminal prosecutions. Only eyewitnesses of the crime were competent. Under English and American law a crime may be proven by any number of witnesses, each of whom testifies to a separate fact which constitutes a link in the chain of circumstantial evidence. But this method of proof was forbidden by both the Pentateuch and the Talmud. Under Hebrew law the capital crime of kidnaping was made up of the two elements of Abduction and Selling. The testimony of two witnesses—one to the fact of Abduction, the other to the fact of Selling—was insufficient to convict. Each had to testify to the facts of both Abduction and Selling. This Talmudic rule of criminal procedure was undoubtedly based upon a supreme regard for the sanctity of human life and upon the fact that the Hebrews rejected circumstantial evidence altogether in proving crime. The extreme of the rule is declared by Mendelsohn when he says: "And even where there appeared a legal number of duly qualified witnesses, the testimony was insufficient to convict, unless they agreed not only with regard to the prisoner's offense, but also with regard to the mode of committing it. Rabbinic law does not subject a person to capital, nor even to corporal punishment, unless all witnesses charge him with one and the same criminal act, their statements fully agreeing in the main circumstances, and declaring that they saw one another, while seeing him engaged in the crime."[139]

No Oath Required.—An oath, in the modern sense, was never administered to a Hebrew witness.

Testimony was given under the sanction of the Ninth Commandment: "Thou shalt not bear false witness against thy neighbor." This solemn prohibition of bearing false witness was regarded by both Moses and the Talmudists as a sufficient safeguard against perjury. It was a settled maxim of Talmudic law that: "Whosoever will not tell the truth without an oath, would not scruple to assert falsehood with an oath." The doctrine was carried still further by some of the Jewish philosophers who declared that swearing was injurious in itself; and that he who consents to swear should *ipso facto* be suspected of lacking credibility.[140]

In the place of an oath, the following solemn warning or adjuration was administered to each witness in the presence of the entire court:

Forget not, O witness, that it is one thing to give evidence in a trial as to money and another in a trial for life. In a money suit, if thy witness-bearing shall do wrong, money may repair that wrong. But in this trial for life, if thou sinnest, the blood of the accused and the blood of his seed to the end of time shall be imputed unto thee.... Therefore was Adam created one man and alone, to teach thee that if any witness shall destroy one soul out of Israel, he is held by the Scripture to be as if he had destroyed the world; and he who saves one such soul to be as if he had saved the world.... For a man from one signet ring may strike off many impressions, and all of them shall be exactly alike. But He, the King of the kings of kings, He the Holy and the Blessed, has struck off from His type of the first man the forms of all men that shall live, yet so that no one human being is wholly alike to any other. Wherefore let us think and believe that the whole world is created for a man such as he whose life hangs on thy words. But these ideas must not deter thee from testifying to what thou actually knowest. Scripture declares: "The witness who hath seen or known, and doth not tell, shall bear his iniquity." Nor must ye scruple about becoming the instrument of the alleged criminal's death. Remember the Scriptural maxim: "In the destruction of the wicked, there is joy."[141]

It will be observed that the two elements of this preliminary caution were, first, a solemn warning against injustice to the accused through false swearing and a reminder of the inevitable retribution of Heaven upon the perjured swearer and his remote descendants; second, a pointed admonition against timidity or fear in testifying.

Bound by this tremendous sanction, the Hebrew witness was prepared to testify. The method was unique, but seems to have been thoroughly effective. Students of law will not be struck by its peculiarity. They are well aware that any plan or mode is legal and effective that binds the conscience of the witness. Even under modern codes that impose an oath, no fixed form is imperatively demanded. In King *v.* Morgan, I Leach C. L. 54, a Mahometan was sworn upon the Koran; in Omychund *v.* Baker, I Atk. 21, a Gentoo was sworn by touching the foot of a Brahmin; in Reg. *v.* Entrehman, I Car. & M. 248, a Chinese witness took an oath by kneeling down and breaking a saucer, the oath being administered through an interpreter in these words: "You shall tell the truth, the whole truth; the saucer is cracked, and if you do not tell the truth, your soul will be cracked like the saucer."

Examination of Witnesses.—As an act of caution against the admission of irrelevant testimony, and as a means of placing before the entire court, in the first instance, only such evidence as was deemed strictly legal, a preliminary examination of witnesses was conducted in private by a special committee of the Sanhedrin appointed for that purpose. All irrelevant testimony developed at this private examination was immediately declared inadmissible and was cast aside. The necessary result of this most sensible proceeding was the discovery, in advance, of discrepancies in the statements of witnesses and the eradication of all illegal testimony. The full court sitting in regular session were not, therefore, exposed to the danger of being prejudiced by the recital of facts that had no legal connection with the case. Modern jurists might easily learn something from the ancient Hebrews in this regard. Every sensible lawyer is perfectly well aware of the absurdity and injustice of the modern method of criminal procedure in allowing skilled and designing attorneys to propose certain kinds of irrelevant testimony in the presence of the jury, knowing very well that it will be overruled by the court. These attorneys frequently deliberately draw out such testimony from the witness with the expectation and understanding that it will be ordered stricken out. The rule of practice that allows incompetent testimony to be temporarily introduced upon a promise that a foundation will be laid or relevancy shown, is abortive instead of productive of justice. The mere clerical act of striking out incompetent testimony does not, as a matter of fact, remove the impression of prejudice from the brain of the judge or juror. The ancient Sanhedrists were men of brilliant education and superior natural endowments. They were trained in powers of logical analysis, and yet they were unwilling to trust themselves with the possession of prejudicial facts arising from incompetent testimony. It is respectfully submitted that the modern average juror, whose mind is usually undisciplined in logic and legal matters, is not able to sift and disentangle the relevant from the irrelevant in the record of a civil or criminal trial of two or more weeks' duration. Theoretically, he is; but practically, he is not. Every impression, good or bad, legal or illegal, received at the trial, affects his judgment and enters into the general summary of the case in reaching a verdict.

Separation of Witnesses.—The witnesses were required to give their testimony separately and always in the presence of the accused.

Daniel said to the people concerning the two old men who testified against Susanna: "*Separate* them, and I will examine them."[142]

By this was meant that witnesses could not be examined until they had been separated in conformity with law. Under modern practice in most jurisdictions, witnesses may be separated and examined one at a time out of the presence of each other. The rule of separation is, however, generally optional with the litigant and discretionary with the court; the ruling of the court being usually reversed only in case of abuse of discretion. But among the Hebrews the requirement was mandatory and imperative. It had to be observed in every case.

Mode of Examination of Witnesses.—The mode employed by the Hebrew judges in examining witnesses is without a precedent or parallel in the jurisprudence of the world. Two distinct sets of questions constituted the examination. The first set consisted of a series of interrogations relating to the *time* and *place* of the alleged crime. These questions were prescribed by law and could not be varied in the slightest. The technical name applied to the first set of questions was Hakiroth. The second set was termed Bedikoth[143] and included all interrogations touching the investigation of relevant circumstances and corroborative facts surrounding the case. The following seven questions, constituting the Hakiroth, the first set of questions, were propounded to each witness: "Was it during a year of jubilee? Was it in an ordinary year? In what month? On what day of the month? At what hour? In what place? Do you identify this person?"[144]

These seven questions were framed and applied in conformity with a fundamental principle of the Hebrew law of evidence that the testimony of any witness, if false, should admit of being impeached and overthrown by proof of an *alibi* against the witness. It seems, indeed, that proof of an *alibi* against the witness was the only method of impeachment known to Hebrew law. It may be readily seen that the only statements capable of being thus contradicted were confined to those relating to the details of *time* and *place*. To illustrate: Suppose that two witnesses had testified that the alleged crime was committed in a certain town at a certain hour; suppose that it subsequently appeared in evidence that, at the stated time, one or both these witnesses were in a neighboring town. In such a case, the witness or witnesses stood impeached, their testimony was overthrown and they, themselves, became subject to the pains and penalties of perjury.

The failure of any witness to answer satisfactorily any of the seven questions above mentioned entitled the accused to immediate acquittal. Any material disagreement between two or more witnesses required by the law in answer to any one of these questions, likewise entitled the prisoner to immediate discharge. These seven questions seem to have been framed not so much to develop truthful testimony and to promote the ends of justice from the standpoint of the State as to enable the defendant to attack and destroy the testimony of hostile witnesses. The rule and the reason thereof are thus clearly and succinctly stated by Mendelsohn:

The several particulars referring to time and place must be furnished with the greatest possible precision and certainty, and that by the whole party of witnesses. The slightest disagreement on the part of the witnesses in regard to any one of these particulars invalidates the entire testimony. Even where a number of witnesses greater than that required by law, as three, appear, and two agree on every point, but the third differs from them as to more than one day, or more than one hour in the day, the whole testimony is invalidated. For time and place are the only points which affect the person of the witness himself; he not being able to be at more than one spot at any one time; time and place are, accordingly, the only grounds on which the witness may be confuted and duly punished.

The second set of questions, termed the Bedikoth, embraced all matters not brought out by the Hakiroth, such as would form the basis of legitimate modern direct or cross examination. The following kinds of evidence, however, were not admissible under either set of questions: Evidence of character, good or bad; previous convictions of the accused; and evidence as to the prisoner's antecedents. Such matters were not relevant, under Hebrew law, and could not be urged against the prisoner.[145]

False Witnesses.—Hebrew law provided that false witnesses should suffer the penalty provided for the commission of the crime which they sought by their testimony to fix upon the accused.

The Scriptural authority for this rule is the following:

"And the judges shall make diligent inquisition; and, behold, if the witness be a false witness and hath testified falsely against his brother, then shall ye do unto him as he had thought to do unto his brother.

... And thine eye shall not pity, but life shall go for life, eye for eye, tooth for tooth, hand for hand, foot for foot."[146]

"And they arose against the two elders, for Daniel had convicted them of false witness, by their own mouth; and according to the law of Moses, they did unto them in such a sort as they maliciously intended to do their neighbor; and they put them to death."[147]

The Accused as Witness.—The accused was never compelled, under Hebrew law, to testify against himself; but was permitted and encouraged to offer testimony in his own behalf. His confession of guilt was accepted in evidence and considered in connection with other facts of the case, but was never permitted, standing alone, to form the basis of a conviction.

The following is the commentary of Maimonides on this rule of law:

We have it as a fundamental principle of our jurisprudence that no one can bring an accusation against himself. Should a man make a confession of guilt before a legally constituted tribunal, such confession is not to be used against him, unless properly attested by two other witnesses. It is, however, well to remark that the death sentence issued against Achan was an exceptional case, brought about by the nature of the circumstances attending it, for our law never condemns on the single confession of an accused party.[148]

It is needless to suggest that the accused was never put under oath. His position in this regard was exactly the same as that of any other Hebrew witness. A special reason assigned for not swearing the accused is that offered in the celebrated maxim: "In most men religion is silent when interest speaks." Again, the inducement to perjury was so great that it was thought imprudent to allow the accused to confess under the solemnity of an oath.

The principle of law which rejects a bare confession of guilt as a basis of criminal conviction is one of the most merciful and benign known to jurisprudence. It is intended to protect the commonwealth against perjury and deception on the part of the accused. It is also intended to protect the prisoner against ignorance and rashness. It is a well-known fact that the masses of mankind are ignorant of law, both civil and criminal. Not one in a thousand in the most enlightened commonwealths can define successfully the elements of the crimes of the state of which he is a citizen. By refusing to allow an uncorroborated confession to be made the basis of a conviction, the State simply throws the mantle of charity and protection around the ignorance of the prisoner who confesses. It is also well known that men will frequently confess guilt when they are not guilty; sometimes, when they are even ignorant of the facts constituting the offense. This is one of the strangest things known to psychology and mental philosophy.[149] It is derived from the well-known and universally recognized weakness of the human will when confronted with a charge that threatens to blight and destroy life and character at a single blow. A celebrated modern writer, while discussing this rule of Hebrew law, wrote the following observations upon the origin and motive of confession of guilt under criminal charges:

The confession of the accused made no exception to the rule, showing how a confession could be made the result of weakness, or folly, or of interest— yes, even of interest. Some homicide on one occasion confessed himself to be guilty of robbery or arson in order to obtain proof of his innocence of some greater crime which he had committed at the same time; a husband persisted in declaring himself guilty of outrage upon a woman, really committed by some unknown person, in order that, by being sentenced on this account, he might prove his marital efficiency, which had been disputed by his wife, who was contemplating steps to annul her marriage. Some weak-minded people, unable to support the torture of a harassing examination, and eager to regain their liberty, make a full confession, accusing themselves in order not to be indicted, like those persons who, crossing a river on a plank bridge, throw themselves, through nervousness, into the rushing water, in order not to fall in. Fools, from want of responsibility, or through a boastful nature, accept, affirm, or confess everything of which they know nothing.[150]

The reasons above stated lie at the foundation of all modern provisions framed for the protection of the accused against precipitate self-condemnation. But, strange to say, these reasons were not urged by the framers or interpreters of Hebrew law. The explanation offered by the Talmud was simply this: "He is his own kin"; and, as we have seen, relatives were never permitted to be witnesses. A modern Jewish writer has assigned the following reason for the rule forbidding a confession to form the basis of a conviction: that, if the prisoner were innocent, he should not be permitted to incriminate himself by a false confession; if he were guilty, he was a wicked person, and, therefore, incompetent to testify under Hebrew law.[151] This rule was not enforced, however, against the defendant when testifying in his own behalf; an additional proof of the merciful regard of Hebrew law for the unfortunate position of a human being charged with crime. His testimony, though self-serving, was given due weight when urged in his own defense. Little attention was paid to it when he testified against himself.

Relevancy of Hebrew Evidence.—*Hearsay evidence was irrelevant under Hebrew law.* "Hearsay evidence was barred equally in civil as in criminal cases, no matter how strongly the witness might believe in what he heard and however worthy and numerous were his informants."[152]

Circumstantial evidence was irrelevant under Hebrew law. "The sages had very little more confidence in circumstantial evidence given for the purpose of 'taking money out of' the defendant's pocket, than in that given for the purpose of inflicting the penalty of death or stripes. Ket. ii. 10 has been cited, according to which a witness may testify that, when a boy, he saw a woman walk about in maidenly attire; the object being to prove that she married as a maiden, not as a widow, and is therefore entitled to a greater sum for her jointure. In discussing this clause, the Talmud remarks that this is only arguing from the majority of cases; for though in most cases those wearing maidens' attire are not widows, occasionally they are; and money ought not to be taken out of a man's pocket on reasoning from the greater number of cases. In fact, circumstantial evidence was generally rejected."[153]

There were occasional exceptions to the rule in the administration of Hebrew civil law, but none in criminal law. In criminal cases no Hebrew prisoner could be convicted upon circumstantial evidence. Every link in the chain of testimony had to be forged by the direct evidence of at least two competent witnesses; else the accused was acquitted and discharged.

Written, or documentary evidence, was not relevant, under Hebrew law, in criminal prosecution. The reason of this rule was derived from a literal interpretation of the Mosaic ordinance: "Whoso killeth any person, the murderer shall be put to death by the *mouth of witnesses.*"[154] The expression, "mouth of witnesses," was construed by the interpreters of the law to require oral testimony and to exclude writing in all criminal prosecutions.

Kinds of Oral Testimony.—Hebrew oral testimony is divided by the Mishna into three leading classes:[155]

- (1) Vain testimony.

- (2) Standing testimony.

-     (3) Adequate testimony.

"Vain testimony" seems to have been wholly immaterial and irrelevant. It was not even conditionally admitted, but was instantly and permanently rejected. The New Testament seems to indicate that such testimony was rendered against Jesus by the "many false witnesses" who first came, and that testimony was rejected.

"Standing testimony" seems to have been conditionally admitted and to have been allowed to remain in evidence until it was properly confirmed by and joined to other evidence which the law required. It was not valid, however, until so connected and confirmed. We must remember that at least two witnesses, agreeing in all essential details, were needed, under Hebrew law, to convict a prisoner. It is evident then that the testimony of the first witness against the accused was necessarily regarded as "standing testimony," until the second or confirming witness, which the law required, had testified. This testimony is also referred to in the New Testament when it is said that: "At the last, came two false witnesses, And said, This fellow said, I am able to destroy the temple of God and to build it in three days."[156] The testimony of the first of these witnesses was doubtless allowed to stand until it was shown that the second witness did not render testimony in agreement with it. Contradictory testimony was thrown out under Hebrew criminal procedure; and this was done regardless of the number of witnesses who testified against the accused. It seems that a rigid application of the principle of exclusion based upon contradictory statements would have shut out the testimony of any number of agreeing witnesses, if said testimony had been contradicted in a radical and material way by even a single witness. The sifting of evidence and the weighing of the credibility of witnesses, which is the peculiar prerogative of the modern jury, were no part of the duties of the ancient Sanhedrists. The testimony of all the witnesses against the accused had to agree in all material respects, else it was wholly rejected. Now it necessarily follows that all testimony against a prisoner was of the "standing" or provisional kind until the last witness had testified, and it was found that the evidence in its entirety was in legal agreement. Mark, using the almost exact technical expression of the law, tells us, concerning the false testimony against Jesus, that "their witness agreed not together."[157] This disagreement caused the "standing testimony" of the first witness to fall and the charge of threatening or attempting to destroy the Temple was abandoned, as we shall see in a later part of this work.

"Adequate testimony," under Hebrew criminal procedure, was evidence that was competent, material, and in legal agreement. When two or more witnesses, being the entire number, against the accused agreed in all essential details, their testimony was considered adequate, and if the judges believed it to be true they based a conviction upon it.

Antecedent Warning.—It is deemed appropriate in this chapter to call attention to and briefly discuss a very striking peculiarity of the law of evidence under Hebrew criminal procedure. In the chapter on Mosaic and Talmudic law, reference was made to the celebrated proviso, called "Antecedent Warning." This proviso was unknown to the Mosaic Code, being a creation of Talmudic law, and is without a parallel in the jurisprudence of the world. Briefly stated, Antecedent Warning, under Hebrew law, meant simply this: That no person charged with crime involving life and death, or even corporal punishment, could be convicted, unless it was shown by competent testimony that immediately before the commission of the crime the offender was warned that what he was about to do was a crime, and that a certain penalty was attached thereto. The warning was not effective if any time elapsed between the admonition and the commission of the offense. Furthermore, the warning was of no force unless it was shown that the alleged criminal had duly acknowledged it and had expressed a willingness to suffer corporal punishment or to die for the act. It must have been shown that, having received the warning, the would-be offender turned to his monitor and said, "I am very well aware of the nature of the act I am about to commit, of the rules of law applicable thereto, and of the inevitable consequences of my misdeed"—else the court could not consider the condition complied with.

This peculiar proviso seems to have been intended to serve three distinct purposes: (1) To protect the would-be offender against his own ignorance and rashness and to prevent the commission of crime by a timely warning; (2) to aid in establishing guilty intention, that is, criminal intent, at the trial of the prisoner, after the commission of the offense; (3) to enable the judges to determine the exact penalty to assess. The first two purposes are self-evident. The third merits a brief consideration. To complete the warning, it was essential that the offender be told the exact penalty attached to the crime which he was about to commit; whether the punishment was capital or corporal, and the exact kind, if capital; that is, whether beheading, burning, stoning, or strangling. Now, it often happened that two crimes were committed by the same person in one day; the penalty for one of which being flagellation and the other death. And it sometimes happened that two different crimes were the result of one criminal transaction. In such a case, the nature of the Antecedent Warning would guide the judges in decreeing punishment. To illustrate: The Mosaic Code forbids the killing of either a cow or a ewe "and her young both in one day";[158] and a violation of this prohibition, according to Rabbinic law, entails the punishment of flagellation. Another Mosaic ordinance imposes the penalty of death on the Jewish idolater.[159] Now, it might have happened that the last two offenses mentioned were committed by the same person at the same time, as when an Israelite slaughtered a ewe and her young and sacrificed them as an offering to an idol. The question would at once arise: Which penalty should be assessed, death for idolatry, or flagellation for killing the ewe and her young both on the same day? Here, the nature of the Warning would determine. If the prisoner had been told that flagellation would be the punishment, then stripes were administered. If he had been warned that death was the penalty, then capital punishment was meted out to him. If the caution had included both death and flagellation, then death would have been administered, because of the enormity of the crime of idolatry and for the reason that all lesser punishments are merged in death.

Another illustration of the third purpose above mentioned, that is, to enable the judges to determine the exact punishment to administer, is this: The ancient Nazarites made solemn vows of abstemiousness.[160] And when any Israelite took the Nazarite vow and violated it, he subjected himself to the penalty of flagellation if he drank a certain measure (¼ log) of wine. If he drank several such measures in succession, the question would arise how he was to be punished. Again, the antecedent caution would decide. If the testimony showed that he had received due warning before each drink, then he was punished for each drink separately. If he had been admonished only once, he was punished only once for the whole debauch.[161]

The enforcement of this proviso established a rule of criminal procedure peculiar to the Hebrews, and recognized by no other nation. Such a requirement seems to be utterly subversive of the celebrated maxim that has found place in every other enlightened system of law: *Ignorantia juris, quod quisque tenetur scire, neminem excusat.* Among modern civilized nations, ignorance or mistake of fact in criminal law, as well as ignorance or mistake of the meaning and effect of civil or private law, has sometimes been permitted to operate as an excuse in favor of the victim of the ignorance or mistake; but ignorance of the criminal or public law has never been permitted to be pleaded as a defense to an indictment for crime. Such a plea would threaten the very existence of the state by rendering the proof of crime and the conviction of criminals impossible.

Other reasons besides those assigned above have been advanced to explain the invention of such a proviso by the Talmudists. None of them is entirely satisfactory. Rabbinowicz has urged with great force that the enactment was the offspring of a constantly increasing tendency on the part of the framers of the Talmud to mitigate the rigors of the Mosaic Code, and to abolish altogether the punishment of death by making the conviction of criminals practically impossible.[162] But this view has been ably and probably successfully combated by Benny and others. To say the least, it was a senseless provision when viewed from the standpoint of the state in maintaining order and preserving the commonwealth. The Rabbins framed several exceptions to its operation which were doubtless designed to stay the progress of certain forms of crime and to preserve the state. The false witness was excluded from the benefit of this proviso, as were also the instigator to idolatry and the burglar. The false witness was denied the benefit because of the impossibility of foreseeing that he would swear falsely and of forewarning him; the idolater was excepted because of the heinousness of the crime of idolatry under a theocratic commonwealth; and the burglar was denied the benefit of the caution for the very peculiar reason that the "breaking in," while committing the crime of burglary, was sufficient warning.[163]

Such a rule is utterly without foundation in logic or reason from the simple fact that crime in every age has been committed with every circumstance of caution and concealment that criminal ingenuity could devise; usually under the cover of night, often with a mask, frequently by the aid of accomplices to give notice of the appearance of the officers of the law, and nearly always with subsequent attempts to wipe out evidences of the commission of the offense. To require a preliminary caution, such as the Antecedent Warning of the Jews, was to handicap the state most seriously and to render almost impossible the apprehension and punishment of public malefactors.

CHAPTER V

HEBREW CRIMINAL LAW—MODE OF TRIAL AND EXECUTION IN CAPITAL CASES

THE administration of Hebrew criminal law was marked by lofty conception of right and wrong, and was pervaded by a noble sentiment of justice and humanity. From the framing of the Decalogue to the latest years of Jewish nationality, each succeeding generation witnessed some humane and merciful modification of existing rules. Talmudic interpretation invented a series or collection of sayings that gave form and character to the whole body of later Hebrew law. These maxims were intended to mitigate the rigors of the Mosaic Code and to establish safeguards against negligence or injustice to the defendant in criminal trials. Indeed, every possible precaution was taken to render impossible the wrongful conviction of an accused person. The student of Hebrew law is at times astonished by the excessive caution inculcated in criminal procedure. Certain cautionary rules are no less than pedantic, and may be justly and aptly styled Judaical. The judges leaned always to the side of the defendant and gave him the advantage of every possible doubt. They went a step farther and sought pretext after pretext that would result in an acquittal. A sense of awful responsibility weighed upon the hearts and consciences of the judges. The services of the synagogue were not conducted with deeper fervor or greater religious solemnity than were the proceedings of a capital trial in the great Judgment Hall of the Sanhedrin. Certain sacred maxims flamed forever like beacon lights along the pathway of the members of the court during the solemn deliberations. "A judge," says the Talmud, "should always consider that a sword threatens him from above, and destruction yawns at his feet." The ancient adage, "the pen of the law fears the thunder of Heaven," though of Chinese origin, is Hebraic in spirit. "Thou shalt do no unrighteousness in judgment" was the leading aphorism of Hebrew jurisprudence. Among the earliest traditions of the Fathers, we read this maxim: "When a judge decides not according to truth, he makes the majesty of God to depart from Israel. But if he judges according to the truth, were it only for one hour, it is as if he established the whole world, for it is in judgment that the divine presence in Israel has its habitation." Hebrew horror of capital punishment and dread of taking human life are well expressed in the celebrated maxim of the Mishna: "The Sanhedrin, which so often as once in seven years, condemns a man to death, is a slaughter-house."[164] And more striking and startling still is the terrible sentence of Rabbi Meir: "What doth God say (if one may speak of God after the manner of men) when a malefactor suffers the anguish due to his crime? He says, *My head and my limbs are pained.* And if he so speaks of the suffering even of the guilty, what must he utter when the righteous is condemned?" The whole spirit of Talmudic caution is well illustrated by the principal rule of the Pirke Aboth, which says: "Be cautious and slow in judgment, send forth many disciples, and *make a fence round the law.*"[165]

In addition to the maxims above mentioned, which were more religious than legal, four cardinal rules of criminal procedure—"strictness in the accusation, publicity in the discussion, full freedom granted to the accused, and assurance against all dangers or errors of testimony"[166]—molded the judgment and guided the consciences of Hebrew judges. These sayings of the Fathers and maxims of the law were the touchstones of all their judicial inquiries and meditations at the trial of capital cases. With prayer in their hearts and these maxims upon their lips, they applied themselves to the solemn duties of their office.

A most interesting passage in the Mishna draws a striking contrast between capital trials and those involving questions of money only. The relevancy of the passage to this chapter is so great that it is deemed best to quote it entire:

Money trials and trials for life have the same rule of inquiry and investigation. But they differ in procedure in the following points: The former require only three, the latter three-and-twenty judges.

In the former it matters not on which side the judges speak who give the first opinions; in the latter, those who are in favor of acquittal must speak first.

In the former, a majority of one is always enough; in the latter, a majority of one is enough to acquit, but it requires a majority of two to condemn.

In the former, a decision may be quashed on review (for error), no matter which way it has gone; in the latter, a condemnation may be quashed, but not an acquittal.

In the former, disciples of the law present in the court may speak (as assessors) on either side; in the latter, they may speak in favor of the accused, but not against him.

In the former, a judge who has indicated his opinion, no matter on which side, may change his mind; in the latter, he who has given his voice for acquittal may not change.

The former (money trials) are commenced only in the daytime, but may be concluded after nightfall; the latter (capital trials) are commenced only in the daytime, and must also be concluded during the day.

The former may be concluded by acquittal or condemnation on the day on which they have begun; the latter may be concluded on that day if there is a sentence of acquittal, but must be postponed to a second day if there is to be a condemnation. And for this reason capital trials are not held on the day before a Sabbath or a feast day.[167]

The principal features of a Hebrew capital trial before the Great Sanhedrin were: (1) The Morning Sacrifice; (2) the Assembling of the Judges in the Lishkath haggazith, or the Hall of Hewn Stones; (3) the Examination of Witnesses; (4) the Debates and Balloting of the Judges on the guilt or the innocence of the accused. These successive steps will be briefly considered in this chapter.

The Morning Sacrifice.—It is not positively known what legal connection, if any, the morning sacrifice had with the trial of a capital case before the Great Sanhedrin at Jerusalem. Several writers contend that there was no essential legal connection; that the sacrifice was offered at the break of day whether a capital case was to be tried or not; and that the court was not dependent upon this religious observance for jurisdiction in the trial of criminal cases. Other writers hold opposite views, and contend that the morning sacrifice was essential to give jurisdiction to the court. MM. Lémann consider it an error in the trial of Jesus that the morning sacrifice was not offered before the commencement of proceedings.[168] Certain passages from the Mishna very strongly support this second view: that the court could not legally convene until the morning sacrifice had been offered. "The Sanhedrin sat from the close of the morning sacrifice to the time of the evening sacrifice."[169] ... "Since the morning sacrifice was offered at the break of day, it was hardly possible for the Sanhedrin to assemble until an hour after that time."[170] These passages seem to indicate that the morning sacrifice was necessary before the court could legally convene. This question will be found more fully discussed under Point V of the Brief in this volume. The method of offering the morning sacrifice was as judicial in its precision as it was religious in its solemnity.

The Assembling of the Judges.—At the close of the morning sacrifice, the members of the court entered the judgment hall in solemn procession. They took their seats, "turbaned, on cushions or pillows, in oriental fashion, with crossed legs, and unshod feet, in a half-circle."[171] The high priest sat in the center with the other members of the court to the right and left of him. "His head was crowned with a turban of blue inwrought with gold. On his bosom hung the priestly breastplate, in which glittered twelve precious stones, emblems of the twelve tribes of Israel. A flowing robe of blue, gathered about his waist by a girdle of purple, scarlet, and gold embroidery, enveloped his person and set off the pure white linen of his capacious sleeves. The buttons of this costly robe were onyx stones. His slippered feet were half concealed beneath the long fringe of his pontifical vestments, which were curiously embroidered with pomegranates in gold and scarlet and crimson. No Roman Catholic pontiff ever wore robes more resplendent than those in which the high priest was attired on public and state occasions. Immediately before him sat the scribes or clerks of the court. The one on his left hand wrote down whatever testimony was adduced against the accused; what votes were cast for his condemnation. The one on the right transcribed what appeared in his favor."[172]

According to most writers, including Dr. Lyman Abbott, only two scribes were present having seats at each end of the semicircle. According to Benny, however, "three scribes were present; one was seated on the right, one on the left, the third in the center of the hall. The first recorded the names of the judges who voted for the acquittal of the accused and the arguments upon which the acquittal was grounded. The second noted the names of such as decided to condemn the prisoner and the reasons upon which the conviction was based. The third kept an account of both the preceding, so as to be able at any time to supply omissions or check inaccuracies in the memoranda of his brother reporters."

The prisoner was placed in front of the high priest, in a conspicuous position, where he could see all and could be seen by all.

Thus organized and arranged, the Sanhedrin began the work of the day.

Examination of Witnesses.—The examination of witnesses, who were also accusers, marked the beginning of proceedings. It is doubtful if the indictment against criminals was in writing. The first witness who was to testify was led into an adjoining room and solemnly warned. He was asked questions similar to the following: Is it not probable that your belief in the prisoner's guilt is derived from hearsay or circumstantial evidence? In forming your opinions concerning the guilt of the accused, have you or not been influenced by the remarks of persons whom you regard as reputable and trustworthy? Are you aware that you will be submitted to a most searching examination? Are you acquainted with the penalty attached to the crime of perjury?

After this preliminary warning, conveyed in these questions, had been given, the most learned and venerable of the judges administered to the witness the following impressive adjuration:

Forget not, O witness, that it is one thing to give evidence in a trial as to money, and another in a trial for life. In a money suit, if thy witness-bearing shall do wrong, money may repair that wrong. But in this trial for life, if thou sinnest, the blood of the accused, and the blood of his seed to the end of time, shall be imputed unto thee.... Therefore was Adam created one man and alone, to teach thee that if any witness shall destroy one soul out of Israel, he is held by the Scripture to be as if he had destroyed the world; and he who saves one such soul to be as if he had saved the world.... For a man from one signet-ring may strike off many impressions, and all of them shall be exactly alike. But He, the King of the kings of kings, He the Holy and the Blessed, has struck off from His type of the first man the forms of all men that shall live; yet so, that no one human being is wholly alike to any other. Wherefore let us think and believe that the whole world is created for a man such as he whose life hangs on thy words. But these ideas must not deter you from testifying from what you actually know. Scripture declares: "The witness who hath seen or known, and doth not tell, shall bear his iniquity." Nor must ye scruple about becoming the instrument of the alleged criminal's death. Remember the Scriptural maxim: "In the destruction of the wicked, there is joy."

At the close of this solemn exhortation, the examination of the witness commenced. The Hakiroth, seven questions prescribed by law, touching the identity of the prisoner and fixing the elements of time and place, were asked. They were as follows: Was it during a year of jubilee? Was it an ordinary year? In what month? On what day of the month? At what hour? In what place? Do you identify this person?

These questions being satisfactorily answered, the next step was a rigid examination into the facts and circumstances attending the commission of the crime and the connection of the accused therewith. This process of examination and cross-examination was termed the Bedikoth and embraced all questions not included in the Hakiroth which tended to establish the guilt or innocence of the prisoner at the bar.

When the witnesses for the Commonwealth of Israel had been examined, witnesses for the defendant were heard. The accused was also urged to say anything he wished in his own behalf. As we have before pointed out, the Hakiroth questions as to time and place could be rebutted only by establishing an alibi against the witnesses for the state. If such an alibi was proved, the defendant was acquitted and at once discharged. A contributor to the "Jewish Encyclopedia," discussing this point of procedure, says: "It has been shown under Alibi how a 'set' of witnesses may be convicted as 'plotters' by another set or sets proving an alibi on them. But the opposite party may prove an alibi on the convicting set or in some other way show that the facts testified to by the first set were impossible or untrue. Under such circumstances, a modern judge or jury would weigh the credibility of the witnesses and the probability of their stories and decide between them accordingly. The sages did not trust themselves or their successors with this discretion. If there were no indicia or fraud, they held that as some one was evidently lying they could not decide which of them it was, and that there was no evidence on the point."[173] The result was an acquittal.

If material contradictions in the testimony of the witnesses were shown by the Bedikoth, the trial was at once terminated and the accused was free. The failure of any witness to answer satisfactorily any of the seven questions above mentioned entitled the accused to immediate acquittal. Any material disagreement between the two or more witnesses required by the law in answer to any of these questions likewise entitled the prisoner to an immediate discharge. If the prosecuting witnesses relied upon documentary, circumstantial or hearsay evidence to convict, their testimony was at once rejected and the defendant was released.

But if the accused failed to establish an alibi against the prosecuting witnesses in the matter of the Hakiroth; and if the Bedikoth developed evidence fairly consistent and uncontradictory; and if the testimony of the witnesses was purely oral, that is, was not documentary, hearsay or circumstantial, then there was legally admissible evidence to lay before the Sanhedrin. The competent witnesses who could render relevant testimony were then led, one at a time, before the general body and required to testify.

The Debates and Balloting of the Judges.—All the evidence, pro and con, having been adduced, the tribunal began a full discussion of the case, preliminary to casting ballots. Arguments could be begun only on behalf of the accused. Nothing was permitted to be said against him until one of the judges had urged something in his behalf, and had said: "As I view the matter, and according to such and such evidence, it seems to me that the prisoner should be acquitted." The discussion became general for and against the accused. The entire record was then overhauled. Each item of evidence was carefully considered and subjected to the minutest criticism. Contradictions were noted and extenuating facts pleaded. If one of the disciples occupying one of the three rows of seats could offer any cogent or valid reason why the prisoner should not be convicted, he was invited to take his seat among the judges, and was regarded as a member of the court during the remainder of the day. If his argument resulted in the acquittal of the accused and saved a human life he was made a permanent member of the court. On the other hand, if one of the disciples had anything to say that would tend to injure the defendant he was not permitted to raise his voice.

When the entire case had been exhaustively discussed, the argument was closed and the balloting on the guilt or innocence of the accused commenced. The scribes were in readiness to record the votes and note the reasons assigned therefor. The youngest members of the tribunal were required to vote first, in order that they might not be unduly influenced by the example of their seniors in age and authority. The high priest, who was generally president of the Sanhedrin, addressed a gentle admonition to the youngest member, who was never less than forty years of age, to render a free and untrammeled verdict, and not to be awed or influenced by the patriarchs of the court. This admonition was repeated in the case of each youthful member of the tribunal. When the balloting commenced, each judge arose in his place and voted; at the same time making a short speech explanatory of his ballot. To secure a conviction it was not necessary that the members of the Sanhedrin should be unanimous. Indeed a peculiar rule of Hebrew law provided that if the verdict was instantaneous and unanimous it was invalid and could not stand. If the prisoner had not a single friend in court, the element of mercy was wanting in the verdict, said the ancient Hebrews, and the proceedings were regarded in the light of conspiracy and mob violence. A majority vote of at least two members was necessary to convict. A majority vote of one in his favor would acquit. Any majority amounting to two or more that did not reach unanimity was sufficient to condemn. If the accused was tried before a Minor Sanhedrin of three-and-twenty members or before the Great Sanhedrin with a bare quorum (twenty-three members, the same number as the full membership of a Minor Sanhedrin), a vote of thirteen members was necessary, in either case, to convict. If eleven judges were for conviction and twelve for acquittal, the prisoner was discharged at once; a majority of one vote being sufficient for that purpose. If twelve were in favor of conviction and eleven for acquittal, the condemnation of the accused was impossible; a majority of at least two being required to condemn. According to some writers, an acquittal was the result in such a case. According to others, in such a contingency the following novel expedient was employed to reach a verdict: From the first row of disciples two additional judges were selected and added to the original twenty-three members. Balloting then commenced anew. If the vote resulted in a majority of at least two against the prisoner, he stood convicted. If not, two more disciples were added from the first row in front and this process of increasing by twos the number of the Sanhedrin was continued until the requisite majority was secured. If it happened that the constant additions finally raised the number to seventy-one, the membership of the Great Sanhedrin, the process of increasing by twos was discontinued, and final balloting then began. If thirty-six voted for conviction and thirty-five for acquittal, the whole case was reargued for a reasonable time until one of the thirty-six yielded and declared in favor of acquittal. In case the thirty-six members persevered in their determination to convict, the prisoner was discharged.

At any stage of the trial, from the beginning with the three-and-twenty judges through all the successive additions of new members, a majority vote of one or more in favor of the accused would acquit; a majority of two or more, not amounting to unanimity, would convict.

In case of an acquittal the prisoner was immediately released and the trial was closed. In the event of conviction sentence could not be pronounced until the next afternoon and the session of the court was accordingly adjourned until the following day. Upon adjournment the members of the Sanhedrin with measured step and solemn mien left the chamber in which the trial had been conducted. Outside the judgment hall, in the open street, the judges formed themselves into groups or knots of five or six to discuss the trial and to lament the awful misfortune impending over Jerusalem; for such was the Hebrew conception of the execution of a son of Israel. The nucleus of each group was formed of elders of the Sanhedrin; the younger members came up from behind, leaned over between the shoulders of the patriarchs, and listened attentively and devoutly to what they were saying about the case. Gradually the groups broke up and the judges linked arm in arm, by twos, walked slowly homeward, still discussing the facts and arguments adduced at the trial. Finally they parted and retired to their respective homes. No heavy food, like meat, and no intoxicating beverage, were taken for the remainder of the day or during the night. Nothing was done that would incapacitate them for correct thinking. At sunset they began to make calls upon each other for the purpose of examining more carefully and debating more fully the issues of the case. When these visits were concluded, in the early evening, each judge retired to the privacy of his own home to sleep, meditate, and pray. At the dawn of day, they arose and prepared to resume again the solemn responsibilities of their office. The morning sacrifice was offered and the judges again assembled at sunrise in the hall of justice. They reseated themselves in the form of a semicircle; the prisoner was again led to the bar of the court; the witnesses were again produced; and the scribes, bringing with them the minutes of the former meeting, again took seats in their accustomed places.

The second part of the trial then began. It must be remembered that there were two trials of every Hebrew capital case. The second day was not a trial *de novo*; but was a proceeding in the nature of an appeal and was intended to accomplish a review of the proceedings of the previous day. Additional testimony, however, which had been discovered after the close of the first trial, might be introduced. But the record of facts seems not to have been considered so important as the question of the fixed opinions of the judges. Each member of the Sanhedrin was required, on the second day, to vote again and to declare anew his notions concerning the guilt or innocence of the accused. The statements of each judge were carefully noted by the scribes and compared with his statements at the previous day. If any judge voted for conviction at the second trial and founded his judgment on reasons and arguments radically different from those of the first day, his verdict was rejected. A member who had voted for acquittal on the first day was not permitted to change his vote for conviction on the second day. But one who had voted for condemnation at the first trial, might, by giving valid reasons, vote on the second day for acquittal.[174]

A most striking peculiarity of Hebrew law is to be noted in their method of counting votes and arriving at sums total in favor of or against the accused. Certain peculiar rules were to be strictly applied in determining the ultimate result. When upon examination of the record it was discovered that two or more judges had advanced identical arguments, though each supported his contention by different Biblical citations, their collective opinions were regarded as the common expression of a single mind and all their votes were counted only as one. Father and son, teacher and pupil, being members of the same court, counted also as one, provided their votes and opinions were arrayed on the same side, but not when they were placed in antagonism.[175]

When the balloting was complete the number for and against the prisoner was again announced. If a majority of at least two votes were registered against him he stood convicted a second time. But the humane and indulgent spirit of Hebrew law continued to operate and deferred immediate sentence. The judges continued to deliberate. No one thought of quitting the judgment hall on the second day of the trial. No one ate anything, no one drank anything on this second day; for the day that was to condemn an Israelite to death was to be a fast day for those who condemned him. It was to be a day of prayerful meditation. Ancient maxims of the Fathers, framed for the protection of the accused, were reconsidered. All the merciful tendencies of Talmudic interpretation were invoked and pleaded by the judges, the defenders of the accused. It was hoped that a few hours' time would discover facts favorable to the doomed man. New arguments, it was thought, might be offered and new witnesses might be forthcoming in his behalf. As they continued to deliberate, the fatal hour approached. There was to be no thirty or sixty days, as in America, between sentence and execution, during which time the condemned man could make peace with God. The moment that saw the judgment finally pronounced witnessed the beginning of its execution. Sunset, Nature's symbol of the extinguishment of the light of life, was the time fixed for both.

The death march and the final circumstances attending the execution of a Hebrew prisoner are without parallel in the jurisprudence of the world. As the culprit was led away to his doom, a man, carrying in his hand a flag, was stationed at the entrance of the Sanhedrin Hall. A mounted officer of the court followed the procession at a convenient distance and kept his eyes constantly turned in the direction of the flag bearer on the hill. A herald, carrying aloft a staff from which fluttered a crimson banner, made proclamation to the gazing multitude along the way that a human being was about to be executed. He cried aloud: "AB is to be put to death on the testimony of CD and XY, on such and such a charge. If any man knows anything favorable to the accused, in the name of God let him come forth and speak, in order that the prisoner may be led back to the Sanhedrin Hall to be again confronted and tried by his judges."

If any witness, friend or stranger, came forth to furnish new evidence in favor of the condemned man, the procession was halted and the accused was led back to the Sanhedrin Chamber. If any member of the court still sitting in the hall of judgment bethought himself of any new argument in behalf of the accused that had not been offered at the trial, he arose quickly in his place and stated it to his fellow-judges. The flag at the gate was then waved and the mounted messenger, chosen for such an emergency, saw it waving and galloped forward to stop the execution.

The culprit himself could delay or prevent the accomplishment of the death sentence if he could give to the Rabbins who escorted him any valid reason why he should not be put to death. He was led back as often as he gave any good excuse, not exceeding five times, the number prescribed by law. If no new witnesses appeared and if the prisoner made no further plea for life, the procession proceeded to within a short distance of the place of execution. The convict was then exhorted to declare himself guilty of the crime of which he was charged and to make full confession of all his sins. He was told that a full confession would entitle him to a happy existence beyond this life, since the flood of death would wash away all stains of sin and cleanse the soul of all the iniquities of existence in this world. If the condemned man still refused to confess that he was guilty of the crime with which he was charged, he was then urged to say: "May my death prove an atonement for all my transgressions."

He was then led to the ground of execution. The death draught, consisting of a mixture of frankincense and myrrh, poured into a cup of vinegar or light wine, was then given him. Stupefaction followed, rendering the culprit unconscious of his impending doom and insensible to the agonies of death. In Jerusalem, this benumbing and stupefying mixture was furnished by the Hebrew women, whose tender and merciful regard for the wretched and unfortunate of earth has in all ages been a striking characteristic of the sex. As soon as the draught had been administered the execution took place. The prisoner was either stoned, strangled, burned, or beheaded, according to the nature of his crime. In case of blasphemy or idolatry the dead body was afterwards hung upon a gallows until dusk. But ordinarily the corpse was immediately interred after execution. On the outskirts of every town there were two graveyards for criminals; in one of these those who had been burned or stoned were buried; in the other were interred those who had been hanged or beheaded. As soon as decomposition had taken place—that is, when the flesh had decayed and fallen from the bones—the relatives were allowed to remove the skeleton and to deposit it in the family burial ground.

Soon after the execution the friends and relatives of the dead man made friendly calls upon the judges who had tried and sentenced him. These visits were intended to show that the visitors harbored no feelings of bitterness or revenge against those who, in condemning one of their loved ones to death, had only performed the high and righteous duties of just and honorable judges of Israel.

PART III
THE BRIEF

THE LAST SUPPER (DA VINCI)

THE BRIEF

A NUMBER of difficult and confusing questions present themselves at the very beginning of any extensive and impartial investigation of the trial of Jesus.

Did the Great Sanhedrin exist at the time of Christ? If it existed, was it still a legally constituted court, having jurisdiction to try capital offenses? Did it have jurisdiction of the particular offense with which Jesus was charged? If the Great Sanhedrin was actually in existence, had criminal jurisdiction in capital cases, and was judicially empowered to try the offense with which Jesus was charged, did it actually try Him? Were the rules of criminal procedure, prescribed in the Mishna and cited in this Brief, in existence and actively in force in Judea at the time of the trial of Jesus? What was the nature of the charge brought against the Christ? Was He guilty as charged? Were forms of law duly observed in the trial of the accusation against Him? Answers to these questions, which will be considered in the Brief in the order above enumerated, will cover the legal aspects of the Hebrew trial of Jesus.

Did the Great Sanhedrin exist at the time of Christ? The answer to this question is of prime importance, since the existence of a court having jurisdiction of the person and subject matter of the suit is a fundamental consideration in all litigation. It is generally supposed that the Hebrew trial of Jesus took place before the Great Sanhedrin in Jerusalem. But many able writers, both Jewish and Gentile, deny that this court had any existence at the time of Christ. In the "Martyrdom of Jesus," Rabbi Wise says: "But this body did positively not exist at the time when Jesus was crucified, having been dissolved 30 A.C. In nowise, then, any passages of the Gospels must be understood to refer to the Great Sanhedrin." Many Jewish and several eminent Gentile authors agree with this contention, which is founded upon a passage in Josephus in which it is declared that King Herod had all the members of the Sanhedrin put to death.[176] It is contended by these writers that the supreme tribunal of the Jews was then abolished and was not restored until subsequent to the crucifixion. Opposed to this assertion, however, is the weight of both reason and authority. Schürer is of the opinion that Josephus did not mean literally "all" (πάντας) when he wrote that Herod had destroyed all the members of the Great Sanhedrin; since in the following book he relates that the same king caused to be put to death the forty-five most prominent members of the party of Antigonus, who must themselves have been members of this court; and forty-five are twenty-six fewer than seventy-one, the full membership of the Great Sanhedrin.[177] The same author asserts the existence and discusses the jurisdiction of this court in the following language: "As regards the area over which the jurisdiction of the Great Sanhedrin extended, it has already been remarked above that its civil authority was restricted, in the time of Christ, to the eleven toparchies of Judea proper. And, accordingly, for this reason it had no judicial authority over Jesus Christ so long as He remained in Galilee. It was only as soon as He entered Judea that He came directly under its jurisdiction."[178]

Again, Salvador, who may be justly styled the Jewish Blackstone, wrote concerning the condemnation of Jesus: "The *senate* declared that Jesus, son of Joseph, born at Bethlehem, had profaned the name of God in usurping it for himself, a simple citizen. The capital sentence was then pronounced." Now, the word "senate" is properly applied nowhere in literature to any other Hebrew court than the Great Sanhedrin. This High Court of the Jews has been frequently compared to the senate of Rome, to the Areopagus of the Greek and to the parliament of England. It should be noted in this connection that the great Jewish writer not only styled the body that tried Jesus "senate" (Great Sanhedrin) but stated that it pronounced a capital sentence, thus declaring that the supreme tribunal of the Jews not only existed at the time of Jesus but had the right to decree capital punishment.

Edersheim, discussing the alleged abolition of the Sanhedrin by Herod, says: "The Sanhedrin did exist during his reign, though it must have been shorn of all real power, and its activity confined to ecclesiastical or semi-ecclesiastical causes. We can well believe that neither Herod nor the procurators would wish to *abolish* the Sanhedrin, but would leave to them the administration of justice, especially in all that might in any way be connected with purely religious questions. In short, the Sanhedrin would be accorded full jurisdiction in inferior and in religious matters; with the greatest show, but with the least amount of real rule or of supreme authority."[179] This is a powerful voice in favor of the existence of the supreme tribunal of the Jews at the time of Christ; for Edersheim's "Life and Times of Jesus the Messiah" is the best and most reliable biography of the Savior in any language.

Keim bases his advocacy of the existence of the Sanhedrin at the time of Christ on New Testament authority. "Not only," he says, "does the New Testament speak of Synedria in the time of Jesus and the Apostles, but Jesus Himself, in a well-established utterance, mentions the Synedrion (Sanhedrin) as the highest legally constituted tribunal and as having the right to pass the sentence of death."[180]

The strongest passage in the New Testament supporting the contention of the existence of the Great Sanhedrin at the time of the crucifixion is contained in Acts v. 21: "But the high priest came, and they that were with him, and called the *council* together, and all the *senate* of the children of Israel, and sent to the prison to have them brought." Here, the use of the words "high priest," "council," and "senate" in the same connection, strongly suggests, almost accurately describes, the president and members of the Great Sanhedrin; and besides, the words, "sent to the prison to have them brought," indicate that this body was exercising judicial functions.

Again, the utterance of Jesus above referred to by Keim is found in two passages of Matthew. The first is in Chap. xvi. 21: "From that time forth began Jesus to shew unto His disciples, how that He must go unto Jerusalem, and suffer many things of the *elders* and *chief priests* and *scribes*, and be killed and be raised again the third day." The second is in Chap. xx. 18: "Behold, we go up to Jerusalem; and the Son of man shall be betrayed unto the chief priests and unto the scribes, and they shall condemn him to death." The "elders" and "chief priests" and "scribes" were the characteristic constituent elements of the Great Sanhedrin; and the prophecy, "they shall condemn him to death," ascribed to them the highest judicial prerogative, the right of passing the death sentence. In his brilliant essay on the Talmud, Emanuel Deutsch emphatically says: "Whenever the New Testament mentions the 'Priests, the Elders, and the Scribes' together, it means the Great Sanhedrin."[181] It is impossible to refrain from contrasting this statement of a most eminent and learned Jewish writer with that of Rabbi Wise, also very scholarly and pious, "In no wise, then, any passages of the Gospels must be considered to refer to the Great Sanhedrin." Suffice it to say that the weight of authority is with Emanuel Deutsch. And that which seems to conclusively disprove the whole theory of the nonexistence of the Great Sanhedrin at the date of the crucifixion, is the fact that Josephus—whose account of the alleged killing of all the members of the Sanhedrin by Herod is the very basis of the theory—in a subsequent chapter, relating to a subsequent event, describes the summoning of Hyrcanus, former king and high priest, before the Sanhedrin to be tried by them. As a result of the trial, Hyrcanus was put to death.[182] Such a personage could have been tried and condemned only by the Great Sanhedrin, which was in existence subsequent to the alleged destruction of all its members by Herod.

It is believed that enough has been said to show that the contention that the Great Sanhedrin did not exist at the time of Christ is not well founded. As a matter of reason, the mere destruction of the members of the court by Herod did not, of necessity, abolish the court itself. From what we know of the character and policy of Herod, he simply had the members of an old and unfriendly aristocracy put to death in order that he might make room in the court for an entirely new body friendly to him and devoted to his interests. Again, it is entirely improbable that the Roman masters, of whom Herod was but a subject prince and tool, would have permitted the destruction of the most important local institution of a conquered state. The policy of the Romans in this regard is well known. Whenever it was consistent with the dignity and safety of the Roman empire, local institutions were allowed to remain intact and undisturbed. We are not aware of any good historical reason why the Great Sanhedrin, the national parliament, and the supreme tribunal of the Jews, should have been abolished thirty years before Christ, as Rabbi Wise and other eminent scholars and theologians have contended. After all, it seems to be more a matter of dogma than of history. The majority of Jewish writers rest their case upon Josephus, with their peculiar construction of the passage; the majority of Christian writers quite naturally prefer the New Testament. But the line is not closely drawn. Dr. Geikie, the eminent Gentile author, supports the Jewish opinion, without reference, however, to the passage in Josephus. On the other hand, Salvador, Edersheim, and Deutsch, all writers of Jewish blood, support the Christian contention.

The assertion of Graetz that Jesus was arraigned before one of the Minor Sanhedrins,[183] of which there were two in Jerusalem, is not to be taken seriously, since these minor courts had no jurisdiction of the crime with which Jesus was charged.[184] It is very evident from the weight of authority that Jesus was tried before the Great Sanhedrin, and that this court had authority to pass sentence of death. Upon this theory, the author will proceed in framing the Brief.

Did the Great Sanhedrin have jurisdiction to try capital offenses at the time of the crucifixion? This question, involving great difficulty and much confusion in discussing the trial of Jesus, arises from the divergent opinions of Bible scholars as to the exact legal and political status of the Jews at the time of Christ. Many concede the existence of the Great Sanhedrin at this time, but insist that it had been shorn of its most important judicial attributes; that the right to try capital cases had been wholly taken from it; and that it retained the legal right to try only petty crimes and religious offenses not involving the death penalty. The Jews contend, and indeed the Talmud states that "forty years before the destruction of the Temple the judgment of capital causes was taken away from Israel." The great weight of authority, however, is registered against this view. The New Testament teachings on the subject have just been discussed in the beginning of the Brief. The opinion generally held by Bible scholars is that the Great Sanhedrin continued to exist after the Roman conquest of Judea and after the time of Herod; that its legislative, executive, and judicial powers remained substantially unimpaired in local matters pertaining to the internal affairs of the Jews; and that the Roman representatives intervened only when Roman interests required and the sovereignty of the Roman State demanded. The question of sovereignty presented itself, indeed, whenever the question of life and death arose; and Rome reserved to herself, in such cases, the prerogative of final judicial determination. Both Renan and Salvador hold the view that the Sanhedrin had the right of initiative, the *cognitio causæ*; that is, the right to try the case.

In the event of the acquittal of the accused the matter was finally ended without Roman interference, but in case of conviction the Roman legate or procurator certainly might review and probably was required to review the matter, and either affirm or reverse the sentence. This is the prevalent opinion among the best writers; and is plausible because it is at once consistent with the idea of the maintenance of Roman sovereignty and of the preservation of the local government of the Jews. However, many able writers, among them Rosadi and Dupin, assert that the Jews had lost the right, by virtue of Roman conquest, even to try capital cases. And it must be admitted that the logic of law is in their favor, though the facts of history and the weight of authority are against them.

Did the Great Sanhedrin have jurisdiction of the particular offense with which Jesus was charged? Admitting the existence of the Great Sanhedrin at the time of Christ, and its right to initiate and try proceedings in capital cases with reference to Roman authority, had it jurisdiction, under Hebrew law, of the special accusation against Christ? On this point there is little difference of opinion. Jesus was brought before the Sanhedrin on the charges of sedition and blasphemy, both of which crimes came within the cognizance of the supreme tribunal of the Jews.[185]

Was there a regular legal trial of Jesus before the Great Sanhedrin? Admitting that this court was in existence at the time of Christ, that it had competence, with reference to Roman authority, to try capital cases, and that it had jurisdiction under Hebrew law of the crime with which Jesus was charged, did it actually conduct a regular, formal trial of the Christ? Many able critics give a negative answer to this inquiry. Jost, one of the greatest and most impartial of Jewish historians, designates the crucifixion of Jesus "a private murder (Privat-Mord) committed by burning enemies, not the sentence of a regularly constituted Sanhedrin."[186] Edersheim supports this view as to the nature of the trial.[187]

A certain class of writers base their objection to a regular trial on the ground of the nonexistence of the Great Sanhedrin at the time of Christ. If this court did not exist, they say, there could not have been any regular judicial proceeding, since this body was the only Hebrew tribunal that had jurisdiction to try the offense with which Jesus was charged. Others, who hold similar views, maintain that the errors were so numerous and the proceedings so flagrant, according to the Gospel account, that there could have been no trial at all, and that it was simply the action of a mob. These writers contend that the members of the Sanhedrin acted more like a vigilance committee than a regularly organized tribunal. Of this opinion is Dr. Cunningham Geikie.

Still another class of critics insist that the Hebrew judges exercised only accusatory functions, and that the examination of Jesus at night was merely preparatory to charges to be presented to Pilate.

Others still apparently reverse the order, and insist that the Hebrew trial was the only one; that the duty of Pilate was merely to review, sanction, and countersign the verdict of the Sanhedrin. Of this class is Renan, who says: "The course which the priests had resolved to pursue in regard to Jesus was quite in conformity with the established law. The plan of the enemies of Jesus was to convict him, by the testimony of witnesses and by his own avowals, of blasphemy and of outrage against the Mosaic religion, to condemn him to death according to law, and then to get the condemnation sanctioned by Pilate."[188] Salvador and Stapfer agree with Renan that the Hebrew trial was regular and that the proceedings were legal. On the other hand, Rosadi, Dupin, Keim and many others denounce the proceedings in the trial of Jesus as outrageously illegal.

As to the number of trials, the authorities above cited seem to be exceptions to the rule. By far the greater number contend that there were two distinct trials: a Hebrew and a Roman, separate and yet dependent. The opinion of this class of writers is most clearly expressed by Innes, who says: "Whether it was legitimate or not for the Jews to condemn for a capital crime on this occasion, they did so. Whether it was legitimate or not for Pilate to try over again an accused whom they had condemned, on this occasion, he did so. There were certainly two trials."[189] This is the view of the writer of these pages; and he has, accordingly, divided the general subject into two trials, devoting a volume of the work to each. It may be answered, then, that there was a regular trial of Jesus before the Great Sanhedrin. The relation of this trial to the Roman proceeding will be more fully discussed in the second volume of this treatise.

Were the rules of criminal procedure prescribed in the Mishna and cited in this Brief, in existence and actively in force in Judea at the time of the trial of Jesus? This question has been answered in the negative by several writers of repute. Others have answered that the matter is in doubt. But it is very generally agreed that an affirmative answer is the proper one. Out of this question, two others arise: (1) Were the rules of criminal law, herein cited, obsolete at the time of the crucifixion? (2) Were they the legal developments of an age subsequent to that great event? In either case, their citation, in this connection, is without reason or justification.

It is a sufficient answer to the first of these questions that none of the standard works on Hebrew criminal law classes any of the rules herein stated as obsolete at the time of Christ. In support of a negative answer to this question, it may be urged that all of the aforesaid rules were the essential elements of an enlightened and humane criminal procedure in capital cases at the date of the crucifixion.

The answer to the second question above suggested is a more serious matter. It is historically true that the Mishna was not reduced to writing until two hundred years after the beginning of our era. The Jerusalem Talmud was not redacted until 390 A.D.; and the Babylonian Talmud, about 365-427 A.D. The question at once arises: Were the rules of criminal procedure, which we have herein invoked in the discussion of this case, the growth of the periods intervening between the crucifixion of Jesus and these dates? Two valid reasons give a negative answer to this question. In the first place, the criminal rules applied in the Brief are in nearly every case traceable to Mosaic provisions which were framed more than a thousand years before the trial of Jesus. In the second place, they could not have been the developments of a time subsequent to the crucifixion, because less than forty years, a single generation, intervened between that event and the fall of Jerusalem, which was followed by the destruction of Jewish nationality and the dispersion of the Jews. This short interval was a period of national decay and disintegration of the Jewish people and could not have been, under Roman domination, a formative period in legal matters. After the fall of Jerusalem, the additions and developments in Hebrew law were more a matter of commentary than of organic formation—more of Gemara than of Mosaic or Mishnic growth. The decided weight of authority, then, as well as the greater reason, is in favor of the proposition that the Hebrew criminal law had reached its full development and was still in active force at the time of which we write.

What was the nature of the charge brought against Christ at the trial before the Sanhedrin? Was He guilty as charged? The questions preceding these were secondary, though important. If the Great Sanhedrin did not exist at the time of Christ, we are forced to believe and admit that the men who arrested and examined Jesus at night were nothing more than an irresponsible rabble, acting without judicial authority or legal excuse. If it was without criminal jurisdiction, though in existence, we have erroneously spoken of a Hebrew trial. If the rules of criminal procedure which we have invoked were not in existence at the time of the crucifixion, we have proceeded upon a false hypothesis. Fortunately, the weight of authority, in every case, is so overwhelmingly in our favor, and our contention is, in each case, so well founded in reason, that we feel justified in now proceeding to a discussion of the real merits of the case, involved in answers to the questions: What was the nature of the charge or charges brought against Jesus at the Hebrew trial? Was He guilty as charged?

The accusations against Christ were numerous, both in and out of court; and it will help to simplify matters and to arrive at a clear understanding, if, in the very beginning, the distinction be made and held in mind between *judicial* and *extra-judicial* charges. By judicial charges are meant those made at the time of the examination of Jesus by the Sanhedrin, assembled at night in the palace of Caiaphas. By extra-judicial charges are meant those made out of court at divers times and places in Jerusalem, Galilee, and elsewhere by the accusers of the Christ, and especially by the spies who dogged His footsteps during the last days of His ministry on earth. Ordinarily, it would be proper, in a work of this kind, to consider only charges made after the trial of the accused had begun, and jeopardy had attached. All others are extra-judicial and are entitled to only passing notice. It would be proper to omit them altogether, if they did not serve to throw much light upon the specific charges at the trial. An excellent summary of the extra-judicial charges brought against Jesus at various times in His career, is given in Abbott's "Jesus of Nazareth," p. 448: "It was charged that He was a preacher of turbulence and faction; that He flattered the poor and inveighed against the rich; that He denounced whole cities, as Capernaum, Bethsaida, Chorazin; that He gathered about Him a rabble of publicans, harlots, and drunkards, under a mere pretense of reforming them; that He subverted the laws and institutions of the Mosaic commonwealth, and substituted an unauthorized legislation of His own; that He disregarded not only all distinctions of society, but even those of religion, and commended the idolatrous Samaritan as of greater worth than the holy priest and pious Levite; that, though He pretended to work miracles, He had invariably refused to perform them in the presence and at the request of the Rabbis of the Church; that He had contemned the solemn sanctions of their holy religion, had sat down to eat with publicans and sinners with unwashen hands, had disregarded the obligations of the Sabbath, had attended the Jewish feasts with great irregularity or not at all, had declared that God could be worshiped in any other place as well as in His Holy Temple, had openly and violently interfered with its sacred services by driving away the cattle gathered there for sacrifice."

These different charges were doubtless present in the minds and hearts of the members of the Sanhedrin at the time of the trial, and probably influenced their conduct and entered into their verdict. But only one or two of these accusations can be said to have any direct connection with the record in this case, and, consequently, can be only indirectly considered in discussing its merits.

We come now to examine the actual charges made at the night trial before the Sanhedrin. The subsequent charges before Pilate have no place in this volume. A review of the proceedings at the time of the examination in the palace of Caiaphas reveals two distinct charges: one preferred by witnesses who had been summoned by the Sanhedrin, the other preferred by Caiaphas himself.

First, according to Matthew, "At the last came two false witnesses, and said, This fellow said, I am able to destroy the temple of God, and to build it in three days."[190] The same testimony is thus reported by Mark: "And there arose certain, and bare false witness against him, saying, We heard him say, I will destroy this temple that is made with hands, and within three days, I will build another made without hands."[191] Luke and John do not discuss the night trial before the Sanhedrin, and therefore make no reference to the charges brought forward by the false witnesses. The second accusation made against Jesus is that by Caiaphas himself, who embodies his charge in the form of an oath or adjuration which he administered to the accused: "I adjure thee by the living God that thou tell us whether thou be the Christ, the Son of God." Then came the confession and condemnation. "Jesus said unto him, Thou hast said: nevertheless I say unto you, Hereafter shall ye see the Son of man sitting on the right hand of power, and coming in the clouds of heaven. Then the high priest rent his clothes, saying, He hath spoken *blasphemy*; what further need have we of witnesses? behold, now ye have heard his blasphemy. What think ye? They answered and said, He is guilty of death."[192]

These few words of Scripture are the essential parts of the record of fact of the most awful trial in the history of the universe. An analysis of the evidence shows the existence of two distinct charges: that preferred by the false witnesses, accusing Jesus of sedition; and that of blasphemy made by Caiaphas himself.

Concerning the testimony adduced in support of the first charge, Mark says: "For many bare false witness against him, but their witness agreed not together."[193] Now, we have seen that the concurrent testimony of at least two witnesses, agreeing in all essential details, was necessary to sustain a conviction under Hebrew law. If one witness against the accused contradicted any other witness against the accused, all were rejected. Under this rule of law, when "their witness agreed not together," according to Mark, the charge of sedition was abandoned, and the accusation of blasphemy then followed, which resulted in a confession and condemnation. Later on, in another place, we shall discuss the illegality of a double accusation, in the same breath and at the same trial. But at this point we have no further interest in the abandoned charge, except to say that the false witnesses, in their ignorance and blindness, failed to grasp the Master's allegorical language in reference to the destruction of the Temple. Their worldly-mindedness and purely physical conception of things centered their thoughts upon the Temple at Jerusalem, and gave a purely temporal and material interpretation to His words. "Forty and six years was this temple in building, and wilt thou rear it again in three days?"[194] This question asked by the original auditors, shows a total misconception of the true meaning of the language of Jesus. The spiritual allusion to the resurrection of His own body seems never to have penetrated their thoughts. Then, again, their general statement was, in effect, an absolute misrepresentation. By perverting His language, He was made to utter a deliberate threat against a national institution, around which clustered all the power, sanctity, and glory of the Hebrew people. He was made to threaten the destruction of the Temple at Jerusalem. But it is most reasonable to infer from the entire evidence as contained in the Sacred Writings that the words imputed to Jesus by the false witnesses were not those which He actually used. In reality, He did not say: "I *can destroy*," or "I *will destroy*"; but, simply, "*Destroy*." "Destroy this temple, and in three days I will raise it up."[195] This is evidently a purely hypothetical expression and is equivalent to "*Supposing you destroy this temple*." St. John, in whose presence, it seems, this language was used, correctly interprets the Savior's meaning when he says: "He spake of the temple of his body."[196]

The evidence of the false witnesses was so contradictory that even wicked judges were forced to reject it and to conduct the prosecution on another charge.

We come now to consider more closely the real accusation upon which Jesus was condemned to death. At first glance, there seems to be no difficulty in determining what this accusation was, since the Gospel record specifically mentions the crime of blasphemy. It was for this offense that Caiaphas pronounced judgment against Jesus with the unanimous approval of his fellow-judges. "Then the high priest rent his clothes and saith, What need we any further witnesses? ye have heard the *blasphemy*: what think ye? and they all condemned him to be guilty of death." But what had they heard that constituted blasphemy? Nothing more than His own confession that He was "the Christ, the Son of God." This seems simple enough upon its face; but a vast mass of acrimonious discussion has resulted from these few passages of the Scripture. The main difficulty turns upon the meaning of the word "blasphemy," as used by the high priest in passing condemnation upon Jesus. The facts adduced at the trial, or rather the facts suggested by the oath or adjuration addressed to Jesus, as to whether or not He was "Christ, the Son of God," did not, in the opinion of many, constitute blasphemy under the definition of that term given in the Mosaic Code and interpreted by the Rabbinic writers whose opinions have been embodied in commentaries upon the Mishna. Eminent Jewish writers have ridiculed the idea of attempting to make a case of blasphemy out of a mere claim of being a "Son of God." Rabbi Wise, in "The Martyrdom of Jesus," has very tersely stated the Jewish position on the subject. "Had Jesus maintained," he says, "before a body of Jewish lawyers to be the Son of God, they could not have found him guilty of blasphemy, because every Israelite had a perfect right to call himself a son of God, the law (Deut. xiv. 1) stating in unmistakable words, 'Ye are sons of the Lord, your God.' When Rabbi Judah advanced the opinion, 'If ye conduct yourselves like the sons of God, ye are; if not, not,' there was Rabbi Mair on hand to contradict him: 'In this or in that case, ye are the sons of the Lord your God.' No law, no precedent, and no fictitious case in the Bible or the rabbinical literature can be cited to make of this expression a case of blasphemy. The blasphemy law is in Leviticus (xxiv. 15-20), which ordains, 'If any man shall curse his God (i.e., by whatever name he may call his God), he shall bear his sin,' but the law has nothing to do with it, dictates no punishment, takes no cognizance thereof. 'But he who shall curse the name of Jehovah, he shall surely be put to death,' be the curser native or alien. Another blasphemy law exists not in the Pentateuch. The ancient Hebrews expounded this law, that none is guilty of blasphemy in the first degree, unless he curses God himself by the name of Jehovah; or, as Maimonides maintains, by the name Adonai. The penalty of death is only threatened in the first degree. The Mishna states expressly as the general law, 'The blasphemer is not guilty, unless he (in cursing the Deity) has mentioned the name itself' (of Jehovah or Adonai), so that there can be no doubt whatever that such was the law in Israel. It is clear that the statements made by Mark, in the name of Jesus, had nothing in the world to do with the blasphemy laws of the Jews."[197]

Rabbi Wise was concededly an able and accomplished theologian; and in a general way the above extract states the truth. But it does not state the whole truth, and in one or two places is certainly erroneous. Leviticus xxiv. 15-20 is undoubtedly the blasphemy statute of the Mosaic Code. But Mr. Wise was assuredly wrong when he stated that "another blasphemy Law exists not in the Pentateuch." For, if this were a correct statement, other eminent Jewish authorities, as well as many Gentile authors, would be all at sea. Besides, the New Testament use of the word "blasphemy," in many places, would only serve to illustrate the dense ignorance of the Jews of the time of Jesus as to the meaning of the term, if the author of "The Martyrdom of Jesus" were right.

In this connection, let us now consider another Jewish authority, as able and even more famous than the one just cited. In Salvador's celebrated treatise entitled "Histoire des Institutions de Moïse," he devotes a chapter to the question of the judgment and condemnation of Jesus. Touching the nature of the charge against Christ and the real cause of His conviction, he says: "But Jesus, in presenting new theories and in giving new forms to those already promulgated, speaks of himself as God; his disciples repeat it; and the subsequent events prove in the most satisfactory manner that they thus understood him. This was *shocking blasphemy* in the eyes of the citizens: the law commands them to follow Jehovah alone, the only true God; not to believe in gods of flesh and bones, resembling men or women; neither to spare or listen to a prophet who, even doing miracles, should proclaim a new god, a god neither they nor their fathers had known. The question already raised among the people was this: Has Jesus become God? But the Senate having adjudged that Jesus, son of Joseph, born in Bethlehem, had profaned the name of God by usurping it to himself, a mere citizen, applied to him the law in the 13th Chapter of Deuteronomy and the 20th verse in Chapter 18, according to which every prophet, even he who works miracles, must be punished when he speaks of a god unknown to the Jews and their fathers: the capital sentence was pronounced."

Here we have the doctors divided; Wise saying that "another blasphemy law exists not in the Pentateuch," and Salvador contending that Jesus was legally convicted of blasphemy under the Mosaic Law as it was laid down, not in Leviticus xxiv. 15-20, but in Deuteronomy xiii.

The law in Deuteronomy is peculiarly impressive in its relationship to the charges against Jesus.

"If there arise among you a prophet, or a dreamer of dreams, and giveth thee a sign or a wonder, And the sign or the wonder come to pass, whereof he spake unto thee, saying, Let us go after other gods, which thou hast not known, and let us serve them; Thou shalt not hearken unto the words of that prophet, or that dreamer of dreams: for the Lord your God proveth you, to know whether ye love the Lord your God with all your heart and with all your soul. Ye shall walk after the Lord your God, and fear Him, and keep His commandments, and obey His voice, and ye shall serve Him, and cleave unto Him. And that prophet, or that dreamer of dreams, shall be put to death; because he hath spoken to turn you away from the Lord your God, which brought you out of the land of Egypt and redeemed you out of the house of bondage, to thrust thee out of the way which the Lord thy God commanded thee to walk in."[198]

The position of Rabbi Wise cannot be defended by trying to identify this passage with the one in Leviticus. The law in Deuteronomy has reference to that form of blasphemy which is nearly identical with idolatry, that is, seducing the people from their allegiance to Jehovah, and inducing them to go off after strange gods. The law in Leviticus applies peculiarly to profane epithets and to curses hurled at Jehovah Himself.

Again, Rabbi Wise ridicules the notion that Caiaphas and the Sanhedrists attempted to twist the use of the words "Son of God" into a crime. He is right when, quoting Deuteronomy xiv. 1, he says that "every Israelite had a perfect right to call himself a son of God." But here again the eminent theologian has stopped short of the entire truth. It is not at all probable that he would have contended that "every Israelite had a perfect right to call himself the son of God" in the sense of being equal with God Himself. Should reply be made that such would be an unwarranted construction of Christ's confession that he was "the Christ, the Son of God," then the opinion of Salvador would be again invoked. In a note to the "Jugement de Jesus," he says: "I repeat that the expression 'Son of God' includes here the idea of God Himself."

We are not in a position, nearly two thousand years after the event occurred, to tell exactly what was in the mind of Caiaphas at the time. But, in view of the condemnation which he passed, and of the language which he used in passing it, we are certainly justified in supposing that he deliberately and designedly connected the two titles—"the Christ" and "the Son of God"—to see if Jesus would assume responsibility for both, or if He would content himself with the simple appellation, "son of God," to which every pious Israelite was entitled. The reply of Jesus, "Thou hast said," meaning "I am" the Christ, the Son of God, was an affirmation of His identity with the Father. The condemnation for blasphemy immediately followed. Such a sentence would have been inconsistent with any other theory than the assumption that Jesus had claimed equality with God, or had arrogated to Himself power and authority which belonged alone to Jehovah. This definition of blasphemy is certainly different from that laid down in Leviticus xxiv. 15-20.

As a matter of history, it is really true that both the Old and New Testaments reveal not only the existence of more than one blasphemy statute in the Mosaic Code, but also more than one conception and definition of blasphemy at different periods in the development of the Hebrew people.

In II Samuel xii. 14 the word "blaspheme" is used in the sense "to despise Judaism." In I Macc. ii. 6 blasphemy means "idolatry." In Job ii. 5; II Kings xix. 4-6; Hosea vii. 16, the term indicates "reproach," "derision."

Not only might God be blasphemed, but the king also, as his representative. The indictment against Naboth was: "Thou didst blaspheme God and the king."[199] The people of Jehovah and his Holy Land might also become victims of blasphemy.[200]

The New Testament writers frequently charge the Jews with blaspheming Jesus, when they use insulting language toward Him, or deny to Him the credit that is His due.[201]

In Revelation, St. John tells that he "saw a beast rise up out of the sea, having seven heads and ten horns, and upon his horns ten crowns, and upon his heads the name of blasphemy. And he opened his mouth in blasphemy against God, to blaspheme his name, and his tabernacles, and them that dwell in heaven."[202] This beast was the symbolical Antichrist, and his blasphemy was simply the treasonable opposition of the antichristian world to God and His kingdom.

A comprehensive meaning of "blasphemy," in the various senses above suggested, is conveyed by the definition of the term "treason" under the governments of Gentile commonwealths. A single statute, 25 Edw. iii. c. 2, defines seven different ways of committing treason against the king of England.[203] The *lex Julia majestatis*, promulgated by Augustus Cæsar, was a single statute which comprehended all the ancient laws that had previously been enacted to punish transgressors against the Roman State.[204] There was no particular statute, as Rabbi Wise would have us believe, among the ancient Hebrews, that defined all forms of blasphemy against Jehovah. But a very clear notion of the various phases of blasphemy may be had if we will keep in mind the various definitions of treason under modern law.

It should not be forgotten that the ancient Hebrew Commonwealth was a pure theocracy; that Jehovah was king; that priests, prophets, and people were merely the subjects and servants of this king; that its government and its institutions were the products of his brain; and that the destinies of the people of Israel, the "chosen seed," were absolutely in his keeping and subject to his divine direction and control. It should also be remembered that the God of Israel was a most jealous God; that the greatest irritant of His wrath was any encroachment upon His rights as ruler of men and creator of the universe; that for the protection of His sovereignty, He had proclaimed to His people through His servant Moses the most stringent statutes against any profanation of His name or disloyalty to His person. The Decalogue was the great charter of Jehovah for the government of His children. The first three commandments were special statutes intended to excite their gratitude and insure their attachment. He reminds them of the circumstances of their deliverance, and warns them, under severe penalty, against going off after strange gods.

But, not content with these, He had still other statutes proclaimed, furnishing safeguards against idolatry and insuring loyalty to His person.[205] At the time of the establishment of the Hebrew theocracy, idolatry was everywhere to be found. Not only were the neighboring peoples worshipers of idols, but the Israelites themselves were prone to idolatry and to running off after strange gods. The worship of the Golden Calf is a familiar illustration of this truth. Thus the Commonwealth of Jehovah was threatened not only with idolatrous invasion from without but with idolatrous insurrection from within. Hence the severity of the measures adopted for the protection of His kingdom, His person, and His name, not only against idolaters but against necromancers, witches, sorcerers, and all persons who pretended to supernatural powers that did not proceed directly from Jehovah Himself. The enforcement of and obedience to these various statutes required an acknowledgment of the power and authority of Jehovah in every case where prophecies were foretold, wonders worked, and supernatural powers of any kind exhibited. And throughout the Sacred Scriptures, in both the Old and New Testaments, we find traces of the operation of this law. Sometimes it is an instance of obedience, as when Pharaoh wanted to credit Joseph with the power of interpreting dreams. "And Joseph answered Pharaoh, saying, It is not in *me*: God shall give Pharaoh an answer of peace."[206] At other times, it is an act of disobedience. To satisfy the thirsty multitude Moses smote the rock and brought forth water at Meribah. But instead of giving the Lord credit for the act, Moses claimed it for Aaron and himself, saying, "Hear now, ye rebels: must *we* fetch you water out of this rock?" Whereupon Jehovah grew very angry and said to Moses and Aaron: "Because ye believe me not, to sanctify *me* in the eyes of the children of Israel, therefore ye shall not bring this congregation into the land which I have given them."[207] As punishment for this blasphemous conduct, neither Moses nor Aaron was permitted to enter the Promised Land.[208] And that this omission to give due acknowledgment to the Lord for the miraculous flow of water was treasonable or blasphemous under the wider interpretation of the term, cannot be doubted.

From the foregoing remarks it is clear that blasphemy among the ancient Hebrews was subject to a twofold classification: (1) A verbal renunciation and profane speaking of the name of Jehovah. To this kind of blasphemy the provision in Leviticus xxiv. 15-20 was applicable. This was blasphemy in its generally accepted but narrower and more restricted sense. This kind of blasphemy indicated a most depraved and malignant state of mind, and to secure a conviction it was necessary to show that the word "Jehovah" or "Adonai" had been pronounced. (2) "Every word or act, directly in derogation of the sovereignty of Jehovah, such as speaking in the name of another god, or omitting, on any occasion that required it, to give to Jehovah the honor due to His own name."[209] This form of blasphemy was nearly the same as treason under modern governments, and included all offenses that threatened the usurpation of the throne of Jehovah, the destruction of His institutions, and that withheld from Him due acknowledgment of His authority and authorship in all matters of miracle and prophecy.

Returning to the trial in the palace of Caiaphas, let us again consider the question: Was Jesus guilty of blasphemy under any of the definitions above given? Had He ever cursed the name of Jehovah and thereby brought Himself within the condemnation of the law, as laid down in Leviticus xxiv. 15-20? Certainly not. Every word uttered by Him at the trial, as well as every other expression elsewhere uttered at any time or place, was said with reverence and awe and love in praise and glorification of the name and person of Jehovah. Rabbi Wise ridicules the notion that Jesus was ever tried upon the charge of blasphemy, because it is not recorded anywhere that He ever used any but tender and affectionate language in speaking of the Heavenly Father.

Had Jesus blasphemed, in the sense of "despising Judaism," and thereby brought Himself within the purview of the rule as exemplified in II Sam. xii. 14? Certainly not. There is no record anywhere that He despised Judaism. Jesus revered both the Law and the Prophets. He claimed that He came to fulfill, not to destroy them.[210] He frequently denounced Pharisaic formalism and hypocrisy, but at the same time He was a most loyal Jew and a devoted son of Israel.

Had He blasphemed by working wonders in His own name, and omitting to give Jehovah credit for them; and did He thereby bring Himself within the condemnation of the rule exemplified by Moses and Aaron in the matter of striking water from the rock at Meribah? We are forced to answer this question in the affirmative. If we regard Jesus as a mere man, a plain citizen, like Moses, the New Testament discloses many infractions of the Law in His prophecies and miracles. It is true that in John v. 19 it is said, "Verily, verily, I say unto you, The Son can do nothing of himself, but what he seeth the Father do." Here He affirmed that the power was from God and not from Himself. Again, having raised Lazarus from the dead, Jesus said, "Father, I thank thee that thou hast heard me,"[211] thus acknowledging the intervention of Jehovah in the performance of the miracle. In several other places He gave the Father credit for the act of the Son. But these were exceptions, isolated cases. The law required an express acknowledgment in every case of prophesy or miracle working. "Thus saith the Lord" was either the prologue or epilogue of every wonder-working performance. In all the miracles wrought by him in Egypt Moses had given due credit to Jehovah. But this was not enough. He was made an example for all time when he failed to make acknowledgment in the matter of striking the water from the rock. Now Jesus worked many miracles in no other name than His own, and in so doing brought Himself within the operation of the rule and of the precedent established in the case of Moses and Aaron. The curing of the bloody issue,[212] the stilling of the tempest,[213] the chasing of the devils into the sea,[214] the raising of Jairus' daughter,[215] and of the son of the widow of Nain[216] from the dead, were done without any mention of the power and guidance of Jehovah.

But these transgressions were extra-judicial offenses and have been discussed merely as an introduction throwing light upon the specific charge at the trial, that Jesus had claimed to be "the Christ, the Son of God." The question of the high priest is meaningless, unless interpreted in the light of knowledge which we know the members of the Sanhedrin had regarding the wonder-working performances of the Christ. The failure of Jesus to acknowledge the power of Jehovah in working miracles might be interpreted as a tacit avowal that He Himself was Jehovah, and that therefore no acknowledgments were necessary. The silence itself was a proclamation of the divinity that was in Him, which placed Him above a law intended to govern the conduct of men like Moses and Aaron.

We are now prepared to consider the final question: Had Jesus blasphemed, when He confessed to the high priest that He was "the Christ, the Son of God"? Had He blasphemed in that wider sense which Salvador has interpreted as being the Jewish notion of blasphemy at the time of Christ; that is, by claiming at once the attributes of the Messiah and the Son of God? Had He asserted an equality with God which looked to a usurpation of His power and the destruction of His throne; that is, did the confession of Jesus that He was "Christ, the Son of God," suggest a rivalry between Him and Jehovah which might result in the dethronement of the latter and the substitution of the former as the Lord and King and Ruler of Israel? Regarding Jesus as a mere man, a plain citizen, an affirmative answer to any one of these questions would convict Him of blasphemy, according to the Jewish interpretation of that term at the time of Christ; for the Hebrew Jehovah had repeatedly proclaimed that He was a jealous God, and that He would brook neither rivals nor associates in the government of His kingdom.

That Jesus had more than once identified Himself with Jehovah, and had claimed divine attributes and powers; and that the Jews regarded all these pretenses as blasphemous, is evident, and can be ascertained from more than one passage of New Testament Scripture. On one occasion the Savior said to one sick of palsy: "Son, be of good cheer; thy sins be forgiven thee. And, behold, certain of the Scribes said within themselves, This *man* blasphemeth."[217] According to Luke, they said: "Who is this man which speaketh blasphemies? Who can forgive sins but God alone?"[218] Here, according to the Scribes and Pharisees, Jesus had blasphemed by claiming the power which alone belonged to Jehovah, that of forgiving sins; or, at least, by exercising a supernatural power without acknowledging the authorship and guidance of the Almighty. It should be remembered that in this instance of alleged blasphemy Jesus had not remotely cursed or profaned the name of Jehovah; but, according to Jewish notions of the times, had exercised a prerogative, that of forgiving sins, which belonged solely to Jehovah, without giving credit.

Again, we read this passage in the New Testament: "Therefore Jews sought the more to kill him, because he not only had broken the Sabbath, but said also that God was his father, making himself equal with God."[219] Here we see that the Jews of the days of Jesus, as well as Salvador in our own day, construed the claims of Jesus to be "the Christ, the Son of God," as an assertion of equality with Jehovah.

Again, on another occasion, Jesus said emphatically: "I and my Father are one. Then the Jews took up stones again to stone him. Jesus answered them, Many good works have I shewed you from my Father; for which of those works do ye stone me? The Jews answered him, saying, For a good work, we stone thee not; but for blasphemy; and because that thou, being a man, makest thyself God."[220] Even before this bold declaration of His identity with Jehovah, He had intimated that He was of Heavenly origin and had enjoyed a divine preëxistence. He had declared that He was the "Bread which came down from Heaven,"[221] and that "Before Abraham was, I am."[222] The Jews regarded His statement that He had lived before Abraham as blasphemy, and "took up stones to cast at him," this being the usual punishment for blasphemous conduct.

We have said enough to emphasize the point that there was another kind of blasphemy known to the Jews of the days of Jesus than that prescribed in Leviticus; and that the confession of being "Christ, the Son of God," as the Jews and Caiaphas interpreted the term, brought Jesus within the meaning of blasphemy, in its wider signification—that of assuming equality with God. The numerous illustrations above furnished were given to provide means of clear interpretation of the term blasphemy, as used in the condemnatory sentence of the high priest. For it is clearly evident that he and the other judges must have had many charges against Jesus in mind other than those that appear in the record of the trial. But we repeat, these extra-judicial charges must be considered only for purposes of correct interpretation and as a means of throwing light upon the actual proceedings in the night trial before the Sanhedrin. We further repeat that the New Testament furnishes abundant evidence that Jesus the man, the Jewish citizen, had, at divers times and places, committed blasphemy against Jehovah, under a strict interpretation of the law of God.

Mr. Simon Greenleaf, the great Christian writer on the Law of Evidence and the Harmony of the Gospels, has thus tersely and admirably summarized the matter from the lawyer's point of view: "If we regard Jesus simply as a Jewish citizen, and with no higher character, this conviction seems substantially right in point of law, though the trial were not legal in all its forms. For, whether the accusation were founded on the first or the second command in the Decalogue, or on the law laid down in the thirteenth chapter of Deuteronomy, or on that in the eighteenth chapter and the twentieth verse, he had violated them all by assuming to himself powers belonging alone to Jehovah. It is not easy to perceive on what ground his conduct could have been defended before any tribunal, unless upon that of his superhuman character. No lawyer, it is conceived, would think of placing his defense upon any other basis."[223]

But, at this point, the reader would do well to discriminate very carefully between certain matters touching the most vital features of the controversy. Certain well-defined distinctions must be observed, else an erroneous conclusion will inevitably follow.

In the first place, proper limitations must be applied to the person and character of Jesus before it can be truthfully said that His conviction by the Sanhedrin was "substantially right in point of law." It must be remembered that, in this connection, Jesus is regarded merely as a man, "a Jewish citizen," to use Greenleaf's phrase. His divine character, as the only-begotten Son of God, as the Second Person of the Trinity, as the Savior of the human race, is not considered. But the reader may object, and with reason, that this is begging the question; and is therefore an inexcusable evasion; since the real issue before the Sanhedrin was this: Is Jesus God? And to strike the Godhead of Jesus from the discussion is to destroy the real issue, and to place the judgment of the Sanhedrin upon an irrelevant and immaterial basis. There is much truth in this contention, since it is clearly evident that if Jesus was actually God, "manifest in the flesh," He was not guilty; if He was not God, He was guilty.

Fortunately for the purposes of this treatise, the legality or the illegality of the proceedings in the trial of Christ is not so much related to the question of substance as to that of form. Whether Jesus were God or not is a question involving His divinity, and is a problem peculiarly within the domain of the theologian. Whether legal rules were duly observed in the trial of Christ, were He man or God, is a question involving His civil rights, and belongs to the domain of the lawyer. Unless this distinction be recognized and held in mind, the treatment of this theme from a legal standpoint has no justification. This contention is all the more certainly true, since proof of the divinity of Jesus, a spiritual problem, would rest more upon the basis of religious consciousness and experience, than upon historical facts and logical inferences.

The author of these volumes believes that Jesus was divine, and that if He was not divine, Divinity has not touched this globe. The writer bases his conviction of this fact upon the perfect purity, beauty, and sinlessness of Jesus; upon the overwhelming historical evidence of His resurrection from the dead, which event "may unhesitatingly be pronounced that best established in history";[224] as well as upon the evident impress of a divine hand upon genuine Christian civilization in every age.

But the historic proofs of the divinity of Christ that have come down to us through twenty centuries were not before the Sanhedrin. A charitable

Christian criticism will be slow in passing unmerciful judgment upon the members of that court for denying the claims of Jesus to identify with God, when His own disciples evidently failed to recognize them. The incidents of the Last Supper clearly prove that those who had been intimately associated with Him during three eventful years did not, at the close of His ministry, fully comprehend His character and appreciate His message and His mission.[225] Were comparative strangers to Him and His teachings expected to be more keenly discerning? After John had baptized Jesus in the Jordan and the Spirit of God, in the form of a dove, had descended upon Him, the Baptist seems to have had some doubts of the Messiahship of Christ and sent an embassy to Him to ask, "Art thou he that should come, or do we look for another?"[226] If the Forerunner of the Messiah did not know, are we justified in demanding perfect prescience and absolute infallibility of Caiaphas?

The most perfect proof of the divinity of Jesus is the fact of His resurrection from the dead, attested by Matthew, Mark, Luke, John, Peter, James, and Paul. And yet, although He had frequently foretold to them that He would rise again, Jesus had to personally appear before them and submit to physical tests before they would believe that His prophecies had been fulfilled.[227] And it must be remembered that the great proof of His divinity, His resurrection from the dead, was not before Caiaphas and his colleagues at the time of the trial.

The preceding suggestions and observations have not been made in order to excuse or palliate the conduct of the members of the Sanhedrin for their illegal conduct of the proceedings against Jesus. Under Point XI of the Brief we shall prove by Jewish testimony alone the utterly wicked and worthless character of these judges. Under Point XII we shall elaborate the proofs in favor of the Messiahship of Jesus and of His divine Sonship of the Father, as far as the scope of this work will permit. We have suggested above the perplexity of the members of the Sanhedrin and of the disciples of Jesus, concerning the divinity of the Nazarene, to illustrate to the reader how futile would be the task of attempting in a treatise of this kind to settle the question of the identity of Jesus with God, and thereby fix upon His judges in the palace of Caiaphas the odium of an unrighteous judgment. The question, after all, is one to be settled in the forum of conscience, illuminated by the light of history, and not at the bar of legal justice.

But whether Jesus were man or God, or man-God, we are justified in passing upon the question of the violation of forms of law which He was entitled to have observed in the trial of His claims. And at this point we return to a consideration of the phrase, "substantially right in point of law." This language is not intended to convey the notion that Jesus was legally convicted. It means simply that the claim of equality with God by a plain

Jewish citizen was, under Hebrew law, blasphemy; the crime which Caiaphas and the Sanhedrin believed that Jesus had confessed, and for which they condemned Him.

Another distinction that must be made is that relating to the kind of law that is meant, when it is said that the conviction of Jesus was "substantially right in point of law." Ancient Hebrew law is meant, and as that law was interpreted from the standpoint of ancient Judaism. The policy and precepts of the New Dispensation inaugurated by Jesus can hardly be considered, in a legal sense, to have been binding upon Caiaphas and the Sanhedrin, since the very claims of Jesus to Messiahship and identity with God were to be tested by the provisions of the Mosaic Code and in the light of Hebrew prophecy. The Pentateuch, the Prophets, and the Talmud were the legal guides, then, of the judges of Israel in judicial proceedings at this time, and furnished rules for determining the genuineness of His pretensions.

Mr. Greenleaf, the author of the phrase, "substantially right in point of law," asserts that the trial was not legal in all its forms, but he fails to enumerate the errors. The purpose of the Brief in this work is to name and discuss the errors and irregularities of the Hebrew trial, that is, the trial before the Sanhedrin.

But the question may be asked: Why be guilty of the inconsistency of discussing illegalities, when admission has already been made that the decision was "substantially right in point of law"? The answer is that a distinction must be made between that which is popularly and historically known or believed to be true, and that which has not been or cannot be proved in a court of law. Every lawyer is familiar with this distinction. The court may know that the accused is guilty, the jury may know it, the attorneys may be perfectly sure of it, but if the verdict of guilt returned by the jury into court is not based upon testimony that came from the witness stand from witnesses who were under oath, and that had submitted to cross-examination, such verdict would hardly be sustained on appeal. In other words, the lives and liberties of alleged criminals must not be endangered by extra-judicial and incompetent testimony. A legal verdict can be rendered only when a regular trial has been had before a competent court, having jurisdiction of the crime charged, and after all legal rules have been observed which the constitution and the laws have provided as safeguards for the protection of the rights of both the people and the prisoner. However heinous the offense committed, no man is, legally speaking, a criminal, until he has been legally tried and declared a criminal. The presumption of innocence, a substantial legal right, is thrown around him from the very beginning, and continues in his favor until it is overthrown by competent and satisfactory evidence. Unless such evidence is furnished, under legal forms, no man, however morally guilty, can be denominated a criminal, in a juristic sense, in the face of the perpetual continuance of this presumption of innocence.

If these rules and principles be applied to the trial of Jesus, either before the Sanhedrin or before Pilate, it can be easily demonstrated that while He might have been abstractly and historically guilty of the crime of blasphemy, in the wider acceptation of that term, He was not remotely a criminal, because He was never legally tried and convicted. In other words, his condemnation was not based upon a legal procedure that was in harmony with either the Mosaic Code or the Mishna. The pages of human history present no stronger case of judicial murder than the trial and crucifixion of Jesus of Nazareth, for the simple reason that all forms of law were outraged and trampled under foot in the proceedings instituted against Him. The errors were so numerous and the proceedings so flagrant that many have doubted the existence of a trial. Others have sought to attack the authenticity of the Gospel narratives and the veracity of the Gospel writers by pointing to the number of errors committed as evidence that no such proceedings ever took place. As Renan would say, this is a species of "naïve impudence," to assert that a trial was not had, because numerous errors are alleged; as if a Hebrew court could not either intentionally or unintentionally commit blunders and many of them. Every lawyer of extensive practice anywhere knows from experience that judges of great ability and exalted character conduct lengthy trials, in both civil and criminal cases, with the most painstaking care, and are aided by eminent counsel and good and honest jurors; the whole purpose of the proceedings being to reach a just and righteous verdict; and yet, on appeal, it is frequently held that not one but many errors have been committed.

At this point, a few preliminary observations are necessary as a means of introduction to the discussion of errors. Certain elementary principles should be clearly understood at the outset. In the first place, an analysis of the word "case," used in a juristic sense, shows the existence of two cardinal judicial elements: the element called Fact, and the element called Law. And whether the advocate is preparing a pleading at his desk, is making a speech to the jury, or addressing himself to the court, these elements are ever present in his mind. He is continually asking these questions: What are the facts of this case? What is the law applicable to these facts? Do the facts and law meet, harmonize, blend, according to the latest decision of the court of last resort? If so, a case is made; otherwise, not.

It is impossible to frame any legal argument upon any other basis than that of the agreement or nonagreement of law and fact, in a juristic sense; and upon this plan errors will be discussed and the Brief will be framed.

In the second place, it must not be forgotten that, in matters of review on appeal, errors will not be presumed; that is, errors will not be considered that do not appeal affirmatively upon the record. The law will rather presume and the court will assume that what should have been done, has been done. In conformity with this principle, only such errors will be discussed in these pages that affirmatively appear in the New Testament Gospels which form the record in this case. By "affirmatively appear" is meant that the error is clearly apparent or may be reasonably inferred.

In Part II of the preceding pages of this volume, Hebrew criminal law, which was actively in force at the time of Christ, was outlined and discussed. In Part I the Record of Fact was reviewed in the light of judicial rules. It is the present purpose, in Part III, to enumerate, in the form of a Brief, the errors committed by the Hebrew judges of Jesus, as the result of their failure to make the facts of their trial conform with the legal rules by which they were bound in all criminal proceedings where human life was at stake. The plan proposed is to announce successive errors in brief statements which will be designated "Points," in imitation of the New York method on appeal. Following the statement of error will be given a short synopsis of the law applicable to the point suggested. Then, finally, will follow the fact and argument necessary to elaboration and proof. Accordingly, in pursuance of this method, let us consider the points in order.

POINT I

THE ARREST OF JESUS WAS ILLEGAL

LAW

"Now the Jewish law prohibited *all proceedings by night*."—DUPIN, "Jesus Devant Caïphe et Pilate."

"The testimony of an accomplice is not permissible by Rabbinic law both *propter affectum* and *propter delictum*, and no man's *life*, nor his *liberty*, nor his *reputation* can be endangered by the malice of one who has confessed himself a criminal."—MENDELSOHN, "Criminal Jurisprudence of the Ancient Hebrews," n. 274.

"Thou shalt not go up and down as a talebearer among thy people: neither shalt thou stand against the blood of thy neighbor. Thou shalt not hate thy brother in thine heart: Thou shalt not avenge or bear any grudge against the children of thy people, but thou shalt love thy neighbor as thyself."—LEVITICUS xix. 17, 18.

FACT AND ARGUMENT

THE Bible record discloses three distinct elements of illegality in the arrest of Jesus: (1) The arrest took place at night in violation of Hebrew law; (2) it was effected through the agency of a traitor and informer, in violation of a provision in the Mosaic Code and of a Rabbinic rule based thereon; (3) it was not the result of a legal mandate from a court whose intentions were to conduct a legal trial for the purpose of reaching a righteous judgment. These elements of illegality will be apparent when the facts of the arrest are briefly stated.

It was the 14th Nisan, according to the Jewish calendar; or April 6th, A.D. 30, according to our calendar. The Paschal Feast was at hand. The eyes of all Israel were centered upon the Metropolis of Judaism. From Judea, from Samaria, from Galilee and Perea, from all parts of the world where Jews were resident, pilgrims came streaming into the Holy City to be present at the great national festival. It was to be an occasion of prayer and thanksgiving, of sweet memories and happy reunions. Then and there offerings would be made and purifications obtained. In the great Temple, with its gorgeous ritual, Judaism was to offer its soul to Jehovah. The national and religious feelings of a divinely commissioned race were to be deeply stirred by memories that reminded them of the first, and by hopes that looked forward to the final great deliverance.

It was probably in the home of Mark, on the outskirts of Jerusalem, that Jesus gathered with the Twelve, on the evening of this day, to eat the Paschal lamb. In the Upper Room, the sacred feast was spread and the little band were gathered. Only the genius of a da Vinci could do justice to that scene. There was Peter, hot-headed, impetuous, bravado-like. There was John, as gentle, pure-minded, and loving as a woman. There was Judas, mercenary, low-browed, and craven-hearted. There were others who, with Peter and John, were to have temples dedicated in their names. In their midst was the Master of them all, "God manifest in the flesh," who "with His pierced hands was to lift empires off their hinges, and turn the stream of centuries from its channel." No moment of history was so fraught with tragic interest for the human race. There the seal of the New Covenant was affixed, the bond of the new human spiritual alliance was made. The great law of love was proclaimed which was to regenerate and sanctify the world. "These things I command you, that ye love one another. And I have declared unto them thy name, and will declare it; that the love wherewith thou hast loved me, may be in them, and I in them." Thus the great law of love was to be the binding tie, not only among the little brotherhood there assembled but was to be the cementing bond between the regenerate of earth, the Mediator, and the great Father of love, Himself. There, too, was given the great example of humility which was to characterize true Christian piety throughout the ages. The pages of history record no other spectacle so thrilling and sublime, and at the same time tender and pathetic, as that afforded by the Paschal Meal, when Jesus, the Savior of men, the Son of God, the Maker of all the shining worlds, sank upon His knees to wash the feet of ignorant, simple-minded Galilean fishermen, in order that future ages might have at once a lesson and an example of that genuine humility which is the very life and soul of true religion.

During the evening, a bitter anxiety, an awful melancholy, seized the devoted band, whose number, thirteen, even to-day inspires superstitious dread. In the midst of the apprehension the heart of the Master was so deeply wrung with agony that He turned to those about Him and said: "Verily, verily, I say unto you that one of you shall betray me." This prediction only intensified the sadness that had already begun to fall over the Sacred Meal and the loving disciples began to ask: "Lord, is it I?" Even the betrayer himself joined with the others, and, with inconceivable heartlessness and effrontery, asked: "Lord, is it I?" At the moment of greatest dread and consternation, Peter, bolder than the rest, leaned across the table and whispered to John, who was resting upon the bosom of Jesus, and suggested that he ask the Master who it was. Accordingly, John whispered and asked the Savior: "Lord, who is it?" "Jesus answered, He it is, to whom I shall give a sop, when I have dipped it. And when he had dipped the sop, he gave it to Judas Iscariot, the son of Simon. And after the sop Satan entered into him. Then said Jesus unto him, That thou doest, do quickly." Judas then arose from the feast and vanished from the room. When he was gone, the Master began to deliver to His "little children,"[228] to those who had loved and followed Him, those farewell words which St. John alone records, and that are so "rarely mixed of sadness and joys, and studded with mysteries as with emeralds."

There, too, doubts and fears began to burst from the hearts and lips of the members of the little company. The knowledge that the gentle Jesus, whose ministry had thrilled and glorified their simple peasant lives, and promised to them crowns of glory in the world to come, was about to leave them, and in a most tragic way, filled them with solicitude and dread. Their anxiety manifested itself by frequent questioning which excites our wonder that men who had been with Him so long in the Apostolic ministry should have been so simple-minded and incredulous. "They said, therefore, What is this that he saith, A little while? We cannot tell what he saith." This verse is a simple illustration of the continued misapprehension, on this night, upon the part of the Apostles, of everything said by the Master. Peter was anxious to know why he could not follow the Lord. Thomas wanted to know the exact way, evidently failing to comprehend the figurative language of the Christ. Judas Lebbæus also had his doubts. He became muddled by mixing the purely spiritual with the physical powers of sight. "Lord, how is it," he asked, "that thou wilt manifest thyself to us and not to the world?" Philip of Bethsaida desired to see the Father. "Lord, show us the Father," he said, "and it sufficeth us." Philip seems to have been so dense that he had no appreciation of the spiritual attributes and invisible existence of the Father.

It was thus that several hours were spent in celebrating the great Feast; in drinking wine; in eating the Paschal lamb, the unleavened bread, and the bitter herbs; in singing hymns, offering prayers, and performing the sacred rites; in delivering discourses which in every age have been the most precious treasures of Christians, and in expressing doubts and fears that have excited the astonishment and even the ridicule of the exacting and supercilious of all the centuries.

At the approach of midnight, Jesus and the Eleven left the Upper Chamber of the little house and stepped out into the moonlight of a solemn Passover night. They began to wend their way toward the Kedron that separated them from the olive orchard on the Mount. Less than an hour's journey brought them to the Garden of Gethsemane. The word "Gethsemane" means "oil press." And this place doubtless derived its name from the fact that in it was located an oil press which was used to crush olives that grew abundantly on the trees that crowned the slopes. Whether it was a public garden or belonged to some friend of Jesus, we do not know, but certain it is that it was a holy place, a sanctuary of prayer, where the Man of Sorrows frequently retired to pray and commune with His Heavenly Father. At the gateway Jesus left eight of the Apostles and took with Him the other three: Peter, James, and John. These men seem to have been the best beloved of the Master. They were with Him at the raising of Jairus' daughter, at the Transfiguration on the Mount, and were now selected to be nearest Him in the hour of His agony. Proceeding with them a short distance, He suddenly stopped and exclaimed: "My soul is exceedingly sorrowful, even unto death: tarry ye here, and watch with me." Then, withdrawing Himself from them a stone's cast, He sank upon His knees and prayed; and in the agony of prayer great drops of sweat resembling blood rolled from His face and fell upon the ground. Rising from prayer, He returned to His disciples to find them asleep. Sorrow had overcame them and they were mercifully spared the tortures of the place and hour. Three times did He go away to pray, and as many times, upon His return, they were found asleep. The last time He came He said to them: "Rise, let us be going; behold he is at hand that doth betray me." At this moment were heard the noise and tramp of an advancing multitude. "Judas then, having received a band of men and officers from the chief priests and Pharisees, cometh thither with lanterns and torches and weapons." This midnight mob, led by Judas, was made up of Roman soldiers, the Temple guard, and stragglers from along the way. It is probable that the traitor walked ahead of the mob by several paces. "And forthwith he came to Jesus, and said, Hail, master, and kissed him and Jesus said unto him, Friend, wherefore art thou come? Then came they and laid hands on Jesus and took him." But the arrest was not accomplished without incidents of pathos and of passion. "Whom seek ye?" asked the Master. "Jesus of Nazareth," they answered. "I am he," replied the Savior. Then, dazed and bewildered, they fell backward upon the ground. "Then asked he them again, whom seek ye? and they said, Jesus of Nazareth. Jesus answered, I have told you that I am he: if, therefore, ye seek me, let these go their way." John says that this intercession for the disciples was to the end that prophecy might be fulfilled.[229] Doubtless so; but this was not all. Nowhere in sacred literature do we find such pointed testimony to the courage and manliness of Jesus. His tender solicitude for the members of the little band, for those who had quit their homes and callings to link their destinies with His, was here superbly illustrated. He knew that He was going to immediate condemnation and then to death, but He ardently desired that they should be spared to live. And for them He threw Himself into the breach.

The furious and the passionate, as well as the tender and pathetic, mark the arrest in the garden. "Then Simon Peter having a sword drew it, and smote the high priest's servant, and cut off his right ear. The servant's name was Malchus." This was bloody proof of that fidelity which Peter loudly proclaimed at the banquet board, but which was soon to be swallowed up in craven flight and pusillanimous denial.

"Then the band and the captain and officers of the Jews took Jesus, and bound him."

At this point the arrest was complete, and we now return to the discussion of the illegalities connected with it.

It was a well-established and inflexible rule of Hebrew law that proceedings in capital trials could not be had at night. This provision did not apply simply to the proceedings of the trial after the prisoner had been arraigned and the examination had been begun. We have it upon the authority of Dupin that it applied to the entire proceedings, from the arrest to the execution. The great French advocate explicitly states that the arrest was illegal because it was made at night.[230] Deference to this rule seems to have been shown in the arrest of Peter and John on another occasion. "And they laid hands upon them and put them in hold unto the next day: for it was now *eventide.*"[231] That Jesus was arrested at night is clearly evident from the fact that those who captured Him bore "*lanterns* and *torches* and *weapons.*"

The employment of Judas by the Sanhedrin authorities constitutes the second element of illegality in the arrest. This wretched creature had been numbered among the Twelve, had been blessed and honored, not merely with discipleship but with apostleship, had himself been sent on holy missions by the Master, had been given the power to cast out devils, had been appointed by his Lord the keeper of the moneys of the Apostolic company, and, if Edersheim is to be believed, had occupied the seat of honor by the Master at the Last Supper.[232] This craven and cowardly Apostate was employed by the Sanhedrin Council to betray the Christ. It is clearly evident from the Scriptures that the arrest of Jesus would not have taken place on the occasion of the Passover, and therefore probably not at all, if Judas had not deserted and betrayed Him. The Savior had appeared and preached daily in the Temple, and every opportunity was offered to effect a legal arrest on legal charges with a view to a legal determination. But the enemies of Jesus did not want this. They were waiting to effect His capture in some out-of-the-way place, at the dead of night, when His friends could not defend Him and their murderous proceedings would not reach the eye and ear of the public. This could not be accomplished as long as His intimates were faithful to Him. It was, then, a joyful surprise to the members of the Sanhedrin when they learned that Judas was willing to betray his Master. "And when they heard it, they were glad, and promised to give him money."

In modern jurisdictions, accomplice testimony has been and is allowed. The judicial authorities, however, have always regarded it with distrust, and we might say with deep-seated suspicion. At the common law in England a conviction for crime might rest upon the uncorroborated testimony of an accomplice, after the jury had been warned that such testimony was to be closely scrutinized. In the American States the testimony of an accomplice is admissible, but must be corroborated in order to sustain a conviction. This is the general rule. The weakness of such evidence is shown by the nature of the corroboration required by several states. In some of them the corroborating testimony must not only tend to prove the commission of the crime but must also tend to connect the defendant with such commission. Another evidence of the untrustworthiness of such testimony is that in several states an accomplice is not permitted to corroborate another accomplice, so as to satisfy the statutes.[233] The admission of such testimony seems to rest, in great measure, upon the supreme necessity of the preservation of the state, which is only possible when the punishment of crime is possible; and in very many instances it would be impossible to punish crime if guilty confederates were not allowed and even encouraged to give state's evidence.

But notwithstanding this supreme consideration of the necessity of the preservation of the state, the ancient Hebrews forbade the use of accomplice testimony, as we have seen from the extract from "The Criminal Jurisprudence of the Ancient Hebrews," by Mendelsohn, cited on page 219.

The arrest of Jesus was ordered upon the supposition that He was a criminal; this same supposition would have made Judas, who had aided, encouraged, and abetted Jesus in the propagation of His faith, an accomplice. If Judas was not an accomplice, Jesus was innocent, and His arrest was an outrage, and therefore illegal.

The Hebrew law against accomplice testimony must have been derived, in part at least, from the following rule laid down in Leviticus xix. 16-18: "Thou shalt not go up and down as a talebearer among thy people: neither shall thou stand against the blood of thy neighbor. Thou shalt not hate thy brother in thine heart: Thou shalt not avenge, or bear any grudge against the children of thy people, but thou shalt love thy neighbor as thyself." It may be objected that this is only a moral injunction and not a legal rule; to which reply must be made that there was no difference between morality and law among the ancient Hebrews. Their religion was founded upon law, and their law upon religion. The two ideas of morality and law were inseparable. The ancient Hebrew religion was founded upon a contract of the strictest legal kind. The Abrahamic covenant, when properly interpreted, meant simply that Jehovah had agreed with the children of Israel that if they would obey the law as He gave it, they would be rewarded by Him. The force of this contention will be readily perceived when it is reflected that the Decalogue is nothing but ten moral injunctions, which are nevertheless said to be the law which God gave to Moses.

Every provision in the rule laid down in Leviticus is, moreover, directly applicable to the character and conduct of Judas, and seems to have been intended as a prophetic warning to him. Let us consider the different elements of this rule in order.

"Thou shalt not go up and down as a talebearer among thy people."

Was not Judas a talebearer among his people? Did he not go to the chief priests to betray his Master unto them? Was he not a 'talebearer" if he did nothing more than communicate to the chief priests the whereabouts of the Savior, that Gethsemane was His accustomed place of prayer and that He might be found and arrested there at midnight? Are we not justified in supposing that Judas told the enemies of Jesus much more than this? Is it not reasonable to infer that the blood-money was paid to secure more evidence than that which would merely lead to the arrest of the Nazarene? Is it not probable that Judas detailed to the chief priests many events in the ministry of Jesus which, it is known, He communicated only to the Twelve? If he did these things, was he not a "talebearer" within the meaning of the rule?

"Neither shalt thou stand against the blood of thy neighbor."

Did not Judas stand against the blood of his nearest and dearest neighbor when he consented to be the chief instrument of an arrest which he knew would result in death?

"Thou shalt not hate thy brother in thy heart."

Is it possible to suppose that anything less than hatred could have induced Judas to betray the Christ? This question is important, for it involves a consideration of the real character of the betrayer and the main motive for the betrayal. Judas was from Kerioth in Judea and was the only Judean among the Twelve. Why Judas was selected as a member of the Apostolic company is too deep a mystery to be solved by the author of these pages. Besides, the consideration of the elements of predestination in his case is foreign to the purpose of this work. His character as a purely human agency is sufficient to answer the present design. Judas had undoubtedly demonstrated business capacity in some way before his appointment to the treasury portfolio of the little band. It cannot be doubted that greed was his besetting sin. This trait, coupled with political ambition, undoubtedly accounts for his downfall and destruction. He was one of those simple-minded, short-sighted individuals of his day who believed that a political upheaval was at hand which would result in the restoration of the independence of Israel as a separate kingdom. He believed that this result would be brought about through the agency of a temporal Messiah, an earthly deliverer of almost divine qualities. He thought at first that he saw in Jesus the person of the Messiah, and in the Apostolic band the nucleus of a revolution. He was gratified beyond measure at his appointment to the treasury position, for he felt sure that from it promotion was in sight. He was perfectly contented to carry for a while the "little bag," provided there was reasonable assurance that later on he would be permitted to carry a larger one.

As the months and years rolled by, heavy scales began to fall from his stupid eyes and he began to be deceived not by but in Jesus. We are justified in believing that Judas never even remotely appreciated the spiritual grandeur of the Christ. He probably had intellect and soul enough to be charmed and fascinated by the lofty bearing and eloquent discourse of Jesus, but after all he perceived only the necessary qualifications of a great republican leader and successful revolutionist. And after a while he doubtless began to tire of all this when he saw that the revolution was not progressing and that there was no possibility of actual and solid results. It is probable that disaffection and treachery were born and began to grow in his mind and heart at Capernaum, when Jesus was deserted by many of His followers and was forced to effect a realignment along spiritual lines. Judas was not equal to the spiritual test, and it was doubtless then that the disintegration of his moral nature began, which stopped only with betrayal, infamy, and death.

But by what process, we may ask, was the mercenary disposition of Judas converted into hatred against Jesus? The process was that of disappointment. When Judas became convinced that all the years of his connection with the Apostolic company had been lost, his will became embittered and his resentment was aroused. In the denseness of his ignorance and in the baseness of his soul he probably thought that Jesus had deceived His followers as to His true mission and he felt enraged because he had been duped. He had looked forward to worldly promotion and success. He had fondly hoped that the eloquence of Jesus would finally call around Him an invincible host of enthusiastic adherents who would raise the standard of revolt, drive the Romans from Judea, and establish the long-looked-for kingdom of the Jews. He had noted with deep disappointment and unutterable chagrin the failure of Jesus to proclaim Himself king when, at Bethphage, the multitude had greeted His entrance into Jerusalem with Hosannas and acclamations. And now, at the Last Supper, he became convinced from the conduct and discourses of the Master that his worst fears were true, that Jesus was sincere in His resolution to offer Himself as a sacrifice for the sake of a principle which he, Judas, did not approve because he could not understand. In other words, he witnessed in the resolve of Jesus to die at once the shipwreck of his hopes, and he made haste to vent his wrath upon the author of his disappointment.

The writer agrees with Renan that the thirty pieces of silver were not the real or leading inducement to this black and monumental betrayal. Having taken the fatal step, by leaving the Upper Room in the home of Mark, to deliver his Lord and Master into the hands of enemies, a bitter hatred was formed at once against the innocent victim of his foul designs, on the well-known principle of human nature that we hate those who have induced us to do that which causes us to despise and hate ourselves.

"Thou shalt not avenge or bear any grudge against the children of thy people."

Where, in the annals of the universe, do we find another such case of vengeance and grudge as this of Judas against Jesus?

"But thou shalt love thy neighbor as thyself."

This commandment of the Mosaic law was also the great commandment of the Master of Galilee, and in violating it by consenting to betray and sacrifice Jesus, Judas assaulted and destroyed in his own soul the cardinal principle of the two great religious dispensations of his race.

And yet this informer, conspirator, and malefactor was employed by the chief priests in effecting the arrest of Jesus. Was not a fundamental rule of Mosaic law violated? Will it be urged that the rule operated against Judas but not against the chief priests? If so, it must be remembered that no wicked instrument could be used in promoting Hebrew justice. Officers of the law were not permitted to require a citizen to do an act which was forbidden by law. If Jesus was innocent, then the arrest was illegal. If He was guilty, then Judas, his Apostle and fellow-worker, was an accomplice; and no accomplice could be utilized in furtherance of justice, under Hebrew law, either in the matter of arrest or in the establishment of guilt as a witness at the trial.

According to the Talmud, there was at least one seeming exception to this rule. Renan describes it with peculiar clearness and succinctness. "The procedure," he says, "against the 'corrupter' (mesith), who sought to attaint the purity of religion, is explained in the Talmud, with details, the naïve impudence of which provokes a smile. A judicial ambush is therein erected into an essential part of the examination of criminals. When a man was accused of being a 'corrupter,' two witnesses were suborned who were concealed behind a partition. It was arranged to bring the accused into a contiguous room, where he could be heard by these two witnesses without his perceiving them. Two candles were lighted near him, in order that it might be satisfactorily proved that the witnesses 'saw him.' (In criminal matters, eyewitnesses alone were admitted. Mishna, Sanhedrin VI, 5.) He was then made to repeat his blasphemy; next urged to retract it. If he persisted, the witnesses who had heard him conducted him to the Tribunal and he was stoned to death. The Talmud adds that this was the manner in which they treated Jesus; that he was condemned on the faith of two witnesses who had been suborned, and that the crime of 'corruption' is, moreover, the only one for which the witnesses are thus prepared."[234]

Most Gentile writers ridicule this statement of the Talmud, and maintain that it was a Rabbinic invention of post-Apostolic days, and was intended to offer an excuse for the outrageous proceedings against the Christ. Schürer dismisses the whole proposition with contempt. Many Jewish scholars also refuse it the sanction of their authority. But even if it was a Talmudic rule of law in force at the time of Christ, its constitutionality, so to speak, might be questioned, in the first place; since it was, in spirit at least, repugnant to and subversive of the Mosaic provision in Leviticus cited above. It must not be forgotten that the Mosaic Code was the constitution, the fundamental law of Judaism, by which every Rabbinic interpretation and every legal innovation was to be tested.

Again, such a law would have been no protection to the chief priests and to Judas against the operation of this Mosaic injunction. If such a rule of procedure could be justified upon any ground, it would require disinterested men acting from honorable motives, in promoting the maintenance of law and order. Officers of the law have sometimes, as pretended accomplices, acted in concert with criminals in order to secure and furnish evidence against them. But they were officers of the law, and the courts have held that their evidence was not accomplice testimony requiring corroboration. It is very clear that Judas was not such a disinterested witness, acting in the interest of public justice. He was a fugitive from the Last Supper of his Master, a talebearer within the meaning of the provision in Leviticus; and his employment by the Sanhedrin was a violation of a fundamental provision in the Mosaic Code.

The third illegality in the arrest of Jesus was that His capture was not the result of a legal mandate from a court whose intentions were to conduct a legal trial for the purpose of reaching a righteous judgment. "This arrest," says Rosadi, "effected in the night between Thursday and Friday, the last day of the life of Jesus, on Nisan 14, according to the Hebrew calendar, was the execution of an illegal and factious resolution of the Sanhedrin. There was no idea of apprehending a citizen in order to try him upon a charge which after sincere and regular judgment might be found just or unfounded; the intention was simply to seize a man and do away with him. The arrest was not a preventive measure such as might lawfully precede trial and condemnation; it was an executive act, accomplished in view of a sentence to be pronounced without legal justification."

POINT II

THE PRIVATE EXAMINATION OF JESUS BEFORE ANNAS (OR CAIAPHAS) WAS ILLEGAL

LAW

"Now the Jewish law prohibited *all proceedings by night*."—DUPIN, "Jesus Devant Caïphe et Pilate."

"Be not a sole judge, for there is no sole judge but One."—MISHNA, Pirke Aboth IV. 8.

"A principle perpetually reproduced in the Hebrew scriptures relates to the two conditions of *publicity* and liberty. An accused man was never subjected to private or secret examination, lest, in his perplexity, he furnish damaging testimony against himself."—SALVADOR, "Institutions de Moïse," pp. 365, 366.

FACT AND ARGUMENT

THE private examination before Annas (or Caiaphas) was illegal for the following reasons: (1) The examination was conducted at night in violation of Hebrew law; (2) no judge or magistrate, sitting alone, could interrogate an accused judicially or sit in judgment upon his legal rights; (3) private preliminary examinations of accused persons were not allowed by Hebrew law.

The general order of events following the arrest in the garden was this: (1) Jesus was first taken to the house of Annas; (2) after a brief delay He was sent by Annas to Caiaphas, the high priest, in whose palace the Sanhedrin, or a part thereof, had already assembled; (3) He was then brought before this body, tried and condemned; (4) He remained, during the rest of the night, in the high priest's palace, exposed to the insults and outrages of His keepers; and was finally and formally sentenced to death by the Sanhedrin which reconvened at the break of day.

That Jesus was privately examined before His regular trial by the Sanhedrin is quite clear. But whether this preliminary examination took place before Annas or Caiaphas is not certainly known. John alone records the private interrogation of Jesus and he alone refers to Annas in a way to connect him with it. This Evangelist mentions that they "led him away to Annas first."[235] Matthew says that after the arrest of Jesus, they "led him away to Caiaphas the high priest,"[236] without mentioning the name of Annas. Mark tells us that "they led Jesus away to the high priest";[237] but he does not mention either Annas or Caiaphas. Luke records that they "took him, and led him, and brought him into the high priest's house,"[238] without telling us the name of the high priest.

"The high priest then asked Jesus of his disciples and of his doctrine."[239] This was the beginning of the examination. But who was the examiner— Annas or Caiaphas? At first view we are inclined to declare that Caiaphas is meant, because he was undoubtedly high priest in that year. But Annas is also designated as high priest by Luke in several places.[240] In Acts iv. 6 he mentions Caiaphas without an official title, but calls Annas high priest. It is therefore not known to whom John refers when he says that the "high priest asked Jesus of his disciples and of his doctrine." For a lengthy discussion of this point, the reader is referred to Andrews's "Life of Our Lord," pp. 505-510.

But it is absolutely immaterial, from a legal point of view, whether it was Annas or Caiaphas who examined Jesus, as the proceedings would be illegal in either case. For whether it was the one or the other, neither had the right to sit alone as judge; neither had the right to conduct any judicial proceeding at night; neither had the right to institute a secret preliminary examination by day or night.

Attention has been called to the matter as involving a question of historical rather than of legal consequence. A knowledge of the true facts of the case might, however, throw light upon the order and connection of the proceedings which followed the same night. For if the private examination recorded by John was had before Annas, it was doubtless separated by a certain interval of place and time from the later proceedings before Caiaphas. Then it is reasonable to suppose that the examination of witnesses, the confession and condemnation which took place at the regular trial before the Sanhedrin over which Caiaphas presided, happened later in the night, or even toward morning, and were of the nature of a regular public trial. If, on the other hand, Annas sent Jesus without delay to Caiaphas, who examined Him, it is reasonable to conclude that witnesses were at once produced, and that the adjuration and condemnation immediately followed. If such were the case, a considerable interval of time must have intervened between these proceedings and the meeting of the Sanhedrin which was had in the morning to confirm the judgment which had been pronounced at the night session. But these considerations are really foreign to the question of legal errors involved, which we come now to discuss.

JESUS IN GETHSEMANE (HOFFMAN)

In the first place, the private examination of Jesus, whether by Annas or Caiaphas, took place at night; and we have learned from Dupin that *all proceedings at night in capital cases* were forbidden.

In the second place, no judge or magistrate, sitting alone, could interrogate an accused person judicially or sit in judgment upon his legal rights. We have seen in Part II of this volume that the Hebrew system of courts and judges provided no single magistrates who, sitting alone, could adjudicate causes. The lowest Hebrew court consisted of three judges, sometimes called the Court of Three. The next highest tribunal was the Minor Sanhedrin of three-and-twenty members. The supreme tribunal of the Jews was the Great Sanhedrin of seventy-one members. There was no such thing among the ancient Hebrews as a court with a single judge. "Be not a sole judge, for there is no sole judge but One," is one of the most famous aphorisms of the Pirke Aboth. The reason of this rule is founded not only in a religious exaction born of the jealousy of Jehovah, but in the principle of publicity which provides for the accused, in the very number of judges, a public hearing. The same principle is suggested by the number of witnesses required by both the Mishna and Mosaic Code for the conviction of a prisoner. At least "two or three witnesses" were required to appear publicly and give testimony against the accused, else a conviction could not follow.

Again, preliminary examinations of accused persons were not allowed by Hebrew law. In the American states and in some other countries, a man suspected of crime and against whom an information or complaint has been lodged, is frequently taken before an examining magistrate to determine whether he should be discharged, admitted to bail, or sent to prison to await the action of a Grand Jury. At such hearing, the prisoner is usually notified that he is at liberty to make a statement regarding the charge against him; that he need not do so unless he desires; but that if he does, his testimony may be subsequently used against him at the regular trial of the case. But such proceedings, according to Salvador, were forbidden by ancient Hebrew law. The preliminary examination, therefore, by Annas or Caiaphas was illegal. The reason of the rule, as above stated, was to protect the prisoner against furnishing evidence that might be used against him at the regular trial of his case. The private examination of Jesus illustrates the justice of the rule and the necessity of its existence, for it was undoubtedly the purpose of Annas or Caiaphas to gather material in advance to lay before the regularly assembled Sanhedrin and thereby expedite the proceedings at the expense of justice.

If it be contended that the leading of Jesus to Annas first, which St. John alone relates, was merely intended to give the aged Sanhedrist an opportunity to see the prisoner who had been causing such commotion in the land for several years; and that there was no examination of Jesus before Annas—the interrogation by the high priest concerning the disciples and the doctrine of Jesus being construed to refer to an examination by Caiaphas, and being identical with the night trial referred to by Matthew and Mark—reply may be made that, under any construction of the case, there was at least an illegal appearance before Annas, as mere vulgar curiosity to see a celebrated prisoner was no excuse for the violation of the spirit if not the letter of the law. It is inconceivable, however, to suppose that Annas did not actually interrogate Jesus concerning His disciples, His doctrine, and His personal pretensions. To suppose that he demanded to see Jesus for no other reason than to get an impression of His looks, is to insult common sense. If Annas examined the prisoner, though only slightly, concerning matters affecting the charges against Him that might endanger His life or liberty, he had violated a very important rule of Hebrew criminal procedure. The question of the amount of examination of the accused is immaterial.

It is not known whether Annas at this time sat in the Great Sanhedrin as a judge. He had been deposed from the high priesthood nearly twenty years before by the procurator Valerius Gratus, for imposing and executing capital sentences. But he was, nevertheless, still all-powerful in the great Council of the Jews. Edersheim says that though "deprived of the Pontificate, he still continued to preside over the Sanhedrin."[241] Andrews is of the opinion that "he did in fact hold some high official position, and this probably in connection with the Sanhedrin, perhaps as occasional president."[242] Basing his criticism upon the words in Luke, "Annas and Caiaphus being the high priests,"[243] Dr. Plummer believes "that between them they discharged the duties, or that each of them in different senses was regarded high priest, Annas *de jure*, and Caiaphas *de facto*."[244] This is a mere supposition, however, since there is no historical evidence that Annas was restored to the pontificate after his deposition by Valerius Gratus, A.D. 14.[245] The phrase, "Annas and Caiaphas being high priests," refers to the fifteenth year of the reign of Tiberius Cæsar, which was A.D. 26.

After all, it is here again an historical more than a legal question, whether Annas was an official or not at the time of the appearance of Jesus before him. In either case his preliminary examination of the Christ was illegal. If he was a member of the Sanhedrin, the law forbade him to hold an informal preliminary examination at night. He certainly could not do this while sitting alone. If he was not a magistrate, as Dupin very properly contends, this fact only added to the seriousness of the illegality of subjecting a prisoner to the whimsical examination of a private citizen.

Whether a member of the Sanhedrin or not, Annas was at the time of Christ and had been for many years its dominating spirit. He himself had been high priest. Caiaphas was his son-in-law, and was succeeded in the high priesthood by four sons of Annas. The writer does not believe that Annas had any legal connection with the Sanhedrin, but, like many American political bosses, exercised more authority than the man that held the office.

He was simply the political tool of the Roman masters of Judea, and the members of the Sanhedrin were simply figureheads under his control.

Again, the private examination of Jesus was marked by an act of brutality which Hebrew jurisprudence did not tolerate. This was not enumerated above as an error, because it was not probably a violation of any specific rule of law. But it was an outrage upon the Hebrew sense of justice and humanity which in its normal state was very pure and lofty.

"The high priest then asked Jesus of his disciples and of his doctrine. Jesus answered him, I spake openly to the world; I ever taught in the Synagogue, and in the Temple, whither the Jews always resort; and in secret have I said nothing. Why askest thou me? ask them which heard me, what I have said unto them: behold, they know what I said." In this reply Jesus planted Himself squarely upon His legal rights as a Jewish citizen. "It was in every word the voice of pure Hebrew justice, founded upon the broad principle of their judicial procedure and recalling an unjust judge to the first duty of his great office."

"And when he had thus spoken, one of the officers which stood by struck Jesus with the palm of his hand, saying, Answerest thou the high priest so?" Again the Nazarene appealed for protection to the procedure designed to safeguard the rights of the Hebrew prisoner. "Jesus answered him, If I have spoken evil, bear witness of the evil: but if well, why smitest thou me?"[246]

We have seen that, under Hebrew law, the witnesses were the accusers, and their testimony was at once the indictment and the evidence. We have also seen that a Hebrew prisoner could not be compelled to testify against himself, and that his uncorroborated confession could not be made the basis of a conviction. "*Why askest thou me? ask them that heard me,* what I have said unto them." This was equivalent to asking: Do you demand that I incriminate myself when our law forbids such a thing? Why not call witnesses as the law requires? If I am an evil-doer, bear witness of the evil, that is, let witnesses testify to the wrongdoing, that I may be legally convicted. If I am not guilty of a crime, why am I thus maltreated?

Is it possible to imagine a more pointed and pathetic appeal for justice and for the protection of the law against illegality and brutal treatment? This appeal for the production of legal testimony was not without its effect. Witnesses were soon forthcoming—not truthful witnesses, indeed—but witnesses nevertheless. And with the coming of these witnesses began the formal trial of the Christ, and a formal trial, under Hebrew law, could be commenced only by witnesses.

POINT III

THE INDICTMENT AGAINST JESUS WAS, IN FORM, ILLEGAL

LAW

"The entire criminal procedure of the Mosaic Code rests upon four rules: *certainty in the indictment*; publicity in the discussion; full freedom granted to the accused; and assurance against all dangers or errors of testimony."—SALVADOR, "Institutions de Moïse," p. 365.

"*The Sanhedrin did not and could not originate charges*; it only investigated those brought before it."—EDERSHEIM, "Life and Times of Jesus the Messiah," vol. i. p. 309.

"*The evidence of the leading witnesses constituted the charge*. There was no other charge: no more formal indictment. Until they spoke, and spoke in the public assembly, the prisoner was scarcely an accused man. When they spoke, and the evidence of the two agreed together, it formed the legal charge, libel, or indictment, as well as the evidence for its truth."—INNES, "The Trial of Jesus Christ," p. 41.

"The only *prosecutors* known to Talmudic criminal jurisprudence are the witnesses to the crime. Their duty is to bring the matter to the cognizance of the court, and to bear witness against the criminal. In capital cases, they are the legal executioners also. Of an official accuser or prosecutor there is nowhere any trace in the laws of the ancient Hebrews."—MENDELSOHN, "The Criminal Jurisprudence of the Ancient Hebrews," p. 110.

FACT AND ARGUMENT

THE Gospel records disclose two distinct elements of illegality in the indictment against Jesus: (1) The accusation, at the trial, was twofold, vague, and indefinite, which Mosaic law forbade; (2) it was made, in part, by Caiaphas, the high priest, who was one of the judges of Jesus; while Hebrew law forbade any but leading witnesses to present the charge.

A thorough understanding of Point III depends upon keeping clearly in mind certain well-defined elementary principles of law. In the first place, it should be remembered that in most modern jurisdictions an indictment is simply an accusation, carries with it no presumption of guilt, and has no evidentiary force. Its only function is to bring the charge against the prisoner before the court and jury, and to notify the accused of the nature of the accusation against him. But not so under the ancient Hebrew scheme of justice. Under that system there was no such body as the modern Grand Jury, and no committee of the Sanhedrin exercised similar accusatory functions. The leading witnesses, and they alone, presented charges. It follows then, of necessity, that the ancient Hebrew indictment, unlike the modern indictment, carried with it a certain presumption of guilt and had certain evidentiary force. This could not be otherwise, since the testimony of the leading witnesses was at once the indictment and the evidence offered to prove it.

Again, in the very nature of things an indictment should, and under any enlightened system of jurisprudence, does clearly advise the accused of the exact nature of the charge against him. Under no other conditions would it be possible for a prisoner to prepare his defense. Most modern codes have sought to promote clearness and certainty in indictments by requiring the charging of only one crime in one indictment, and in language so clear and simple that the nature of the offense charged may be easily understood.

Now Salvador says that "certainty in the indictment" was one of the cardinal rules upon which rested the entire criminal procedure of the Mosaic Code. Was this rule observed in framing the accusation against Jesus at the night trial before the Sanhedrin? If so, the Gospel records do not disclose the fact. It is very certain, indeed, that the learned of no age of the world since the crucifixion have been able to agree among themselves as to the exact nature of the indictment against the Christ. This subject was too exhaustively discussed in the beginning of the Brief to warrant lengthy treatment here. Suffice it to say that the record of the night trial before Caiaphas discloses two distinct charges: the charge of sedition—the threat to destroy a national institution and to seduce the people from their ancient allegiance, in the matter of the destruction of the Temple; and the charge of blasphemy preferred by Caiaphas himself in the adjuration which he administered to Jesus. When the false witnesses failed to agree, their contradictory testimony was rejected and the charge of sedition was abandoned. And before Jesus had time to answer the question concerning sedition, another distinct charge, that of blasphemy, was made in almost the same breath.[247] Did this procedure tend to promote "certainty in the indictment"? Did it not result in the complete destruction of all clearness and certainty? Are we not justified in supposing that the silence of Jesus in the presence of His accusers was at least partially attributable to His failure to comprehend the exact nature of the charges against Him?

Again, the accusation was, in part, by Caiaphas, the high priest, who was also one of the judges of Jesus;[248] while Hebrew law forbade any but leading witnesses to present the charge. Edersheim tells us that "the Sanhedrin did not and could not originate charges; it only investigated those brought before it." If the Sanhedrin as a whole could not originate charges, because its members were judges, neither could any individual Sanhedrist do so. When the witnesses "agreed not together" in the matter of the charge of sedition, this accusation was abandoned. Caiaphas then deliberately assumed the rôle of accuser, in violation of the law, and charged Jesus, in the form of an adjuration, with blasphemy, in claiming to be "the Christ, the Son of God." Confession and condemnation then followed. Only leading witnesses could prefer criminal charges under Hebrew law. Caiaphas, being a judge, could not possibly be a witness; and could not, therefore, be an accuser. Therefore, the indictment against Jesus was illegally presented.

The writer believes that the above is a correct interpretation of the nature and number of the charges brought against the Christ, and that the legal aspects of the case are as above stated. But candor and impartiality require consideration of another view. Several excellent writers have contended that there were, in fact, not two charges preferred against Jesus but only one under different forms. These writers contend that Caiaphas and his colleagues understood that Jesus claimed supernatural power and identity with God when He declared that He was *able* to destroy the Temple and to build it again in three days,[249] and that the question of the high priest, "I adjure thee by the living God, that thou tell us whether thou be the Christ, the Son of God," flowed naturally from and had direct reference to the charge of being able to destroy the Temple. The advocates of this view appeal to the language of the original auditors to sustain their contention. "Forty-and-six years was this temple in building, and wilt thou rear it again in three days?" It is insisted that these words convey the idea that those who heard Jesus understood Him to mean that He had supernatural power. There is certainly much force in the contention but it fails to meet other difficulties. In the first place, it is not clear that a threat to destroy the Temple implied a claim to supernatural power; in which case there would be no connection between the first charge and that in which it was suggested that Jesus had claimed to be the Christ, the Son of God. In the second place, the contention that the two charges are substantially the same ignores the language of Mark, "But neither so did their witness agree together,"[250] which was certainly not injected by the author of the second Gospel as a matter of mere caprice or pastime. This language, legally interpreted, means that the testimony of the false witnesses, being contradictory, was thrown aside, and that the charge concerning the destruction of the Temple was abandoned. This is the opinion of Signor Rosadi and is very weighty.

Those writers who maintain that there was only one charge, that of blasphemy, under different forms, rely upon the passage in Matthew, "I am *able* to destroy the temple of God and to build it again in three days," and interpret it as a claim to supernatural power in the light of the language used by those who heard it: "Forty-and-six years was this temple in building, and wilt thou rear it again in three days?" Those who hold the opposite view, that there were two distinct charges, rely upon the passage in Mark, "I *will* destroy this temple that is made with hands, and within three days I will build another made without hands," and interpret it in the light of a similar accusation against Stephen a few months afterwards: "For we have heard him say, that this Jesus of Nazareth *shall destroy this place*, and *shall change the customs* which Moses delivered us."[251] This second interpretation, which we believe to be the better, establishes the existence at the trial of Christ of two distinct charges: that of sedition, based upon a threat to assault existing institutions; and that of blasphemy, founded upon the claim of equality with God. And, in the light of this interpretation, the illegality in the form of the indictment against Jesus has been urged.

If the first construction be the true one, then the error alleged in Point III is not well founded, since the accusation was presented by witnesses, as the law required; unless it could be successfully urged that the witnesses, being *false* witnesses, were no more competent to accuse a prisoner than to convict him upon their false testimony. In such a case the substance as well as the form of the indictment would be worthless, and the whole case would fall, through failure not only of competent testimony to convict but also of a legal indictment under which to prosecute.

Neither the Mishna nor the Gemara mentions written indictments among the ancient Hebrews. "The Jewish Encyclopedia" says that accusations were probably in writing, but that it is not certain.[252] A passage in Salvador seems to indicate that they were in writing. "The papers in the case," he says, "were read, and the accusing witnesses were then called." "The papers" were probably none other than the indictment. But of this we are not sure, and cannot, therefore, predicate the allegation of an error upon it. From the whole context of the Scriptures, however, we are led to believe that only oral charges were preferred against Jesus.

POINT IV

THE PROCEEDINGS OF THE SANHEDRIN AGAINST JESUS WERE ILLEGAL BECAUSE THEY WERE CONDUCTED AT NIGHT

LAW

"Let a capital offence be tried during the day, but suspend it at night."— MISHNA, Sanhedrin IV. 1.

"Criminal cases can be acted upon by the various courts during day time only, by the Lesser Synhedrions from the close of the morning service till noon, and by the Great Synhedrion till evening."—MENDELSOHN, "Criminal Jurisprudence of the Ancient Hebrews," p. 112.

"The reason why the trial of a capital offense could not be held at night is because, as oral tradition says, the examination of such a charge is like the diagnosing of a wound—in either case a more thorough and searching examination can be made by daylight."—MAIMONIDES, Sanhedrin III.

FACT AND ARGUMENT

HEBREW jurisprudence positively forbade the trial of a capital case at night. The infraction of this rule involves the question of jurisdiction. A court without jurisdiction can pronounce no valid verdict or judgment. A court has no jurisdiction if it convenes and acts at a time forbidden by law.

One is naturally disposed to deride the reason assigned by Maimonides for the existence of the law against criminal proceedings at night. But it should not be forgotten that in the olden days surgery had no such aids as are at hand to-day. Modern surgical apparatus had not been invented and electric lights and the Roentgen Rays were unknown. In the light of this explanation of the great Jewish philosopher the curious inquirer after the real meaning of things naturally asks why the Areopagus of Athens always held its sessions in the night and in the dark.[253]

We have seen that Jesus was arrested in Gethsemane about midnight and that His first ecclesiastical trial took place between two and three o'clock in the morning.[254] St. Luke tells us that there was a daybreak meeting,[255] which was evidently intended to give a semblance of legality and regularity to that rule of Hebrew law that required two trials of the case.

The exact time of the beginning of the night session of the Sanhedrin is not known. It is generally supposed that the arrest took place in the garden between midnight and one o'clock. The journey to the house of Annas must have required some little time. Where this house was located nobody knows. According to one tradition Annas owned a house on the Mount of Olives close to the booths or bazaars under the "Two Cedars." Stapfer believes that Jesus was taken to that place. According to another tradition the house of Annas was located on the "Hill of Evil Counsel." Barclay believes that this was the place to which Jesus was conducted. But the tradition which is most generally accepted is that which places the palace of Annas on Mount Zion near the palace of Caiaphas. It is believed by many that these two men, who were related, Annas being the father-in-law of Caiaphas, occupied different apartments in the same place. But these questions are mere matters of conjecture and have no real bearing upon the present discussion, except to show, in a general way, the length of time probably required to conduct Jesus from Gethsemane to Annas; from Annas to Caiaphas, if the latter was the one who privately examined Jesus; and thence to the meeting of the Sanhedrin. It is reasonable to suppose that at least two hours were thus consumed, which would bring Jesus to the palace of Caiaphas between two and three o'clock, if the arrest in the garden took place between twelve and one o'clock. But here, again, a difference of one or two hours would not affect the merit of the proposition stated in Point IV. For it is beyond dispute that the first trial before the Sanhedrin was had at night, which was forbidden by law.

The question has been frequently asked: Why did the Sanhedrin meet at night in violation of law? The answer to this is referable to the treachery of Judas, to the fact that he "sought opportunity to betray him unto them in the absence of the multitude," and to the thought of the Master: "But this is your hour, and the power of God." Luke tells us that the members of the Sanhedrin "feared the people."[256] Mark informs us that they had resolved not to attempt the arrest and execution of Jesus at the time of the Passover, "lest there be an uproar of the people."[257]

Jesus had taught daily in the Temple, and had furnished ample opportunity for a legal arrest with a view to a legal trial. But His enemies did not desire this. "The chief priests and scribes sought how they might take him by craft, and put him to death."[258] The arrival of Judas from the scene of the Last Supper with a proposition of immediate betrayal of the Christ was a glad surprise to Caiaphas and his friends. Immediate and decisive action was necessary. Not only the arrest but the trial and execution of Jesus must be accomplished with secrecy and dispatch. The greatest festival of the Jews had just commenced. Pilgrims to the feast were arriving from all parts of the Jewish kingdom. The friends and followers of Jesus were among them. His enemies had witnessed the remarkable demonstration in His honor which marked His entrance into Jerusalem only a few days before. It is not strange, then, that they "feared the people" in the matter of the summary and illegal proceedings which they had resolved to institute against Him. They knew that the daylight trial, under proper legal forms, with the friends of Jesus as witnesses, would upset 259their plans by resulting in His acquittal. They resolved, therefore, to act at once, even at the expense of all forms of justice. And it will be seen that this determination to arrest and try Jesus at night, in violation of law, became the parent of nearly every legal outrage that was committed against Him. The selection of the midnight hour for such a purpose resulted not merely in a technical infraction of law, but rendered it impossible to do justice either formally or substantially under rules of Hebrew criminal procedure.

POINT V

THE PROCEEDINGS OF THE SANHEDRIN AGAINST JESUS WERE ILLEGAL BECAUSE THE COURT CONVENED BEFORE THE OFFERING OF THE MORNING SACRIFICE

LAW

"The Sanhedrin sat from the close of the morning sacrifice to the time of the evening sacrifice."—TALMUD, Jerus., Sanhedrin I. fol. 19.

"No session of the court could take place before the offering of the morning sacrifice."—MM. LÉMANN, "Jesus Before the Sanhedrin," p. 109.

"Since the morning sacrifice was offered at the dawn of day, it was hardly possible for the Sanhedrin to assemble until the hour after that time."—MISHNA, "Tamid, or of the Perpetual Sacrifice," C. III.

FACT AND ARGUMENT

THE fact that the Sanhedrin convened before the offering of the morning sacrifice constitutes the fifth illegality. This error is alleged upon the authority of MM. Lémann, who, in their admirable little work entitled "Jesus Before the Sanhedrin," have called attention to it. It is very difficult, however, to determine whether this was a mere irregularity, or was what modern jurists would call a material error. From one point of view it seems to be merely a repetition of the rule forbidding the Sanhedrin to meet at night. The morning sacrifice was offered at the break of day and lasted about an hour. A session of the court before the morning sacrifice would, therefore, have been a meeting at night, which would have been an infringement of the law. But this was probably not the real reason of the rule. Its true meaning is doubtless to be found in the close connection that existed between the Hebrew law and the Hebrew religion. The constitution of the Hebrew Commonwealth was an emanation of the mind of Jehovah, the Temple in which the court met was His residence on earth, and the judges who formed the Great Sanhedrin were the administrators of His will. It is most reasonable, then, to suppose that an invocation, in sacrifice and prayer, of His guidance and authority would be the first step in any judicial proceedings conducted in His name.

It is historically true that a session of the Sanhedrin in the palmiest days of the Jewish Commonwealth was characterized by all the religious solemnity of a service in the synagogue or the Temple. It is entirely probable, therefore, that the morning sacrifice was made by law an indispensable prerequisite to the assembling of the supreme tribunal of the Jews for the transaction of any serious business. On any other supposition the rules of law cited above would have no meaning. We have reason to believe, then, that the offering of the morning sacrifice was a condition precedent to the attachment of jurisdiction, and without jurisdiction the court had no authority to act. That the morning sacrifice was offered each day, whether the court assembled or not, as a religious requirement, does not alter the principle of law above enunciated.

But it may be asked: How do we know that the morning sacrifice was not offered? The answer is that the whole context of the Scriptures relating to the trial shows that it could not have been offered. Furthermore, a simple and specific reason is that the time prescribed by law for conducting the morning service was between the dawn of day and sunrise. Then, if the court convened between two and three o'clock in the morning, it is very certain that the sacrifice had not been offered. It is true that there was a morning session of the Sanhedrin. But this was held simply to confirm the action of the night session at which Jesus had been condemned. In other words, the real trial was at night and was held before the performance of the religious ceremony, which was, in all probability, a prerequisite to the attachment of jurisdiction.

POINT VI

THE PROCEEDINGS AGAINST JESUS WERE ILLEGAL BECAUSE THEY WERE CONDUCTED ON THE DAY PRECEDING A JEWISH SABBATH; ALSO ON THE FIRST DAY OF THE FEAST OF UNLEAVENED BREAD AND THE EVE OF THE PASSOVER

LAW

"Court must not be held on the Sabbath, or any holy day."—"Betza, or of the Egg," Chap. V. No. 2.

"They shall not judge on the eve of the Sabbath, nor on that of any festival."—MISHNA, Sanhedrin IV. 1.

"No court of justice in Israel was permitted to hold sessions on the Sabbath or any of the seven Biblical holidays. In cases of capital crime, no trial could be commenced on Friday or the day previous to any holiday, because it was not lawful either to adjourn such cases longer than over night, or to continue them on the Sabbath or holiday."—RABBI WISE, "Martyrdom of Jesus," p. 67.

FACT AND ARGUMENT

NO Hebrew court could lawfully meet on a Sabbath or a feast day, or on a day preceding a Sabbath or a feast day.

Concerning the Sabbath day provision Maimonides offers the following reason for the rule: "As it is required to execute the criminal immediately after the passing of the sentence, it would sometimes happen that the kindling of a fire would be necessary, as in the case of one condemned to be burned; and this act would be a violation of the law of the Sabbath, for it is written 'Ye shall kindle no fire in your habitations on the Sabbath day.'"[259] (Exodus xxxv. 3.)

Under modern practice, sessions of court may be adjourned from day to day, or, if need be, from week to week. But under the Hebrew system of criminal procedure the court could not adjourn for a longer time than a single night. Its proceedings were, so to speak, continuous until final judgment. As the law forbade sessions of court on Sabbath and feast days, it became necessary to provide that courts should not convene on the day preceding a Sabbath or a feast day, in order to avoid either an illegal adjournment or an infringement of the rule relating to the Sabbath and feast days.

Now Jesus was tried by the Sanhedrin on both a feast day and a day preceding the Sabbath. And, at this point, a clear conception of the ancient Jewish mode of reckoning time should be had. The Jewish day of twenty-four hours began at one sunset and ended with the next. But this interval was not divided into twenty-four parts or hours of equal and invariable length. Their day proper was an integral part of time and was reckoned from sunrise to sunset. Their night proper was likewise a distinct division of time and was measured from sunset to sunrise. An hour of time, according to modern reckoning, is invariably sixty minutes. But the ancient Jewish hour was not a fixed measure of time. It varied in length as each successive day and night varied in theirs at different seasons of the year. Neither did the Jews begin their days and nights as we do. Our day of twenty-four hours always begins at midnight. Their day of twenty-four hours always began at one sunset and ended with the next.

Now Jesus was tried by the Sanhedrin on the 14th Nisan, according to the Jewish calendar; or between the evening of Thursday, April 6th, and the afternoon of Friday, April 7th, A.D. 30, according to our calendar. The 14th Nisan began at sunset on April 6th and lasted until sunset on April 7th. This was a single Jewish day, and within this time Jesus was tried and executed. According to our calendar, the trial and execution of Jesus took place on Friday, April 7th. This was the day preceding the Jewish Sabbath, which came on Saturday, according to our reckoning. And on a day preceding the Sabbath no Jewish court could lawfully convene. This is the first error suggested under Point VI.

Again, it is beyond dispute that the Feast of Unleavened Bread had begun and that the Passover was at hand when Jesus was tried by the

Sanhedrin.[260] This was in violation of a specific provision of Hebrew law, and constitutes the second error alleged under Point VI.

There seems to be some conflict among the authorities as to whether Jesus was tried on the first day of the celebration of the feast of the Passover or on the day preceding. But the question is immaterial from a legal point of view, as the law forbade a trial either on a feast day or on the day preceding, for reasons above stated.

This violation of the law relating to the Sabbaths and feast days, like that relating to night sessions of the Sanhedrin, resulted in still other errors. It is necessary to mention only one of these at this point. The proceedings of the Sanhedrin were recorded by two scribes or clerks. Their records were to be used on the second day of the trial in reviewing the proceedings of the first. But Hebrew law forbade any writing on a Sabbath or a holy day. How was it possible, then, to keep a record of the proceedings, if Jesus was tried on a Sabbath and also on a feast day, without violating a rule of law? If no minutes of the meeting were kept, a most glaring irregularity is apparent.

POINT VII

THE TRIAL OF JESUS WAS ILLEGAL BECAUSE IT WAS CONCLUDED WITHIN ONE DAY

LAW

"A criminal case resulting in the acquittal of the accused may terminate the same day on which the trial began. But if a sentence of death is to be pronounced, it can not be concluded before the following day."—MISHNA, Sanhedrin IV. 1.

FACT AND ARGUMENT

CARE and conservatism, precaution and delay, were the characteristic features of the criminal procedure of the ancient Hebrews. The principal aphorism of the Pirke Aboth is this: "*Be cautious and slow in judgment,* send forth many disciples, and *make a fence around the law.*"[261] The length and seriousness of their deliberations in criminal proceedings of a capital nature were due to their supreme regard for human life. "Man's life belongs to God, and only according to the law of God may it be disposed of." "Whosoever preserves one worthy life is as meritorious as if he had preserved the world." These and similar maxims guided and controlled Hebrew judges in every capital trial. Their horror of death as the result of a judicial decree is shown by the celebrated saying: "The Sanhedrin which so often as once in seven years condemns a man to death, is a slaughter-house."[262]

To assure due deliberation and reflection in a case where a human life was at stake, Hebrew law required that the trial should last at least two days, in case of the conviction of the accused. In case of an acquittal the trial might terminate within a single day. Before condemnation could be finally decreed a night had to intervene, during which time the judges could sleep, fast, meditate, and pray. At the close of the first day's trial they left the judgment hall and walked homeward, arm in arm, discussing the merits of the case. At sunset they began to make calls upon each other, again reviewing among themselves the facts in evidence. They then retired to their homes for further meditation. During the intervening night they abstained from eating heavy food and from drinking wine. They carefully avoided doing anything that would incapacitate them for correct thinking. On the following day they returned to the judgment hall and retried the case. The second trial was in the nature of a review and was intended to detect errors, if there were any, in the first trial.[263] It was not until the afternoon of this day that a final decree could be made and that a capital sentence could follow.

Now the Gospel record very clearly discloses the fact that Jesus was arrested, tried, and executed within the limits of a single day. Neither the exact hour of His arrest, nor of His trial, nor of His execution is known. But it is positively certain that all took place between sunset, the beginning of Nisan 14, and sunset, the beginning of Nisan 15. This was the interval of a single Jewish day, Nisan 14. And within such an interval of time it was illegal to finally condemn a man to death under Hebrew law. Even Stapfer, who contends that the trial was legal and that forms of law were generally observed, admits this error. He asserts that the precipitate conduct of the members of the Sanhedrin was not only opposed to the spirit of Hebrew conservatism in the matter of criminal procedure but was a breach of a specific provision of the criminal code.[264]

It is true that there were two distinct trials: one between 2 and 3 A.M., Friday, April 7th, which is recorded by Matthew[265] and Mark,[266] and a second about daybreak of the same day, recorded by Matthew,[267] Mark,[268] and Luke.[269] But both these trials were had within one day—indeed, within six hours of each other. The judges did not try the case and then retire to their homes for sleep, prayer, and meditation until the following day, as the law required. Even if they had done so, they would not have avoided an illegal procedure, inasmuch as the trial had been illegally begun on a feast day and the eve of the Sabbath, and it would have been impossible to avoid the error alleged in Point VII. For if they had deferred the sentencing and execution of Jesus until the following day it would still have been illegal, since the next day was both a Sabbath and a holy day (the Passover).

Several writers who contend that there was a regular trial of Jesus assert that the morning meeting of the Sanhedrin was intended to give a semblance of legality and regularity to that rule of Hebrew law which required at least two trials. But it will readily be seen that this was a subterfuge and evasion, since both trials were had on the same day, whereas the law required them to be held on different days.

POINT VIII

THE SENTENCE OF CONDEMNATION PRONOUNCED AGAINST JESUS BY THE SANHEDRIN WAS ILLEGAL BECAUSE IT WAS FOUNDED UPON HIS UNCORROBORATED CONFESSION

LAW

"We have it as a fundamental principle of our jurisprudence that no one can bring an accusation against himself. Should a man make confession of guilt before a legally constituted tribunal, such confession is not to be used against him unless properly attested by two other witnesses."—MAIMONIDES, Sanhedrin IV. 2.

"Not only is self-condemnation never extorted from the defendant by means of torture, but no attempt is ever made to lead him on to self-incrimination. Moreover, a voluntary confession on his part is not admitted in evidence, and therefore not competent to convict him, unless a legal number of witnesses minutely corroborate his self-accusation."—MENDELSOHN, "Criminal Jurisprudence of the Ancient Hebrews," p. 133.

FACT AND ARGUMENT

MORE than one system of jurisprudence has refused to permit a conviction for crime to rest upon an uncorroborated confession. But it remained for the ancient Hebrews to discover the peculiar reason for the rule, that the witness who confessed was "his own relative"; and relatives were not competent witnesses under Hebrew law. Modern Jewish writers, however, have assigned other reasons for the rule. Rabbi Wise says: "Self-accusation in cases of capital crime was worthless. For if not guilty he accuses himself of a falsehood; if guilty he is a wicked man, and no wicked man, according to Hebrew law, is permitted to testify, especially not in penal cases."[270] Mendelsohn says that "the reason assigned for this enactment is the wish to avoid the possibility of permitting judicial homicide on self-accusing lunatics, or on persons who, in desperation, wish to cut short their earthly existence, and to effect this falsely accuse themselves of some capital crime."[271]

Modern jurists have assigned still other reasons for the rule as it has existed in modern law.[272] Men have been known to confess that they were guilty of one crime to avoid punishment for another. Morbid and vulgar sentimentality, such as love of newspaper notoriety, have induced persons of inferior intelligence, who were innocent, to assume responsibility for criminal acts.

But whatever the reason of the rule, Jesus was condemned to death upon His uncorroborated confession, in violation of Hebrew law.

"For many bare false witness against him, but their witness agreed not together. And there arose certain, and bare false witness against him, saying, We heard him say, I will destroy this temple that is made with hands, and within three days I will build another made without hands. But neither so did their witness agree together. And the high priest stood up in the midst, and asked Jesus, saying, Answerest thou nothing? what is it which these witness against thee? But he held his peace, and answered nothing. Again the high priest asked him, and said unto him, Art thou the Christ, the Son of the Blessed? And Jesus said, I am: and ye shall see the Son of Man sitting on the right hand of power, and coming in the clouds of Heaven. Then the high priest rent his clothes, and saith, What need we any further witnesses? ye have heard the blasphemy: what think ye? And they all condemned him to be guilty of death. And some began to spit on him, and to cover his face, and to buffet him, and to say unto him, Prophesy."[273]

It will be seen from a perusal of this report of the trial that it was sought to condemn Jesus first on the charge of sedition, that is, that He had threatened the destruction of the Temple and thereby endeavored to seduce the people from their national allegiance. "But their witness agreed not together"; and under Hebrew law they were required to reject contradictory testimony and discharge the prisoner, if the state was unable to prove its case. This is what should have been done at this point in the trial of Jesus. But, instead, the judges, in their total disregard at law, turned to the accused and said: "Answerest thou nothing? what is it which these witness against thee?" "But he held his peace, and answered nothing." By remaining silent, Jesus only exercised the ordinary privilege of a Jewish prisoner to refuse to incriminate himself. The modern rule that the accused cannot be made to testify against himself, unless he first voluntarily takes the witness stand in his own behalf, was substantially true among the ancient Hebrews. But here we find Caiaphas insisting that Jesus incriminate Himself. And he continues to insist in the matter of the second charge, that of blasphemy. "And the high priest asked him, and said unto him, Art thou the Christ, the Son of the Blessed?" That question was illegal, because it involved an irregular mode of criminal procedure, and because it asked for a confession of guilt to be made the basis of a conviction. The false witnesses had failed to agree and had evidently been rejected and dismissed. The judges were then without witnesses to formulate a charge and furnish proof of its truth. They were thus forced to the despicable and illegal method of asking the accused to condemn Himself, when they knew that no confession could be made the basis of a conviction. They were also guilty of the illegality of formulating a charge without witnesses. We have seen that only leading witnesses could present an indictment, but here the judges became the accusers, in violation of law.

In answer to the high priest's question, Jesus, feeling that He could not afford at such an hour and in such a place to longer conceal His Messiahship, answered boldly and emphatically: "I am."[274] "And they all condemned him to be guilty of death." It will thus be seen that upon His own confession and not upon the testimony of at least two competent witnesses agreeing in all essential details, as the law required, was the Nazarene condemned to death.

If it be argued, as it has been, that the two charges of threatening to destroy the Temple and of pretending to be the "Christ, the Son of God," were in fact but different phases of the same charge of blasphemy, and that the two witnesses were the corroborators of the confession of Jesus, then reply must be made that the witnesses were not competent, being false witnesses, nor was their testimony legally corroborated, because it was false and contradictory.

Again, it was the rule of Hebrew law that both witnesses had to testify to all the essential elements of a complete crime. One could not furnish one link, and another another link, in order to construct a chain of evidence. Each had to testify to all the essential elements necessary to constitute the legal definition of a crime. But the false witnesses did not do this. Under any view of the case, then, the testimony of these witnesses was wholly worthless, and the confession of Jesus was the solitary and illegal basis of His conviction.

The failure of the Sanhedrin to secure sufficient and competent evidence to convict Jesus must not be regarded as accidental, or as attributable to the hour and to the surroundings. The popularity of the Nazarene, outside the narrow circle of the Temple authorities, was immense. The friendship of Nicodemus and Joseph of Arimathea is proof that He had standing even in the Sanhedrin itself. It was therefore difficult to find witnesses who were willing to testify against Him. Besides, the acts of His ministry, while in no sense cowardly or hypocritical, had been, in general, very cautious and diplomatic. He seems to have retired, at times, into the desert or the wilderness to avoid disagreeable and even dangerous complications with the civil and ecclesiastical authorities.[275] Jesus was in no sense a politician, but He was not lacking in mother wit and practical resources. He saw through the designs of Herod Antipas, who wished to get Him out of his dominions.

It will be remembered that certain Pharisees, pretending friendship for Him, warned Him to flee from Galilee to avoid being killed by Herod. The courage and manliness of Jesus are shown by the fact that He remained in His native province, and even sent a contemptuous message to the Tetrarch, whom He styled "that fox."[276]

At other times, Christ was compelled to defend Himself against the swarm of spies that hovered over His pathway through Samaria, along the Jordan, and around the Sea of Galilee. In His discussions with His enemies who sought to entrap Him, He displayed consummate skill in debate. His pithy sayings and incomparable illustrations usually left His questioners defenseless and chagrined. Oftentimes in these encounters He proclaimed eternal and universal truths which other nations and later ages were to develop and enjoy. When, holding in His hand a penny with Cæsar's image upon it, He said, "Render therefore unto Cæsar the things which are Cæsar's, and unto God the things that are God's," he foretold and stamped with approval the immortal principle that was to be embodied in the American constitution and to remain the cornerstone of the American Commonwealth; a truth repeated by Roger Williams when in the forests of Rhode Island he declared that the magistrate should rule in civil matters only and that man was answerable for his religious faith to God alone. This declaration of the Nazarene is the spiritual and intellectual basis of the sublime doctrine of civil liberty and religious freedom that finds its highest expression in that separation of the Church and State which enables men of different creeds and different parties to live side by side as patriots and religionists and as comrades, though antagonists.

The replies of Jesus to those who came to "entangle him in his talk" usually left them disconcerted and defeated, and little disposed to renew their attacks upon Him.[277] The efforts of the Pharisees to entrap Him seem to have resulted in failure everywhere and at all times. And at the trial the Sanhedrin found itself in possession of a prisoner but with no competent evidence to establish His guilt. It was least of all prepared to convict Him of the crime of blasphemy as founded upon the claim of Messiahship, for Jesus had been exceedingly cautious, during His ministry, in declaring Himself to be the Messiah. Except in the presence of the woman of Samaria, who came to draw water from the well, there is no recorded instance of an avowal of His Messiahship outside the immediate circle of the disciples.[278] He forbade the devils whom He had cast out, and that recognized Him, to proclaim His Messiahship.[279] When the Jews said to Him, "How long dost thou make us doubt? if thou be the Christ, tell us plainly," Jesus simply referred them to His works, and made no further answer that could be used as testimony against Him.[280] He revealed Himself to His followers as the Messiah, and permitted them to confess Him as such, but forbade them to make the matter public. "Then charged he his disciples that they should tell no man that he was Jesus, the Christ."[281]

It will thus be seen that probably no two witnesses who were legally competent to testify could have been secured to condemn Jesus upon the charge preferred at the trial. In their desperation, then, the members of the Sanhedrin were compelled to employ false testimony and a confession which was equally illegal.

POINT IX

THE CONDEMNATION OF JESUS WAS ILLEGAL BECAUSE THE VERDICT OF THE SANHEDRIN WAS UNANIMOUS

LAW

"A simultaneous and unanimous verdict of guilt rendered on the day of the trial has the effect of an acquittal."—MENDELSOHN, "Criminal Jurisprudence of the Ancient Hebrews," p. 141.

"If none of the judges defend the culprit, i.e., all pronounce him guilty, having no defender in the court, the verdict of guilty was invalid and the sentence of death could not be executed."—RABBI WISE, "Martyrdom of Jesus," p. 74.

FACT AND ARGUMENT

FEW stranger rules can be found in the jurisprudence of the world than that provision of Hebrew law which forbade a conviction to rest upon the unanimous vote of the judges. A comparison instantaneously and almost inevitably arises in the mind between the Saxon and Hebrew requirement in the matter of unanimity in the verdict. The finest form of mind of antiquity, with the possible exception of the Greek and Roman, was the Hebrew. One of the finest types of intellect of the modern world is that of the Anglo-Saxon. The Hebrew organized the Sanhedrin, and, under God, endowed it with judicial and spiritual attributes. The Anglo-Saxon, on the shores of the German Ocean, originated the modern jury and invested it with its distinctive legal traits. With the Anglo-Saxon jury a unanimous verdict is necessary to convict, but with the Hebrew Sanhedrin unanimity was fatal, and resulted in an acquittal. A great modern writer[282] has declared that law is the perfection of reason. But when we contemplate the differences in Hebrew and Saxon laws we are inclined to ask, in seeking the degree of perfection, whose law and whose reason?

But, after all, the Jewish rule is not so unreasonable as it first appears, when we come to consider the reason of its origin. In the first place, as we have seen in Part II, there were no lawyers or advocates, in the modern sense, among the ancient Hebrews. The judges were his defenders. Now if the verdict was unanimous in favor of condemnation it was evident that the prisoner had had no friend or defender in court. To the Jewish mind this was almost equivalent to mob violence. It argued conspiracy, at least. The element of mercy, which was required to enter into every Hebrew verdict, was absent in such a case.

Again, this rule of unanimity was only another form or statement of the requirement that the court defer final action, in case of conviction, to the next day in order that time for deliberation and reflection might intervene. In other words, Hebrew law forbade precipitancy in capital proceedings. And what could be more precipitate than an instantaneous and unanimous verdict? "But where all suddenly agree on conviction, does it not seem," asks a modern Jewish writer, "that the convict is a victim of conspiracy and that the verdict is not the result of sober reason and calm deliberation?"

But how did they convict under Hebrew law? By a majority vote of at least two. A majority of one would acquit. A majority of two, or any majority less than unanimity, would convict.[283] If the accused had one friend in court, the verdict of condemnation would stand, since the element of mercy was present and the spirit of conspiracy or mob violence was absent. Seventy-one constituted the membership of the Great Sanhedrin. If all the members were present and voted, at least thirty-seven were required to convict. Thirty-six would acquit. If a bare quorum, twenty-three members, was present, at least thirteen were required to convict. Twelve would acquit.

This rule seems ridiculous and absurd, when viewed in the light of a brutal and undeniable crime. If the facts constituting such a crime had been proved against a Jewish prisoner beyond any possibility of doubt, if such facts were apparent to everybody, still it seems that the rule above stated required that the defendant have at least one advocate and one vote among the judges; else, the verdict was invalid and could not stand. Such a procedure could be justified on no other ground than that exceptional cases should not be permitted to destroy a rule of action that in its general operation had been found to be both generous and just.

Now the condemnation of Jesus was illegal because the verdict of the Sanhedrin was unanimous. We learn this from Mark, who says: "Then the high priest rent his clothes and saith, What need we any further witnesses? ye have heard the blasphemy: what think ye? And they *all* condemned him to be guilty of death."[284] If they *all* condemned Him, the verdict was unanimous and therefore illegal. The other Evangelists do not tell us that the verdict was unanimous; neither do they deny it. Mark's testimony stands alone and uncontradicted; therefore we must assume that it is true.

Rabbi Wise[285] and Signor Rosadi[286] call attention to the fact that the verdict was unanimous. The former seeks to ridicule Mark as an authority because a unanimous verdict was illegal under Hebrew law, and the distinguished Hebrew writer does not conceive that Hebrew judges could have made such a mistake. Such argument, reduced to ultimate analysis, means, according to Rabbi Wise, that there were certain rules of Hebrew law that could not be and were never violated.

In this connection, it has been frequently asked: Was the entire Sanhedrin present at the night trial of Jesus? Were Nicodemus and Joseph of Arimathea present? If they were present, did they vote against Jesus? These questions can be answered only in the light of the authorities. Only two of the Gospel writers, Matthew and Mark, tell us of the night trial. Both declare that "all the council" were present.[287] The "council" (concilium) is the Vulgate, the Latin New Testament designation of the Great Sanhedrin. Then, if all the "council" were present, the Great Sanhedrin were all present.

THE BETRAYING KISS (SCHEFFER)

Concerning the number of judges at the second or daybreak meeting of the Sanhedrin, both Matthew and Mark again declare that the full membership was present. Matthew says: "When the morning was come, *all* the chief priests and elders of the people took counsel against Jesus to put him to death."[288] Mark says: "And straightway in the morning the chief priests held a consultation with the elders and scribes and the *whole council*, and bound Jesus, and carried him away, and delivered him to Pilate."[289] It should be remembered that neither Luke nor John contradicts even remotely the statements of Matthew and Mark concerning the full attendance of the members of the Sanhedrin at either the night or morning trial. The first and second Gospel writers therefore corroborate each other, and the presumption of the law is that each told the truth.

And yet most commentators and writers seem to be of the opinion that all the members of the Sanhedrin were not present at the night trial of Jesus. They insist that both Matthew and Mark were employing a figure of speech, synecdoche, when they said that "all the council" were present. But these same writers seem to think that these same Evangelists were in earnest and speaking literally when they declared that "*all* the chief priests and elders" and the "*whole* council" were present at the morning trial. We shall not attempt to settle the question but will leave it to the reader to draw his own inferences. Suffice it to say that as far as the rule stated in connection with Point IX is concerned, it was immaterial whether the full council was present at either meeting. The rule against unanimity applied to a bare quorum or to any number less than the full Sanhedrin. It was the unanimity itself, of however few members, that carried with it the spirit and suggestion of mob violence and conspiracy against which Hebrew law protested.

The question of the number of members that were present at the different meetings of the Sanhedrin has been discussed in the light of history, and as bearing upon the conduct of Nicodemus and Joseph of Arimathea, who were friends of Jesus. Nicodemus was certainly a member of the Great Sanhedrin. This we learn from two passages of New Testament scripture.[290] It is also believed that Joseph of Arimathea was a member from a mere suggestion in another passage.[291] Did these friends of the Christ vote against Him? If they were members of the court; if Matthew and Mark wrote literally when they said that "all the council" were present; and if Mark wrote literally and truthfully when he said that "they *all* condemned him to be guilty of death"; then it naturally and inevitably follows that both Nicodemus and Joseph voted against Jesus.

———

THE ARREST OF JESUS (HOFFMAN)

A number of arguments have been offered against this contention. In the first place, it is said that at a previous meeting of the Sanhedrin Nicodemus defended Jesus by asking his fellow-judges this question: "Doth our law judge any man before it hear him and know what he doeth?"[292] It is asserted that there is no good reason to believe that Nicodemus defended Jesus at this meeting and turned against Him at a subsequent one, that there is a presumption of a continuance of fidelity. But is this good reasoning? Did not Peter cut off the ear of the high priest's servant, Malchus, in defense of Jesus at midnight, in the garden, and then within three hours afterwards deny that he knew Jesus? There is no good reason to believe that Nicodemus was braver or more constant than Peter, for the former seems to have been either ashamed or afraid to express his affection for the Master during the daytime, but preferred to do it at night.[293]

Concerning the part taken by Nicodemus in the final proceedings, Rosadi says: "The verdict was unanimous. The members of the Sanhedrin who were secretly favorable to the Accused were either absent or else they voted against him. Nicodemus was amongst the absentees, or amongst those that voted against him. At all events, he did not raise his voice against the pronouncement expressed by acclamation."

If Joseph of Arimathea was a member of the Great Sanhedrin, it seems that he "had not consented to the counsel and the deed of them."[294] But it is impossible to tell certainly to which one of the three meetings of the Sanhedrin, held within the six months preceding the crucifixion, this language refers. The defense of Jesus offered by Nicodemus was certainly not at the final meeting which condemned Jesus. It may be that the reference to the protest of Joseph of Arimathea also referred to a prior meeting. Its connection in Luke seems to make it refer to the last trial, but this is not certain. Neither is it certain that Joseph was a member of the Great Sanhedrin, and his failure to consent, if he were not a member, would not disturb the contention made in Point IX of the Brief. Even if he were a member, his failure to consent would not destroy the contention, since ancient Hebrew judges, like modern American jurors, could have first protested against their action and then have voted with them. The polling of the jury, under modern law, has reference, among other things, to this state of affairs.

But we may admit that both Nicodemus and Joseph of Arimathea, as well as many others, were absent, as Rosadi suggests, and still contend that the verdict against Jesus was illegal because it was unanimous, as Mark assures us, since the number of judges present was immaterial, provided there was a quorum of at least twenty-three and their verdict was unanimous against the accused. According to the second Gospel writer, there seems to be no doubt that this was the case in the judgment pronounced against Jesus.

***

POINT X

THE PROCEEDINGS AGAINST JESUS WERE ILLEGAL IN THAT: (1) THE SENTENCE OF CONDEMNATION WAS PRONOUNCED IN A PLACE FORBIDDEN BY LAW; (2) THE HIGH PRIEST RENT HIS CLOTHES; (3) THE BALLOTING WAS IRREGULAR

LAW

"After leaving the hall Gazith no sentence of death can be passed upon anyone soever."—TALMUD, Bab., Abodah Zarah, or of Idolatry, Chap. I. fol. 8.

"A sentence of death can be pronounced only so long as the Sanhedrin holds its sessions in the appointed place."—MAIMONIDES, Sanhedrin XIV.

"And he that is the high priest among his brethren, upon whose head the anointing oil was poured, and that is consecrated to put on the garments, shall not uncover his head, nor rend his clothes."—LEVITICUS xxi. 10.

"And Moses said unto Aaron, and unto Eleazar, and unto Ithamar, his sons, Uncover not your heads, neither rend your clothes; lest ye die, and lest wrath come upon all the people."—LEVITICUS x. 6.

"Let the judges each in his turn absolve or condemn."—MISHNA, Sanhedrin XV. 5.

"The members of the Sanhedrin were seated in the form of a semicircle at the extremity of which a secretary was placed, whose business it was to record the votes. One of these secretaries recorded the votes in favor of the accused, the other those against him."—MISHNA, Sanhedrin IV. 3.

"In ordinary cases the judges voted according to seniority, the oldest commencing; in a capital trial, the reverse order was followed. That the younger members of the Sanhedrin should not be influenced by the views or arguments of their more mature, more experienced colleagues, the junior judge was in these cases always the first to pronounce for or against a conviction."—BENNY, "Criminal Code of the Jews," pp. 73, 74.

FACT AND ARGUMENT

IN the trial of capital cases, the Great Sanhedrin was required to meet in an apartment of the National Temple at Jerusalem, known as the Hall of Hewn Stones (Lishkhath haggazith). Outside of this hall no capital trial could be conducted and no capital sentence could be pronounced.[295] This place was selected in obedience to Mosaic injunction: "Thou shalt do according to the tenor of the sentence, which they may point out to thee *from the place which the Lord shall choose.*"[296] The Rabbis argued that the Great Council could not try a capital case or pronounce a death sentence, unless it met and remained in the place chosen by God, which, they contended, should be an apartment of the Great Temple. The Lishkhath haggazith was chosen, and continued for many years to be the meeting place of the supreme tribunal.

But Jesus was not tried or condemned to death in the Hall of Hewn Stones, as Hebrew law required. It is clearly evident, from the Gospels, that He was tried and sentenced in the palace of Caiaphas, probably on Mount Zion. It is contended by the Jews, however, that soon after the Roman conquest of Judea the Great Sanhedrin removed from the sacred place to Bethany, and from there to other places, as occasion required. And there is a Jewish tradition that the court returned to the accustomed place on the occasion of the trial and condemnation of Jesus.[297]

In opposition to this, Edersheim says: "There is truly not a tittle of evidence for the assumption of commentators that Christ was led from the palace of Caiaphas into the Council Chamber (Lishkhath haggazith). The whole proceedings took place in the former, and from it Christ was brought to Pilate."[298] St. John emphatically declares: "Then led they Jesus from Caiaphas into the hall of judgment."[299] This Hall of Judgment was the Prætorium of Pilate.

The first irregularity, then, noted under Point X is that Jesus was tried and condemned in the palace of Caiaphas instead of the Hall of Hewn Stones, the regular legal meeting place of the Great Sanhedrin.

The second error noted under Point X is that which relates to the rending of garments by the high priest. "An ordinary Israelite could, as an emblem of bereavement, tear his garments, but to the high priest it was forbidden, because his vestments, being made after the express orders of God, were figurative of his office."[300]

When Jesus confessed that He was Christ the Son of God, Caiaphas seems to have lost his balance and to have committed errors with all the rapidity of speech. "Then the high priest rent his clothes, and saith, What need we any further witnesses? ye have heard the blasphemy: what think ye? And they all condemned him to be guilty of death."[301] In this language and conduct of the son-in-law of Annas there were several irregularities in procedure. The first was the rending of garments reported by Matthew and Mark, which act was forbidden by the provisions of the Mosaic Code, recorded in Leviticus and cited above.

But it is only fair to state the dissenting opinion on this point. In the times of Christ it seems to have been the custom among the Jews to rend the garments as a sign of horror and execration, whenever blasphemous language was heard. Edersheim states the rule: "They all heard it—and, as the law directed, when blasphemy was spoken, the high priest rent both his outer and inner garment, with a rent that might never be repaired."[302] The law here referred to, however, is the Rabbinic or Talmudic and not the Mosaic law. It should be remembered that the Mosaic Code was the constitution or fundamental law of the ancient Hebrews. The Talmudic law embodied in the Mishna was, in a sense, a mere commentary upon the Mosaic law. We have seen in Chapter I of Part II of this volume that the traditional law was based upon, derived from, and inspired by the written law contained in the Pentateuch. It is true that the Talmud, while professing subordination to the Pentateuch, finally virtually superseded it as an administrative code. But the doctors never repealed a Mosaic injunction, since it was an emanation of the mind of Jehovah and could not be abrogated by human intelligence. When an ancient ordinance ceased to be of practical value the Jewish legists simply declared that it had fallen into desuetude. And whenever a new law was proclaimed to meet an emergency in the life of the Hebrew people the Rabbins declared that it was derived from and inspired by some decree which God had handed down to Moses for the benefit of the nation. In other words, the Mosaic Code was Israel's divine constitution which was to serve as a standard for all future legislation. And as the Jewish lawmakers were not permitted to repeal a Mosaic ordinance, neither were they allowed to establish a rule in contravention of it. Now the Pentateuch forbade the rending of garments. Then did the Talmudists have a right to declare that the law might be changed or broken in the case of blasphemy? That they did is denied by many writers.

But admitting the validity of the Talmudic rule, it is nevertheless beyond dispute that the high priest was forbidden to rend his clothes on Sabbaths and holidays. And as Jesus was condemned on both a Sabbath and a festival day, the high priest's action in rending his clothes on that day was illegal.[303]

Again, the proceedings against Jesus were illegal because the balloting was irregular. This is the third error noted under Point X.

The Hebrew law required that each judge, when his time came to vote upon the guilt or innocence of the accused, should rise in his place, declare his vote, and state his reasons for so voting. In capital cases the youngest judge was required to vote first, in order that he might not be unduly influenced by the example of his seniors in age and authority. The balloting continued in this manner from the youngest member to the high priest, who was generally among the oldest. Two scribes—according to some writers, three—were present to record the votes and to note the reasons stated. These records were to be used on the second day of the trial in comparing the arguments of the judges on that day with those offered on the first day. Judges who had voted for acquittal on the first day could not change their votes on the second day. Those who had voted for conviction on the first day might change their votes on the second day, by assigning good reasons. Those who had voted for conviction on the first day could not vote for conviction on the second day, if the reasons assigned on the second day were radically different from those assigned on the first day.[304] It will thus be seen how very essential were the records of the scribes and how important it was that they should be correctly kept. Hence the necessity, according to Benny, of a third scribe whose notes might be used to correct any discrepancies in the reports of the other two.

Now are we justified in assuming that this was the method employed in counting votes at the trial of Jesus? The law will not permit us to presume errors. We must rather assume that this was the method employed, unless the Gospel record indicates, either by plain statement or by reasonable construction, that it was not the method used.

In this connection, let us review the language of the Scriptures. "Ye have heard the blasphemy: what think ye? And they all condemned him to be guilty of death." Is it not clearly evident, from this passage, that the balloting was not done singly, the youngest voting first, as Hebrew law required? Can it not be seen at a glance that the judges voted *en masse*? If they did, was it possible for the scribes to record the votes and make a note of the reasons assigned, as the law required? If these things were not done, were the proceedings regular?

According to Matthew, Caiaphas, before calling for the votes exclaimed: "He hath spoken blasphemy."[305] Instead of doing this should he not, under the law, have carefully concealed his opinion until the younger members of the court had voted? Is it not a matter of history that the opinion of the high priest was regarded as almost infallible authority among the ancient Hebrews? Did not this premature declaration of guilt on the part of the high priest rob the subordinate judges of freedom of suffrage?

The conduct of the case at the close, when the balloting took place, seems to justify the view of those writers who assert that there was no regular trial of Jesus, but rather the action of a mob.

POINT XI

THE MEMBERS OF THE GREAT SANHEDRIN WERE LEGALLY DISQUALIFIED TO TRY JESUS

LAW

"The robe of the unfairly elected judge is to be respected not more than the blanket of the ass."—MENDELSOHN, "Hebrew Maxims and Rules," p. 182.

"As Moses sat in judgment without the expectation of material reward, so also must every judge act from a sense of duty only."—MENDELSOHN, "Hebrew Maxims and Rules," p. 177.

"Nor must there be on the judicial bench either a relation, or a particular friend, or an enemy of either the accused or of the accuser."—MENDELSOHN, "Criminal Jurisprudence of the Ancient Hebrews," p. 108.

"He (the Hebrew judge) was, in the first instance, to be modest, of good repute among his neighbors, and generally liked."—BENNY, "Criminal Code of the Jews," p. 38.

"Nor under any circumstances, was a man known to be *at enmity with the accused person* permitted to occupy a position among his judges."—BENNY, "Criminal Code of the Jews," p. 37.

FACT AND ARGUMENT

THE Gospel records disclose the fact that the members of the Great Sanhedrin were legally disqualified to try Jesus. This disqualification was of two kinds: (1) A general disqualification, under Hebrew law, to act as judges in any case; (2) a special disqualification to sit in judgment upon the life of Jesus.

Among all the great systems of jurisprudence of the world the ancient Hebrew system was the most exacting in the matter of judicial fitness. In the palmiest days of the Hebrew Commonwealth the members of the Great Sanhedrin represented the most perfect mental, moral, and physical development of the Hebrew people. A man could not be a member of this court who had any serious mental, moral, or physical defect. He must have been "learned in the law," both written and unwritten. He must have had judicial experience; that is, he must have filled three offices of gradually increasing dignity, beginning with one of the local courts and passing successively through two magistracies at Jerusalem. He must have been an accomplished linguist; that is, he must have been thoroughly familiar with the languages of the surrounding nations. He must have been modest, popular, of good appearance, and free from haughtiness. He must have been pious, strong, and courageous. And above all, he must have been friendly in his attitude toward the accused.[306]

These were the qualifications of Israel's judges before Roman politics had corrupted them. But at the time of Christ they had grown to be time-serving, degenerate, and corrupt. Judea was then passing through a period of religious and political revolution. At such a time in any state, as all history teaches us, the worst elements of society generally get the upper hand and control the political currents of the day. Many members of the Sanhedrin had themselves been guilty of criminal acts in both public and private life. Many of them held office by purchase—they had bought their seats. They were thus unfitted to be judges in any case; especially in one involving the great question of life and death.

In order to show the general disqualification, under the test of Hebrew law, of the members of the Great Sanhedrin, at the time of Christ, to exercise judicial functions, it is necessary to quote only Jewish authorities. In "The Martyrdom of Jesus," Rabbi Wise says: "The chief priests, under the iron rule of Pilate and his wicked master, Sejan, were the tools of the Roman soldiers who held Judea and Samaria in subjection. Like the high priest, they were appointed to and removed from office by the Roman governor of the country, either directly or indirectly. They purchased their commissions for high prices and, like almost all Roman appointees, used them for mercenary purposes. They were considered wicked men by the ancient writers and must have stood very low in the estimation of the people over whom they tyrannized. The patriots must have looked upon them as hirelings of the foreign despot whose rule was abhorred. Although there was, here and there, a good, pious and patriotic man among them, he was an exception. As a general thing, and under the rule of Pilate, especially, they were the corrupt tools of a military despotism which Rome imposed upon enslaved Palestine."

Again, the Talmud, in which we never look for slurs upon the Hebrew people, where slurs are not deserved, contains this bitter denunciation of the high-priestly families of the times of Christ: "What a plague is the family of Simon Bœthus; cursed be their lances! What a plague is the family of Ananos; cursed be their hissing of vipers! What a plague is the family of Cantharus; cursed be their pens! What a plague is the family of Ismael ben Phabi; cursed be their fists! They are high priests themselves, their sons are treasurers, their sons-in-law are commanders, and their servants strike the people with staves."

In like manner the Talmud, in withering rebuke and sarcasm, again declares that "The porch of the sanctuary cried out four times. The first time, Depart from here, descendants of Eli; ye pollute the Temple of the Eternal! The second time, Let Issachar ben Keifar Barchi depart from here, who polluted himself and profaneth the victims consecrated to God! The third time, Widen yourselves, ye gates of the sanctuary and let Israel ben Phabi, the wilful, enter that he may discharge the functions of the priesthood! Yet another cry was heard, Widen yourselves, ye gates, and let Ananias ben Nebedeus, the gourmand, enter, that he may glut himself on the victims."[307]

It should be borne in mind that the high-priestly families so scathingly dealt with by the Talmud were the controlling spirits in the Great Sanhedrin at the time of Christ. Were they legally qualified, then, under the ancient and honorable tests of Hebrew law, to be members of the highest court in the land? If they bought their offices and used them for mercenary purposes, as Wise asserts, were they worthy of the great exemplar, Moses, who "sat in judgment without the expectation of material reward"? If they thus secured their places and prostituted them to selfish purposes, were their robes to be respected any more than the blanket of the ass?

The ancient Hebrew judges, in the days of Israel's purity and glory, submitted their claims to judicial preferment to the suffrage of a loving and confiding people.[308] They climbed the rungs of the judicial ladder by slow and painful degrees. Integrity and ability marked each advance toward the top. Was this the process of promotion in the case of Caiaphas and his fellow-judges? Did their bought and corrupted places not brand them with the anathema of the law?

We come now to consider the special disqualifications of members of the Sanhedrin to sit in judgment upon the life of Jesus. The reasons for these disqualifications were two: (1) The members of this court were, in the language of Jost, "burning enemies" of Jesus, and were therefore disqualified, under Hebrew law, to act as His judges; (2) they had determined upon His guilt, and had sentenced Him to death before the trial began; and had thus outraged not only a specific provision of Hebrew law but also a principle of universal justice.

The various causes of the hatred of the members of the Sanhedrin for Jesus are too numerous and profound to admit of exhaustive treatment here. A thorough analysis of these causes would necessitate a review of the life of Christ from the manger to the sepulcher. A few reasons will suffice.

But at this point a distinction should be made between that personal hatred which disqualifies and the hatred and loathing of the crime that do not disqualify. Every just and righteous judge should loathe and hate the crime itself; and a certain amount of loathing and dislike for the criminal is most natural and almost inevitable. But no judge is qualified to sit in judgment upon the rights of life, liberty, or property of another whom he hates as the result of a personal grudge, born of personal experience with the prisoner at the bar. The hatred that disqualified the members of the Sanhedrin, under Hebrew law, was that kind of hatred that had been generated by personal interest and experience. The most merciless invective, barbed with incomparable wit, ridicule, and satire, had been daily hurled at them by Jesus with withering effect. With a touch more potent than that of Ithuriel's spear He had unmasked their wicked hypocrisy and had blazoned it to the skies. Every day of His active ministry, which lasted about three years, had been spent in denouncing their shameless practices and their guilty lives. The Scribes and Pharisees were proud, haughty, and conceited beyond description. They believed implicitly in the infallibility of their authority and in the perfection of their souls. How galling, then, to such men must have been this declaration of an obscure and lowly Nazarene: "Verily, I say unto you, That the publicans and the harlots go into the kingdom of God before you."[309] What impetuous invective this: "Woe unto you, scribes and Pharisees, hypocrites! for ye devour widows' houses, and for a pretense make long prayer: therefore ye shall receive the greater damnation. Woe unto you, scribes and Pharisees, hypocrites! for ye compass sea and land to make one proselyte, and when he is made, ye make him twofold more the child of hell than yourselves."[310] We can well imagine how these fiery darts pierced and tore the vanity of a haughty and contemptuous priesthood.

Consider for a moment the difference in the spheres of Jesus and of His enemies. He, an obscure prophet from Nazareth in Galilee; they, the leaders of Israel and the guardians of the Temple at Jerusalem. He, the single advocate of the New Dispensation; they, the manifold upholders of the Old. He, without earthly authority in the propagation of His faith; they, clothed with the sanction of the law and the prestige of a mighty past. Imagine, then, if you can, the intensity of the hatred engendered by the language and the conduct of Jesus.

That we may fully appreciate the tension of the situation let us cast a single glance at the character of the Scribes. Edersheim has written these wonderfully graphic lines about them:

He pushes to the front, the crowd respectfully giving way, and eagerly hanging on his utterances, as those of a recognized authority. He has been solemnly ordained by the laying on of hands; and is the Rabbi, "my great one," Master, amplitudo. Indeed, his hyper-ingenuity in questioning has become a proverb. There is not measure of his dignity, nor yet limit to his importance. He is the "lawyer," the "well-plastered pit," filled with the water of knowledge, "out of which not a drop can escape,' in opposition to the "weeds of untilled soil" of ignorance. He is the divine aristocrat, among the vulgar herd of rude and profane "country people," who "know not the law," and are "cursed." Each scribe outweighed all the common people, who must accordingly pay him every honor.... Such was to be the respect paid to their sayings that they were to be absolutely believed, even if they were to declare that to be at the right hand which was at the left, or vice-versa.[311]

What could, then, be more terrific than the hatred of such a character for an unlettered Galilean who descended from the mountains of His native province to rebuke and instruct the "divine aristocrats" in religious matters and heavenly affairs? Imagine his rage and chagrin when he heard these words: "Woe unto you, scribes and Pharisees, hypocrites! for ye are like unto whited sepulchres, which indeed appear beautiful outward, but are within full of dead men's bones, and all uncleanness.... Woe unto you, scribes and Pharisees, hypocrites! because ye build the tombs of the prophets, and garnish the sepulchres of the righteous, And say, If we had been in the days of our fathers, we would not have been partakers with them in the blood of the prophets. Wherefore ye be witnesses unto yourselves, that ye are the children of them which killed the prophets. Fill ye up then the measure of your fathers. Ye serpents, ye generation of vipers, how can ye escape the damnation of hell?"[312]

"His exquisite irony," says Renan, "His stinging remarks, always went to the heart. They were everlasting stings, and have remained festering in the wound. This Nessus-shirt of ridicule which the Jew, son of the Pharisees, has dragged in tatters after him during eighteen centuries, was woven by Jesus with a divine skill. Masterpieces of fine raillery, their features are written in lines of fire upon the flesh of the hypocrite and the false devotee. Incomparable traits worthy of a Son of God! A god alone knows how to kill in this way. Socrates and Molière only grazed the skin. The former carried fire and rage to the very marrow."[313]

Are we not now justified in asserting, with Jost, that the members of the Sanhedrin, who were none other than the Scribes and Pharisees above described by Jesus, were the "burning enemies" of the prisoner at the bar? If they were, were they legally qualified to be His judges?

But it may be argued that their hatred was simply a form of righteous indignation provoked by His repeated assaults upon the national religion and the national institutions; that it was their duty as guardians of both to both hate and try Him; and that they would have been derelict in duty if they had not done so. But it is apparent from the record and is evident to any fair-minded reader that the enmity of the judges toward Jesus was more personal than political, more a private than a public affair. In support of this contention, in addition to the withering language addressed to them, the matter of the purification of the Temple may be mentioned. It will be remembered how Jesus, with a scorpion lash, scourged the money-changers and traders from the Sanctuary. Now it is historically true that Annas and Caiaphas and their friends owned and controlled the stalls, booths, and bazaars connected with the Temple and from which flowed a most lucrative trade. The profits from the sale of lambs and doves, sold for sacrifice, alone were enormous. When Jesus threatened the destruction of this trade He assaulted the interests of Annas and his associates in the Sanhedrin in a vital place. This grievance was certainly not so religious as it was personal. The driving of the cattle from the stalls was probably more effective in compassing the destruction of the Christ than any miracle that He performed or any discourse that He delivered. But whatever the cause the fact is historic and indisputable that the Sanhedrists were enemies of Jesus, and therefore disqualified under Hebrew law to try Him.

A second reason for the special disqualification of the members of the Sanhedrin to sit as judges at the trial of Christ was the fact that they had determined upon His guilt and had sentenced Him to death before the trial began. This point needs no extensive argument or illustration. Under every enlightened system of justice the first great qualification of judges has been that they should be unbiased and unprejudiced. Judicial proceedings are murderous and no better than mob violence when judges and jurors enter upon the trial of the case with a determination to convict the accused, regardless of the testimony. The principles underlying this proposition are fundamental and self-evident.

Now the Gospel narratives disclose the fact that three different meetings of the Sanhedrin were held in the six months preceding the crucifixion, to discuss the miracles and discourses of Jesus, and to devise ways and means to entrap Him and put Him to death.

The first meeting was held in the latter part of the month of September, A.D. 29, about six months before the night trial in the palace of Caiaphas. This meeting is recorded by St. John in Chap. vii., verses 37-53. The occasion was the Feast of Tabernacles, when Jesus made many converts by His preaching, and at the same time caused much apprehension among the Pharisees, who assembled the Sanhedrin to adopt plans to check His career. It was on this occasion that Nicodemus defended Christ and asked the question that shows the nature of the proceedings at that time. "Doth our law judge any man before it hear him and know what he doeth?" This was the voice, not only of Hebrew but of universal justice demanding a hearing before a condemnation. Nothing definite seems to have been accomplished at this meeting.

The second session of the Sanhedrin took place in the month of February, A.D. 30, about six weeks before the crucifixion. The occasion of this meeting was the resurrection of Lazarus, an account of which is given in John xi. 41-53. The chief priests and Pharisees seem to have been seized with consternation by the reports of the progress of the propaganda of Jesus. They had often listened contemptuously and in sullen silence to the accounts of His miraculous performances. But when He began to raise the dead to life, they decided that it was about time to act. At this meeting Caiaphas appealed to his associates in the name of the common weal. "Ye know nothing at all," he said, "nor consider that it is expedient for us, that one man should die for the people, and that the whole nation perish not."[314] This seems to have been a form of condemnation in which the other judges joined. "Then from that day forth they took counsel together for to put him to death."[315] At this second session of the Sanhedrin the death of Jesus seems to have been decreed in an informal way and an opportunity was awaited for its accomplishment.

The third meeting of the Sanhedrin took place just a few days before the Paschal Feast.

"Now the feast of unleavened bread drew nigh, which is called the Passover. And the chief priests and scribes sought how they might kill him; for they feared the people."[316] "Then assembled together the chief priests, and the scribes, and the elders of the people, unto the palace of the high priest, who was called Caiaphas, and consulted that they might take Jesus by subtilty, and kill him. But they said, Not on the feast day, lest there be an uproar among the people."[317]

At this third session of the court it was agreed that the arrest and execution of Jesus should be accomplished at the earliest possible date.

It will be seen that at these different sessions of the Sanhedrin in the six months preceding the regular trial the judges had resolved that Jesus should be done away with at the first convenient opportunity. In short, and in fact, their hatred was formed and their determination fixed in the matter of the proceedings to be instituted against Him. Were they, then, legally qualified to act as His judges?

Again, besides prejudging Him to death had they not demonstrated their total unfitness for any righteous administration of justice by seeking false witnesses against Him? Hebrew law forbade them to seek for witnesses of any kind. They were the defenders of the accused and, under the Hebrew system, were required to search for pretexts to acquit and not for witnesses to condemn.[318] It was a maxim that "the Sanhedrin was to save, not to destroy life."[319] Much more were they forbidden to seek for false witnesses. Hebrew law denounced false witnesses and condemned them to the very punishment prescribed for those whom they sought to convict.

"And the judges shall make diligent inquisition; and, behold, if the witness be a false witness, and hath testified falsely against his brother; then shall ye do unto him, as he had thought to do unto his brother.... And thine eye shall not pity; but life shall go for life, eye for eye, tooth for tooth, hand for hand, foot for foot."[320]

But here we find the judges actually seeking testimony which the law pointedly prohibited. This matter alone establishes their utter unfitness to try Jesus, and is explicable only on the ground of the degradation into which they had fallen at the time of Christ and on the hypothesis that their burning hatred had overwhelmed their judgment and sense of justice.

If it be objected that the points of disqualification above alleged were not applicable to all the judges, a single sentence of Scripture meets the objection: "And the chief priests and *all the council* sought for witness against Jesus to put Him to death."[321] The fact that "all the council" were willing to outrage a provision of the fundamental law is sufficient proof that they were all disqualified to try Christ.

Another conclusive proof of the total unfitness of the members of the Sanhedrin to try Jesus is the fact that they so far forgot themselves that they abandoned all sense of self-respect and judicial dignity by brutally striking Him and spitting in His face. We would like to believe that this outrageous conduct was limited to the servants of the priests, but the Gospel of St. Mark, Chap. xiv., verse 65, clearly indicates that the judges themselves were also guilty.

POINT XII

THE CONDEMNATION OF JESUS WAS ILLEGAL BECAUSE THE MERITS OF THE DEFENSE WERE NOT CONSIDERED

LAW

"Then shalt thou inquire, and make search, and ask diligently."—DEUTERONOMY xiii. 14.

"The judges shall weigh the matter in the sincerity of their conscience."—MISHNA, Sanhedrin IV. 5.

"The primary object of the Hebrew judicial system was to render the conviction of an innocent person impossible. All the ingenuity of the Jewish legists was directed to the attainment of this end."—BENNY, "Criminal Code of the Jews," p. 56.

FACT AND ARGUMENT

THE actual trial of any criminal case shows, upon the record, two essential parts: (1) The accusation; (2) the defense. The absence of the elements of defense makes the proceeding *ex parte*; and there is really no trial. And it is impossible to conceive a proper administration of justice where a defense is not allowed, since the right to combat the allegations of the indictment is the essential principle of liberty under the law. The destruction of this right is the annihilation of freedom by subjecting the individual citizen to the whims and caprices of the governing power. An ideal code of criminal procedure would embody rules of evidence and practice perfectly adapted to establish truth in the matter at issue between the commonwealth and the prisoner. Neither the people nor the accused would be favored or prejudiced by the admission or exclusion of any kind of evidence. An exact interpretation and administration of this code would result in a perfect intellectual balance between the rights of the state and the defendant. But such a code has never been framed, and if one were in existence, it would be impossible to enforce it, as long as certain judges insisted on aiding the prosecution and others on helping the accused, in violation of standard rules of evidence.

Now, the ancient Hebrew system of criminal procedure was no such ideal one as that above described. It should be remembered that there was no body, under that system, corresponding to our modern Grand Jury, to present indictments. There were no prosecuting officers and no counselors-at-law, in the modern sense. The leading witnesses preferred charges and the judges did the rest. They examined and cross-examined witnesses, did the summing up and were, above all, the defenders of the accused. The rights of the defendant seem to have alone been seriously considered. This startling maxim was a constant menace to the integrity of the government and to the rights of the commonwealth: "The Sanhedrin which so often as once in seven years condemns a man to death, is a slaughter-house."[322] Lightfoot is of the opinion that the Jews did not lose the power of capital punishment as the result of the Roman conquest, but that they voluntarily abandoned it because the rules of criminal procedure which they had from time to time adopted finally became wholly unfitted for convicting anyone. This view is unsupported by historic fact, but it is nevertheless true that the legal safeguards for the protection of the rights of the accused had, in the later years of Jewish nationality, become so numerous and stringent that a condemnation was practically impossible. The astonishing provision of Hebrew law to which we have referred in Part II known as Antecedent Warning had the effect of securing an acquittal in nearly every case. It is contended by many that this peculiar provision was intended to abolish capital punishment by rendering conviction impossible.

In the light of the principles above suggested let us review the action of the Sanhedrin in condemning Jesus to death upon His uncorroborated confession. The standard of thoroughness in investigating criminal matters is thus prescribed in the Mosaic Code: "Then shalt thou inquire, and make search, and ask diligently." The Mishna supplements the fundamental law by this direction: "The judges shall weigh the matter in the sincerity of their conscience." From what we know of the peculiar tendency of the Hebrew system to favor the accused we are justified in assuming that the two rules just cited were framed for the protection of the prisoner more than for the security of the commonwealth.

Now at this point we are led to ask: Were these rules applied in the trial of Jesus in any sense either for or against the accused? Did Caiaphas and the other members of the Sanhedrin "inquire, and make search and ask diligently" concerning the facts involved in the issue between Jesus and the Hebrew people? Did they weigh the whole matter "in the sincerity of their conscience?" Is it not clearly evident from the record that the false witnesses contradicted themselves, were rejected and dismissed, and that Jesus was then condemned upon His uncorroborated confession that He was the Christ, the Son of God? The usual and natural proceeding in a Jewish criminal trial was to call witnesses for the defendant, after the leading witnesses had testified for the people. Was this done in the case of Jesus? His own apostles deserted Him in the garden, although two of them seem to have returned to the scene of the trial. Is it probable, in the light of the record, that witnesses were called for the defendant? We have seen that they could not legally convict Him upon His own confession. And there is nowhere the faintest suggestion that witnesses other than the false ones were called to testify against Him. The record is clear and unequivocal that the conviction of Jesus was upon His uncorroborated confession. This was illegal. When Caiaphas said, "I adjure thee by the living God that thou tell us whether thou be the Christ, the Son of God," Jesus answered, "Thou hast said"; that is, "I am," according to Mark. Here was an issue squarely joined between the Commonwealth of Israel and Jesus of Nazareth. It was incumbent upon the state to establish His guilt by two competent witnesses who agreed in all essential details. If these witnesses were not present, or could not be secured, it was the duty of the court to discharge Christ at once. This the law provided and demanded. But this was not done.

If, as has been contended, the false witnesses were relied upon by the Sanhedrin to corroborate the confession of Jesus, then under Hebrew law the judges should at least have sought witnesses in His behalf, or should have allowed His friends time to find them and bring them in. In other words, His defense should have been considered. However overwhelming the conviction of the judges of the Sanhedrin that the claims of Jesus were false and blasphemous, they were not justified in refusing to consider the merits of His pretensions. If a midnight assassin should stealthily creep into the room of a sleeping man and shoot him to death, a judge would not be legally justified in instructing the jury, at the close of the people's case, to bring in a verdict of guilty, on the ground that nothing that the defendant could prove would help his case. However weak and ridiculous his defense, the prisoner should at least be heard; and a failure to accord him a hearing would certainly result in reversal on appeal. A refusal to consider the defense of a prisoner under ancient Hebrew law was nothing less than an abrogation of the forms of government and a proclamation of mob violence in the particular case, for it must be remembered that Hebrew criminal law was framed especially for the protection of the accused.

It should also be kept in mind that it would not have been incumbent upon Caiaphas and his fellow-judges to acquit Jesus simply because a defense had been made. In other words, they were not bound to accept His explanations and arguments. If they had heard Him and His witnesses, they could have rejected His pretensions as false and blasphemous, although they were truthful and righteous, without incurring the censure of mankind and the curse of Heaven, for it would be preposterous to require infallible judgment of judicial officers. All that can be demanded of judges of the law is that they act conscientiously with the lights that are in front of them. The maledictions of the human race have been hurled at Caiaphas and his colleagues during nineteen centuries, not because they pronounced an illegal judgment, but because they outraged rules of law in their treatment of the Christ; not because they misinterpreted His defense, but because they denied Him all defense.

We should constantly keep in mind that Jesus was entitled to have the two requirements, "Then shalt thou inquire, and make search, and ask diligently," and "The judges shall weigh the matter in the sincerity of their conscience," applied not only for but against Him. That is, before the Hebrew Commonwealth rested its case against Him, He had a right to demand that a *prima facie* case be made, or in case of failure to do so, that He be at once discharged. This rule was as pointed and imperative under ancient as under modern law, and before the merits of the defense were required to be considered the state had to close its case against the defendant, with a presumption of guilt against Him, as a result of the introduction of competent and satisfactory evidence.

If rules of law had been properly observed in the trial of Jesus the question of the merits of His defense would never have been raised; for it was practically impossible to convict Him under the circumstances surrounding the night trial in the palace of Caiaphas. As has been before suggested, Jesus was very popular outside the circle of the Temple authorities. So great was His popularity that it is almost certain that two competent witnesses could not have been secured to convict Him of blasphemy in the sense that He had claimed to be the Messiah. We have seen, under Point VIII, that Jesus had confessed His Messiahship to no one excepting the Samaritan woman, outside the Apostolic company. Judas, then, was probably the only witness who had heard Him declare Himself to be the Messiah that could have been secured; and his testimony was incompetent, under Hebrew law, because, under the supposition that Jesus was a criminal, Judas, His apostle, was an accomplice. As to the charge of blasphemy in the broader sense of having claimed equality with God, upon which, according to Salvador, Jesus was convicted, it seems from the Gospel record that there would have been no difficulty in legally convicting Him, if the Sanhedrin had met regularly and had taken time to summon witnesses in legal manner. For on many occasions Jesus had said and done things in the presence of both friends and enemies that the Jews regarded as blasphemous; such as claiming that He and His Father were one; that He had existed before Abraham; and that He had power to forgive sins. But these charges were not made at the trial, and we have no right to consider them except as means of interpreting the mind of Caiaphas in connection with the meaning of the claim of Jesus that He was the Christ, the Son of God. If Caiaphas was justified in construing these words to mean that Jesus claimed identity with Jehovah, then he was justified in inferring that Jesus had spoken blasphemy, for from the standpoint of ancient Judaism and considering Jesus simply as a Jewish citizen, blasphemy was the crime that resulted from such a claim. But even from this point of view Caiaphas was not justified in refusing Jesus ample opportunity to prove His equality with Jehovah, or at least that He was gifted with divine power. This was all the more true because the claim of Jesus was that of Messiahship, and according to one line of authorities in Hebrew Messianic theology the Messiah was to be clothed with divine authority and power as the messenger and vicegerent of Jehovah on earth.

But it is clearly certain that a *prima facie* case of guilt was not made by the Sanhedrin against Jesus; and, as a matter of law, He was not called upon to make any defense. He could have refused to say a word in answer to the accusation. He could have asserted His legal rights by objecting that a case against Him had not been made, by demanding that the charges against Him be dismissed and that He be set at liberty at once. But Jesus did not do this. He simply confessed His Messiahship and Sonship of the Father. This confession was not legal evidence upon which He could have been convicted, but it did help to create an issue, the truth or falsity of which should have been investigated by the court.

Now, let us suppose, for argument's sake, that a *prima facie* case of guilt against Jesus was made before the Sanhedrin. What was the next legal step under Hebrew law? What should the judges have done after hearing the witnesses against Him? It is beyond dispute that they should have begun at once to "inquire, and make search, and ask diligently" concerning all matters pertaining to the truthfulness and righteousness of His claims to Messiahship. They should have assisted Him in securing witnesses whose testimony would have helped to establish those claims. Having secured such testimony, they should have weighed it "in the sincerity of their conscience." But this they did not do.

It may be asked: What proofs could have been offered that Jesus was "the Christ, the Son of God," if complete rights of defense had been accorded? That question is difficult to answer, nearly two thousand years after the trial. But if a *prima facie* case of guilt had been made against Him, shifting the burden of proof, and requiring that His claims be proved, it may be reasonably contended that a complete defense would have necessitated proofs: (1) That Jesus was the Christ, that is, that He was the Messiah; (2) that He was also the Son of God, that is, that He was identical with God Himself. Let us consider these two phases of the subject and their attendant proofs in order.

And first, what evidence could have been offered that Jesus was the Christ, that is, the Messiah? What method of procedure should have been employed by the Sanhedrin in investigating His claims? Let us suppose that Caiaphas understood that Jesus claimed to be the long-looked-for Messiah who had come from Jehovah with divine authority to redeem mankind and to regenerate and rule the world. Let us not forget that the Jews were expecting a Messiah, and that the mere claim of Messiahship was not illegal. Such a claim merely raised an issue as to its truth or falsity which was to be investigated like any other proposition of theology or law. It was not one to be either accepted or rejected without demonstration. Then when Jesus acknowledged His Messiahship in answer to the high priest's question it was the duty of the court either to admit His claim and discharge Him at once, or to summon competent witnesses, by daylight, to prove that His pretensions were false and blasphemous. Having rested their case, it was their duty to aid the prisoner in securing witnesses to substantiate His claims, and according to the spirit of Hebrew law to view rather favorably than unfavorably such claims. It was also incumbent upon them to apply to Jesus all the Messianic tests of each and every school. It should be remembered that at the time of Christ there were radically different views of the attributes of the expected Messiah. No two schools agreed upon all the signs by which the future Deliverer would be recognized. Only one sign was agreed upon by all—that He would be a scion of the House of David. The followers of Judas of Galilee believed that the Messiah would be an earthly hero of giant stature—a William Tell, a Robert Bruce, an Abraham Lincoln—who would emancipate the Jews by driving out the Romans and permanently restoring the kingdom of David on the earth. The school of Shammai believed that he would be not only a great statesman and warrior, but a religious zealot as well; and that to splendid victories on the battlefield, he would add the glorious triumphs of religion. Radically different from both these views, were the teachings of the gentle Hillel and his disciples. According to these, the Messiah was to be a prince of peace whose sublime and holy spirit would impress itself upon all flesh, would banish all wars, and make of Jerusalem the grand center of international brotherhood and love. But even these conceptions were not exhaustive of the various Messianic ideas that were prevalent in Palestine in the days of Jesus. Some of the Messianic notions were not only contradictory but diametrically opposite in meaning. A "prince of peace" and a "gigantic warrior" could not well be one and the same person. And for this reason it is apparent that, had an examination been made, the claims of Jesus to the Messiahship could not have been rejected by Caiaphas and the Sanhedrin, simply because this or that attribute did not meet the approval of this or that sect or school.

Instead of condemning Him to death for blasphemy, when Jesus answered that He was the Christ, the Son of God, Caiaphas should have asked a second question: "What sign shewest thou then, that we may see and believe thee?" It has been contended by Jewish writers that, far from denying Jesus the privilege of proving His Messiahship, He was frequently asked to give signs and perform wonders. The reply to this is that as far as the legal merits of the case are concerned Jesus was not invited at the trial in the palace of Caiaphas to show signs or give proofs of His Messiahship. And as to the chances afforded Him at other times and places, they were extra-judicial and were mere street affairs in which Jesus probably refused to gratify vulgar curiosity and by which He was not remotely bound legally or religiously. It is only when properly arraigned and accused that a citizen under modern law can be compelled to answer a charge of crime. The rule was more stringent under the ancient Hebrew dispensation. Private preliminary examinations, even by judicial officers, were not permitted by Hebrew law, as Salvador explicitly states. It was only when confronted by proper charges before a legally constituted tribunal in regular session, that a Hebrew prisoner was compelled to answer. And at the regular trial before the full Sanhedrin Jesus was not asked to give evidence that would serve to exculpate Him. What Caiaphas should have done was to notify Jesus, at the time of the arraignment in his own house, that His life was at stake and that now was the time to produce testimony in His own behalf. It was the duty, furthermore, of the high priest and his associates to consult the sacred books to see if the Messianic prophecies therein contained were fulfilled in the birth, life, and performances of Jesus, as these matters were developed at the trial by witnesses duly summoned in His behalf.

It was a matter personally within the knowledge of the judges that the time was ripe for the appearance of the Deliverer. Not only the people of Israel, but all the surrounding nations were expecting the coming of a great renovator of the world. Of such an arrival Virgil had already sung at Rome.[323]

A great national misfortune had already foreshadowed the day of the Messiah more potently than had any individual event in the life of Jesus. When Jacob lay dying upon his deathbed, he called around him his twelve sons and began to pronounce upon each in turn the paternal and prophetic blessing. When the turn of Judah came, the accents of the dying patriarch became more clear and animated, as he said: "Judah, thou art he whom thy brethren shall praise: thy hand shall be in the neck of thine enemies; thy father's children shall bow down before thee. Judah is a lion's whelp: from the prey, my son, thou art gone up: he stooped down, he couched as a lion, and as an old lion; who shall rouse him up? The *sceptre* shall not depart from Judah, nor a lawgiver from between his feet, until Shiloh come; and unto him shall the gathering of the people be."[324] The Jewish Rabbinical commentators of antiquity were unanimously of the opinion that this prophecy of Jacob referred to the day of the Messiah. And for ages the people had been told to watch for two special signs which would herald the coming of the great Deliverer: (1) The departure of the scepter from Judah; (2) the loss of the judicial power.

The Talmudists, commenting on the above passage from Genesis, say: "The son of David shall not come unless the royal power has been taken from Judah"; and in another passage: "The son of David shall not come unless the judges have ceased in Israel."[325] Now both these signs had appeared at the time of the Roman conquest, shortly before the birth of Christ. At the deposition of Archelaus, A.D. 6, Judea became a Roman province with a Roman procurator as governor. Sovereignty then passed away forever from the Jews. And not only was sovereignty taken from them, but its chief attribute, the power of life and death in judicial matters, was destroyed. Thus the legal and historical situation was produced that had been prophesied by Jacob. The *scepter* had passed from Judah and the *lawgiver* from between his feet, when Jesus stood before the Sanhedrin claiming to be the Messiah.

A fair trial in full daylight, it is believed, would have called before His judges a host of witnesses friendly to Jesus, whose testimony would have established an exact fulfilment of ancient Messianic prophecy in His birth, life, arrest, and trial. A judicial record would have been made of which the following might be regarded as an approximately correct transcript:

(1) *That the Messiah was to be born in Bethlehem.*

PROPHECY—But thou, Beth-lehem Ephratah, though thou be little among the thousands of Judah, yet out of thee shall he come forth unto me that is to be ruler in Israel; whose goings forth have been from of old, from everlasting.—MICAH v. 2.

FULFILLMENT—Now when Jesus was *born in Bethlehem* of Judea in the days of Herod the king, behold, there came wise men from the east to Jerusalem.—MATT. ii. 1.

And Joseph also went up from Galilee, out of the city of Nazareth, into Judea, unto the city of David, which is called Bethlehem (because he was of the house and lineage of David), To be taxed with Mary his espoused wife, being great with child. And so it was, that, while they were there, the days were accomplished that she should be delivered. And she brought forth her firstborn son, and wrapped him in swaddling clothes, and laid him in a manger; because there was no room for them in the inn.—LUKE ii. 4-7.

(2) *That the Messiah was to be born of a virgin.*

PROPHECY—Therefore the Lord himself shall give you a sign; Behold, a virgin shall conceive, and bear a son, and shall call his name Immanuel.—ISA. vii. 14.

FULFILLMENT—And in the sixth month the angel Gabriel was sent from God unto a city of Galilee, named Nazareth, To a virgin espoused to a man whose name was Joseph, of the house of David; and the virgin's name was Mary.... And the angel said unto her, Fear not, Mary: for thou hast found favor with God. And, behold, thou shalt conceive in thy womb, and bring forth a son, and shalt call his name Jesus.—LUKE i. 26-30.

Then Joseph being raised from sleep did as the angel of the Lord had bidden him, and took unto him his wife: and knew her not till she had brought forth her firstborn son: and he called his name Jesus—MATT. i. 24, 25.

(3) *That the Messiah was to spring from the house of David:*

PROPHECY—Behold, the days come, saith the Lord, that I will raise unto David a righteous Branch, and a King shall reign and prosper, and shall execute judgment and justice in the earth. In his days Judah shall be saved, and Israel shall dwell safely: and this is his name whereby he shall be called, THE LORD OUR RIGHTEOUSNESS.—JER. xxiii. 5, 6.

FULFILLMENT—He shall be great, and shall be called the Son of the Highest; and the Lord God shall give unto him the throne of his father David.—LUKE i. 32.

But while he thought on these things, behold, the angel of the Lord appeared unto him in a dream, saying, Joseph, thou son of David, fear not to take unto thee Mary thy wife: for that which is conceived in her is of the Holy Ghost.—MATT. i. 20.

(4) *That the Messiah should not come until the scepter had departed from Judah and the lawgiver from between his feet:*

PROPHECY—The Sceptre shall not depart from Judah, nor a lawgiver from between his feet, until Shiloh come.—GEN. xlix. 10.

FULFILLMENT—And he saith unto them, Whose is this image and superscription? They say unto him, Cæsar's. Then saith he unto them, Render therefore unto Cæsar the things which are Cæsar's; and unto God the things that are God's.—MATT. xxii. 20, 21.

Then said Pilate unto them, Take ye him, and judge him according to your law. The Jews therefore said unto him, It is not lawful for us to put any man to death.—JOHN xviii. 31.

(5) *That a forerunner like unto Elijah should prepare the way of the Messiah:*

PROPHECY—Behold, I will send my messenger, and he shall prepare the way before me: and the Lord, whom ye seek, shall suddenly come to his temple, even the messenger of the covenant, whom ye delight in: behold, he shall come, saith the Lord of hosts.—MAL. iii. 1.

The voice of him that crieth in the wilderness, Prepare ye the way of the Lord, make straight in the desert a highway for our God.—ISA. xl. 3.

FULFILLMENT—In those days came John the Baptist, preaching in the wilderness of Judea, And saying, Repent ye: for the kingdom of heaven is at hand. For this is he that was spoken of by the prophet Esaias, saying, The voice of one crying in the wilderness, Prepare ye the way of the Lord, make his paths straight.—MATT. iii. 1-3.

This is he, of whom it is written, Behold, I send my messenger before thy face, which shall prepare thy way before thee. For I say unto you, Among those that are born of women there is not a greater prophet than John the Baptist.—LUKE vii. 27, 28.

(6) *That the Messiah should begin to preach in Galilee.*

PROPHECY—In Galilee of the nations, the people that walked in darkness have seen a great light.—ISA. ix. 1, 2.

FULFILLMENT—Now when Jesus had heard that John was cast into prison, He departed into Galilee.... The people which sat in darkness, saw great light; and to them which sat in the region and shadow of death light is sprung up. From that time, Jesus began to preach, and to say, Repent: for the kingdom of heaven is at hand.—MATT. iv. 12-17.

(7) *That the Messiah should perform many miracles:*

PROPHECY—Then the eyes of the blind shall be opened, and the ears of the deaf shall be unstopped. Then shall the lame man leap as a hart, and the tongue of the dumb sing: for in the wilderness shall waters break out, and streams in the desert.—ISA. xxxv. 5, 6.

FULFILLMENT—Then was brought unto him one possessed with a devil, blind, and dumb, and he healed him, insomuch that the blind and dumb both spake and saw.—MATT. xii. 22.

But that ye may know that the Son of man hath power upon earth to forgive sins (he said unto the sick of the palsy), I say unto thee, Arise, and take up thy couch, and go into thine house. And immediately he rose up before them, and took up that whereon he lay, and departed to his own house, glorifying God.—LUKE v. 24, 25.

Jesus answered and said unto them, Go and shew John again those things which ye do hear and see: The blind receive their sight, and the lame walk, the lepers are cleansed, and the deaf hear, the dead are raised up, and the poor have the gospel preached to them.—MATT. xi. 4, 5.

(8) *That the Messiah should make his public entry into Jerusalem riding upon an ass:*

PROPHECY—Rejoice greatly, O daughter of Zion; shout, O daughter of Jerusalem: behold, thy King cometh unto thee: he is just, and having salvation; lowly, and riding upon an ass, and upon a colt the foal of an ass.— ZECH. ix. 9.

FULFILLMENT—And the disciples went, and did as Jesus commanded them, And brought the ass, and the colt, and put on them their clothes, and they set him thereon. And a very great multitude spread their garments in the way; others cut down branches from the trees, and strewed them in the way. And the multitudes that went before, and that followed, cried, saying, Hosanna to the Son of David: Blessed is he that cometh in the name of the Lord; Hosanna in the highest.—MATT. xxi. 6-9.

(9) *That the Messiah should be betrayed by one of his followers for thirty pieces of silver which would finally be thrown into the potter's field:*

PROPHECY—Yea, mine own familiar friend, in whom I trusted, which did eat of my bread, hath lifted up his heel against me.—PSA. xli. 9.

And I said unto them, If ye think good, give me my price; and if not, forbear. So they weighed for my price thirty pieces of silver. And the Lord said unto me, Cast it unto the potter: a goodly price that I was prized at of them. And I took the thirty pieces of silver, and cast them to the potter in the house of the Lord.—ZECH. xi. 12, 13.

FULFILLMENT—Then one of the twelve, called Judas Iscariot, went unto the chief priests, And said unto them, What will ye give me, and I will deliver him unto you? And they covenanted with him for thirty pieces of silver.—MATT. xxvi. 14, 15.

Then Judas, which had betrayed him, when he saw that he was condemned, repented himself, and brought again the thirty pieces of silver to the chief priests and elders, Saying, I have sinned in that I have betrayed the innocent blood. And they said, What is that to us? see thou to that. And he cast down the pieces of silver in the temple, and departed, and went and hanged himself. And the chief priests took the silver pieces, and said, It is not lawful for to put them into the treasury, because it is the price of blood. And they took counsel, and bought with them the potter's field, to bury strangers in.—MATT. xxvii. 3-8.

(10) *That the Messiah should be a man of poverty and of suffering; and should be despised and rejected of men:*

PROPHECY—He is despised and rejected of men; a man of sorrows, and acquainted with grief: and we hid as it were our faces from him; he was despised, and we esteemed him not.—ISA. liii. 3.

FULFILLMENT—And Jesus said unto him, Foxes have holes, and birds of the air have nests; but the Son of man hath not where to lay his head.—LUKE ix. 58.

And they smote him on the head with a reed, and did spit upon him, and bowing their knees worshipped him. And when they had mocked him, they took off the purple from him, and put his own clothes on him, and led him out to crucify him.—MARK xv. 19, 20.

Through reasonable diligence, witnesses might have been secured to testify to a majority, at least, of the points above enumerated, touching Messianic prophecy and fulfillment. Besides these are many others too numerous to mention in a treatise of this kind.

The question then arises at once: Admitting that all the evidence above suggested, marked "Prophecy" and "Fulfillment," could have been introduced in evidence at the trial before the Sanhedrin; were the judges morally and legally bound to acquit and release Jesus, if they believed this testimony to be true? We answer unhesitatingly, yes; as far as the count in the accusation relating to Messiahship was concerned. But we must remember that the charge against Jesus was not limited to His claims to Messiahship. The indictment against Him was that He claimed to be "the Christ, the Son of God." "Christ" is the English form of the Greek translation of the word meaning "Messiah." The real nature of the charge against the prisoner, then, was that He claimed to be not only the Messiah but also the Son of God. We have seen that "Son of God" conveyed to the Sanhedrin the notion of divine origin and of equality with Jehovah. Even to-day there is no dispute between Jews and Christians in regard to this construction. Jews charge that Jesus made such a claim and Christians agree with them. They are compelled to do so, indeed, or else abjure the fundamental dogma of their faith—the doctrine of the Trinity.

Now we approach the consideration of a phase of the subject where theology and law meet and blend. It has been sought to ridicule the contention that Jesus should have been heard on the charge of being the Son of God, in the sense that He was God Himself, because such a claim was not only ridiculous and frivolous as a plea, but because it was blasphemous upon its face; as being opposed, by bare assertion, to the most fundamental and sacred precept of the Mosaic Code and of the teachings of the Prophets: that God was purely and wholly spiritual; that He was not only incorporeal but invisible, indivisible, and incomprehensible. The advocates of this theory declare that Jesus asserted, in the face of this primary belief of the Hebrews, a plurality of gods of which He was a member, and that this assertion destroyed the very cornerstone of Judaism, founded in the teaching of the celebrated passage: "Hear, O Israel: The Lord our God is one Lord." They further declare that when Jesus presented Himself in the flesh, and declared that He was God, He insulted both the intelligence and religious consciousness of His judges by a complete anthropomorphism; and that when He did this, He was not entitled to be heard.

One of the most radical of this class is Rabbi Wise who, in "The Martyrdom of Jesus," says: "Had Jesus maintained before a Jewish court to be the Son of God, in the trinitarian sense of the terms, viz., that He was part, person, or incarnation of the Deity, He must have said it in terms to be understood to that effect, as ambiguous words amount to nothing. But if even clearly understood, the court could only have found Him insane, but not guilty of any crime." This is strong language, indeed, and deserves serious consideration. It means nothing less than that Jesus, upon His confession of equality and identity with God, should have been committed as a lunatic, and not tried as a criminal. And the real meaning of this too extreme view is that the claims of Jesus, being a man in the flesh, to membership in a plurality of gods was such an outrageous and unheard-of thing that it amounted to insanity; and that an insane person was not one to be listened to, but to be committed and protected. The purpose of the distinguished Hebrew theologian was to show by the absurdity of the thing that Jesus was never tried before a Hebrew court; that He never claimed to be the Son of God, and that the Evangelical narratives are simply false. The same writer thus continues in the same connection: "Mark reports furthermore, that Jesus did not simply affirm the high priest's question but added: 'And ye shall see the Son of Man sitting on the right hand of power, and coming in the clouds of heaven.' Jesus cannot have said these words. Our reasons are: they are not true; none of the judges and witnesses present ever did see him either sitting on the right hand of power or coming in the clouds of heaven. These words could have originated only after the death of Jesus, when the Jewish Christians expected his immediate return as the Messiah and restorer of the kingdom of heaven, so that those very men could see him coming in the clouds of heaven. Besides, Jesus, the Pharisean Jew, could not have entertained the anthropomorphism that God had a *right hand*."[326] It is only necessary to add that Rabbi Wise may be right, if the Gospel writers were untruthful men. Suffice it to say that we have said enough in support of the veracity of the Evangelists in Part I of this volume. If we are right that they were truthful historians when they published these biographies to the world, Rabbi Wise is wrong; for according to these writers the Sanhedrin did not take the view that Jesus was a crazy man, but that He was a criminal. They accordingly tried Him to the extent of bringing an accusation against Him and of supporting it with a certain kind and amount of testimony, and by then leading Him away to be crucified by the Romans. Our contention is that the trial was not complete, in that His judges did not consider the merits of the defense of Jesus in the proceedings which they conducted against Him.

It would be entirely consistent with the plan of this treatise and of the special treatment of this theme to ignore completely the question of the divinity of Jesus; since we have announced a legal and not a theological consideration of the subject. But we repeat that the theological and the legal are inseparably interwoven in a proper handling of Point XII. If Rabbi Wise and others are right that the anthropomorphic pretensions of Jesus robbed Him of the protection of the law, in the sense that His claims to be God in the flesh were not worthy of consideration by a Hebrew court, then we are wrong in making the point that the merits of His defense should have been considered.

Our contention is that the claims of Jesus were not so strange and shocking as to place Him without the pale of the law and to deny Him its ordinary protection; that His pretensions were not those of an insane man; that if He was not the Son of God He was guilty of blasphemy; and that if He was the Son of God He was innocent. We further contend that all these things were subjects of legitimate judicial examination by Hebrew judges under Hebrew law, and that Jesus should have had His day in court.

A very brief examination of the question of anthropomorphism in its connection with the claims of Jesus will demonstrate the fallacy of the arguments of Rabbi Wise and of those who agree with him. Candor compels us to admit that the Jewish conception of Jehovah at the time of the crucifixion was very foreign to the notion of a God of flesh and bone. Hebrew monotheism taught the doctrine of one God who was purely spiritual, and therefore invisible, intangible, and unapproachable. Judaism delighted to lift its deity above the sensual, material, and corporeal things of earth, and to represent Him as a pure and sinless spirit in a state of awful and supreme transcendence. Our first impression, then, is that this dogma of divine unity and spirituality must have received a dreadful shock when Jesus, a carpenter of Nazareth, whose mother, father, brothers, and sisters were known, confronted the high priest and declared to him that He was God. But the shock was certainly not so great that Caiaphas and his colleagues, after a moment's composure and reflection, could not have concluded that the pretensions of Jesus were not wholly at variance with the revelations of Hebrew theology in the earlier years of the Commonwealth of Israel. They might have judged His claims to be unfounded, but they were certainly not justified in pronouncing Him insane, or in ignoring His rights under the law to be heard and to have His defense considered. Their arrest and trial of the prisoner was the consummation of a number of secret meetings in which the astounding personality and marvelous performances of Jesus were debated and discussed with fear and trembling. The raising of Lazarus from the dead had created a frightful panic among the Sadducean oligarchy. Far from regarding Him as an obscure person whose claims were ridiculous and whose mind was unbalanced, the priests feared lest all men might believe on Him, and boldly declared that such was the influence of

His deeds that His single life might be balanced against the existence of a whole nation.[327]

What the judges of the Sanhedrin should have done in examining the merits of the defense of Jesus was: (1) To consider whether, in the light of Hebrew scripture and tradition, a god of flesh and bone, representing the second person of a Duality or a Trinity of gods, was possible; (2) to weigh thoroughly the claims of Jesus, in the light of testimony properly adduced at the trial, that He was this second person of a Duality or Trinity of gods.

In making this examination, let us bear in mind, the members of the court were not to look forward, but backward. They were to examine the past, not the future, in reference to the present. Furthermore, they were not to consider so much a Trinity as a Duality of gods; for it must be remembered that the Holy Ghost was not a feature of the trial. The Athanasian creed and the proceedings of the Nicene Council were not binding upon Caiaphas and his fellow-judges. Nor were the teachings of the New Testament scriptures published to the world more than a generation after the trial. They were to consider the divine pretensions of Jesus in the light of the teachings and revelations of the Law and the Prophets. They were to measure His claims by these standards in the light of the evidence adduced before them.

With a view to a thorough and systematic examination of the merits of the defense of Jesus, Caiaphas, as presiding officer of the Sanhedrin, should have propounded to his fellow-judges the following initial questions: (1) Do the Law and the Prophets reveal the doctrine of a plurality of gods among the Israelites? That is, has Jehovah ever begotten, or has He ever promised to beget, a Son of equal divinity with Himself? Was this Son to be, or is He to be born of a woman; and to have, therefore, the form of a man and the attributes of a human being? Was this Son to be, or is He to be at any time identical with the Father? Do the Law and the Prophets tell us unmistakably that Jehovah ever appeared upon the earth in human form and exhibited human attributes? Do they contain a promise from the Father that He would send His Son to the earth to be the Redeemer of men and the Regenerator of the world? (2) Do the credentials of Jesus, the prisoner at the bar, in the light of the evidence before us, entitle Him to be considered this Son and Ambassador of God, sent from the Father to redeem mankind?

It follows logically and necessarily that if affirmative answers were not given to the first set of questions an examination of the second would be useless. Let us conceive, then, that the judges of the Sanhedrin had employed this method. What answers, we may ask, would they have developed to these questions from the Sacred Books?

At the outset it is safe to say that negative answers would have been given, if the judges had considered the claims of Jesus with reference alone to the prevailing Pharisaic teachings of the days of Jesus. And in this connection let us note that the Hebrew conception of Jehovah had materially changed in the time intervening between the Mosaic dispensation and the coming of the Christ. The spiritual growth of the nation had been characterized at every step by marked aversion to anthropomorphism—the ascription to God of human form and attributes. In the Pentateuch there is a prevailing anthropomorphic idea of Jehovah. He is frequently talked about as if He were a man. Human passions and emotions are repeatedly ascribed to Him. This was inevitable among a primitive people whose crude religious consciousness sought to frame from the analogy of human nature a visible symbol of the Deity and a sensible emblem of religious faith. All early religions have manifested the same anthropomorphic tendencies. Both Judaism and Christianity have long since planted themselves upon the fundamental proposition that God is a spirit. But both these systems of religion have in all ages been compelled to run the gantlet of two opposing tendencies: one of which sought by a living, personal communion with God through Moses and through Christ, by means of human attributes and symbols, an intimate knowledge and immediate benefit of the divine nature; the other, from a horror of anthropomorphism, tending to make God purely passionless and impersonal, thus reducing Him to a bare conception without form or quality, thus making Him a blank negation.

The successive steps in the progress of weeding out anthropomorphisms from the Pentateuch may be clearly traced in later Hebrew literature. The Prophets themselves were at times repelled by the sensuous conceptions of God revealed by the writings of Moses. The great lawgiver had attributed to Jehovah the quality of repentance, a human attribute. "And it *repented* the Lord that he had made man on the earth, and it grieved him at his heart," says Genesis vi. 6. But a later writer, the prophet Samuel, denied that God had such a quality. "And also the Strength of Israel will not lie nor repent: for he is not a man, that he should repent."[328] And the prophet Hosea affirms this declaration when he places in the mouth of Jehovah the affirmation: "For I am God and not man."[329]

At a still later age, when the notion of the supreme transcendence of Jehovah had become prevalent, it was considered objectionable to make God say, "I will dwell in your midst"; as a substitute, "I shall cause you to dwell" was adopted. "To behold the face of God" was not a repulsive phrase in the ancient days of Hebrew plainness and simplicity, but later times sought to eradicate the anthropomorphism by saying instead, "to appear before God."

The Septuagint, the Greek version of the Bible in use at the time of Christ, reveals the same tendency toward paraphrasing or spiritualizing the anthropomorphic phrases of the older Bible. In this translation the "image of God" of the older Hebrew literature becomes "the glory of God," and "the mouth of God" is expressed by "the voice of the Lord."

The Septuagint was written more than a century before the birth of Jesus, and we may safely assert that at the beginning of our era the Jews not only affirmatively proclaimed the doctrine of divine unity and pure spirituality, in relation to the person and character of Jehovah, but that they boldly and indignantly denied and denounced any attempt to make of God a man or to attribute to Him human qualities. But when we say "the Jews," we mean the dominant religious sect of the nation, the Pharisees. We should not forget, in this connection, that the primary difference between the Sadducees and the Pharisees was in the varying intensity with which they loved the Law of Moses and adhered to its teachings. We have seen in Part II of this volume that the Mishna, the oral law, was really more highly esteemed by the Pharisaic Jews than was the Mosaic Code. But the Sadducees planted themselves squarely upon the Pentateuch and denied that the traditions of the Scribes were of binding force. "The Sadducees were a body of aristocrats opposed to the oral law and the later developments of Judaism."

Now what views, we may ask, did the Sadducees entertain of the possibility of God appearing to men in the flesh? In other words, what was their notion, at the time of Christ, of the anthropomorphisms of the Pentateuch, which was their ultimate guide and standard in all matters of legal and religious interpretation? These questions are important in this connection, since Caiaphas and the large majority of his colleagues in the Great Sanhedrin were Sadducees and held the fate of Jesus in their hands. Candor compels us to admit that we believe that the Sadducees agreed with the Pharisees that Jehovah was a pure and sinless spirit. But we feel equally sure that their knowledge of the Pentateuch, in which at times anthropomorphism is strongly accentuated, taught them that Jehovah had not only appeared in the flesh among men in olden times, but that it was not at all impossible or unreasonable that He should come again in the same form. But this much is certain: that in determining whether Jesus could be both man and God the Sadducees would be disposed to ignore the traditions of the Pharisees and "the later developments of Judaism," and appeal direct to the law of Moses. Jesus Himself, if He had been disposed to make a defense of His claims, and His judges had been disposed to hear Him, would have appealed to the same legal standard. Christ more than once manifested a disposition to appeal to the Mosaic Code, as a modern citizen would appeal from mere statutes and the decisions of the courts, to the constitution, as the fundamental law of the land. Mark tells us that in denouncing the Pharisees, He used this language: "And he said unto them, Full well ye reject the commandment of God, that ye may keep your own tradition.... Making the word of God of none effect through your tradition, which ye have delivered: and many such like things do ye."[330] Hebrew sacred literature is filled with anecdotes, often characterized by raillery and jests, of how the Sadducces denounced the Pharisees for their attempts to nullify Mosaic injunction by their peculiar interpretation.

Now in view of what we have just said, are we not justified in assuming that if the judges had accorded Jesus full liberty of defense He would have appealed to the Pentateuch, with the approbation of His judges, to show that God had appeared among men in the flesh, and that a plurality in the Godhead was plainly taught? Would He not then have appealed to the Prophets to show that Jehovah had spoken of a begotten Son who was none other than Almighty God Himself? Would He not have shown from both the Law and the Prophets that the angel of Jehovah, who was none other than Himself, had frequently, in ages past, acted as the ambassador of God in numerous visits to the earth, on missions of love and mercy among men? Would He not have proved to them that this angel of Jehovah had been at certain times in the past none other than Jehovah Himself? Could He not have pointed out to them that their whole sacred literature was filled with prophecies foretelling the coming of this Son and Ambassador of God to the earth to redeem fallen man? Could He not then have summoned a hundred witnesses to prove His own connection with these prophecies, to show His virgin birth, and to give an account of the numerous miracles which He had wrought, and that were the best evidence of His divine character?

Let us imagine that Caiaphas, as judge, had demanded of Jesus, the prisoner, to produce Biblical evidence that God had ever begotten or had promised to beget a Son who was equal with Himself. The following passages might have been produced:

Psa. ii. 7: Thou art my son; this day have I begotten thee.

Isa. ix. 6: For unto us a child is born, unto us a son is given: and the government shall be upon his shoulder: and his name shall be called Wonderful, Counselor, The mighty God, The everlasting Father, The Prince of Peace.

What closer identity, we may ask, could be demanded between the Father and the Son than is revealed by this language of Isaiah, "and his (the son's) name shall be called The mighty God, The everlasting Father?" What more exact equality could be asked than the same words suggest? What stronger proof of plurality in the Godhead could be demanded?

Again, let us suppose that His judges had demanded of Jesus scriptural proof that the divine Son of God was to be born of a woman, and was to have, therefore, the form of a man and the attributes of a human being. The following passages might have been produced:

Isa. vii. 14: Therefore the Lord himself shall give you a sign; Behold, a virgin shall conceive and bear a son, and shall call his name Immanuel.

Gen. iii. 15: And I will put enmity between thee and the woman, and between thy seed and her seed; it shall bruise thy head, and thou shalt bruise his heel.

Enoch lxii. 5: And one Portion of them will look on the other, and they will be terrified, and their countenance will fall, and they will seize them when they see *that Son of Woman* sitting on the throne of his glory.

The first of these passages needs no comment. It is perfectly clear and speaks for itself. Regarding the second, it may be observed that after the fall of Adam and Eve in the Garden of Eden it was announced that the seed of the woman should bruise the serpent's head. This announcement contained, when viewed in the light of subsequent revelations, both a promise and a prophecy; a promise of a Redeemer of fallen man, and a prophecy that He would finally triumph over all the powers of sin and darkness whose father was Satan, who had entered into the serpent. The "seed of the woman" foretold that the Redeemer would have a human nature; His triumph over Satan suggested His divine origin and power.

Again, continuing the examination, let us suppose that Caiaphas had informed Jesus that His pretensions to be God in the flesh were not only not sanctioned by but were offensive to the current teachings of Judaism in relation to the person and character of Jehovah. Let us suppose, further, that the high priest had informed the prisoner that he and his fellow-judges, who were Sadducees in faith and a majority in number of the Sanhedrin, did not feel themselves bound by Pharisaic tradition and "the later developments of Judaism"; that they preferred the Mosaic Code as a standard of legal and religious judgment; that the anthropomorphisms of the Pentateuch were not particularly offensive to them, for the reason that they had not been to Moses; and that if He, the prisoner at the bar, could cite instances related by Moses where Jehovah had appeared among men, having the form of a human being, His case would be greatly strengthened; on the ground that if God had ever appeared in the flesh on one occasion it was not unreasonable, or at least impossible, that He should so appear again.

In proof that God had appeared in the flesh, or at least in human form, among men, the following passages might have been adduced:

Gen. xviii. 1-8: And the Lord appeared unto him in the plains of Mamre: and he sat in the tent door in the heat of the day; And he lifted up his eyes and looked, and, lo, three men stood by him: and when he saw them, he ran to meet them from the tent door, and bowed himself toward the ground,

And said, My Lord, if now I have found favour in thy sight, pass not away, I pray thee, from thy servant: ... And Abraham ran unto the herd, and fetched a calf tender and good, and gave it unto a young man; and he hasted to dress it. And he took butter, and milk, and the calf which he had dressed, and set it before them; and he stood by them under the tree, and they did eat.

Gen. xvi. 10-13: And the angel of the Lord said unto her, I will multiply thy seed exceedingly, that it shall not be numbered for multitude. And the angel of the Lord said unto her, Behold, thou art with child, and shalt bear a son, and shalt call his name Ishmael; because the Lord hath heard thy affliction.... And she called the name of the Lord that spake unto her, Thou God seest me: for she said, Have I also here looked after him that seeth me?

Gen. xxii. 11, 12: And the angel of the Lord called unto him out of heaven, and said, Abraham, Abraham: and he said, Here am I. And he said, Lay not thine hand upon the lad, neither do thou any thing unto him: for now I know that thou fearest God, seeing thou hast not withheld thy son, thine only son, from me.

Ex. iii. 2-6: And the Angel of the Lord appeared unto him in a flame of fire out of the midst of a bush: and he looked, and, behold, the bush burned with fire, and the bush was not consumed. And Moses said, I will not turn aside, and see this great sight, why the bush is not burnt. And when the Lord saw that he turned aside to see, God called unto him out of the midst of the bush, and said, Moses, Moses. And he said, Here am I. And he said, Draw not nigh hither: put off thy shoes from off thy feet; for the place whereon thou standest is holy ground. Moreover he said, I am the God of thy father, the God of Abraham, the God of Isaac, and the God of Jacob. And Moses hid his face; for he was afraid to look upon God.

From the first passage above cited it is clear that Jehovah, in the form of a man, appeared to Abraham in the plains of Mamre. A contributor to "The Jewish Encyclopedia" declares that these three men were angels in the shape of human beings of extraordinary beauty but that they were not at once recognized as angels.[331] The Christian commentators are generally agreed that it was Jehovah who was present in human form.[332] The other members of the company are declared by some of them to be the second and third persons of the Trinity. Plausibility is given to this contention by the fact that Abraham first saw one person, the Lord; then he looked up and saw three; he then advanced to meet the three, and, addressing them, used a singular epithet, "My Lord." The form of the address, together with the movements of Abraham, seem to suggest three in one and one in three. But with this theory we are not seriously concerned, as our present purpose is to show that Jehovah occasionally appeared in human form upon the earth in the olden days. A plurality of gods is suggested, however, by the passage, if

Christian interpretation be applied; for if one of these men was Jehovah, as Abraham's language seems to indicate, and as modern Christian interpretation generally maintains, why could not the other two men have also been gods in the form of the Son and the Holy Spirit? If the Jewish commentator's opinion, to which we have referred heretofore, be plausible—that the three men were angels in human form—why is it not equally as plausible to suppose that a god or gods should also appear in human form? But at all events these three men were not ordinary human beings. He who maintains that they were assaults the intelligence of either the translators of the Bible or of Abraham, or both; for the Hebrew patriarch believed that Jehovah was present as a guest in his house, and he spread a hospitable meal for him. The language of Genesis very clearly indicates as much. And the question may be asked: If Abraham could not recognize Jehovah, who could or can?

In the second of the above extracts from Genesis the angel of the Lord appeared unto Hagar and said to her: "I will multiply thy seed exceedingly, that it shall not be numbered for multitude." And Hagar made reply: "And she called the name of the Lord that spake unto her, Thou God seest me." This passage plainly teaches that the angel of the Lord and Jehovah were sometimes identical.

The third passage heretofore cited from Genesis also teaches the identity of the angel of the Lord and of God Himself, in the matter of the attempted sacrifice of Isaac by Abraham. It was the same voice, that of the angel of the Lord, that said: "For now I know that thou fearest God, seeing thou hast not withheld thy son, thine only son from me."

Again, the identity of the angel of the Lord and of Jehovah is unmistakably shown from the account of the voice that cried from the burning bush: "I am the God of thy father, the God of Abraham, the God of Isaac, and the God of Jacob. And Moses hid his face, for he was afraid to look upon God."

Concerning the manifestation of Jehovah to men in angelic and human form a modern writer says: "Much has been written concerning a certain Mal'akh Yaweh (messenger of Jehovah) who appears in the Old Testament. I say 'a certain' Mal'akh Yaweh, because it is not every Mal'akh Yaweh that appears to which I refer. In most passages the Mal'akh Yaweh is simply an angel sent by the Almighty to communicate his will or purposes to men. These angels are distinctly apprehended as created intelligences, wholly separate and diverse from God. But there is a class of passages in which the Mal'akh Yaweh appears as a self-manifestation of God. He appears indeed in human form and speaks of God in the third person. But those to whom he appears are oppressed by the consciousness that they have seen God and must die. They see in him an impersonation of Deity such as is found in no other angel. He is to their minds not merely a messenger from God but the revelation of the being of God. The Christian fathers for the most part identify him with the Logos of the New Testament. But there is as much reason to adopt the opinion of many modern writers who hold that he is Jehovah himself appearing in human form, for he is explicitly addressed as Jehovah (Judges vi. 11-24)."[333]

The identity of the angel of Jehovah and of Jehovah Himself could not be more conclusively proved than in the appearance to Gideon, related in the passage above cited, Judges vi. 11-24. The absolute identity is revealed in verses 22, 23: "And when Gideon perceived that he was an angel of the Lord, Gideon said, Alas, O Lord God! for because I have seen an angel of the Lord face to face. And the Lord said unto him, Peace be unto thee; fear not: thou shalt not die."

Now let us suppose that Caiaphas and the Sanhedrin had received these passages favorably; that they had become convinced that Jehovah had appeared in the olden days in the form of angels and of men; that at one time He was identical with a man, and at another with an angel whom He had sent. Let us suppose further that the judges of Jesus had demanded of Him a passage of ancient Scriptures connecting Him even remotely with this messenger of God. The following passage might have been produced:

Ex. xxiii. 20, 21: Behold, I send an Angel before thee, to keep thee in the way, and to bring thee into the place which I have prepared. Beware of him, and obey his voice, provoke him not; for he will not pardon your transgressions: for my name is in him.

The concluding paragraph of the last cited passage, "My name is in him," is equivalent to "I am in him." The mere name of God is often used to denote God Himself as manifested. For instance, in I Kings viii. 29 is contained the statement, "My name shall be there"; that is, "There will I dwell." And when it is said that the name of Jehovah would be in the angel of Jehovah it is equivalent to saying that Jehovah Himself would be present in His messenger which He had sent before Him. The passage further teaches that the messenger of Jehovah to the earth bore a commission to pardon sin, or not to, according to his pleasure. The Sanhedrin were undoubtedly aware that Jesus claimed the same power by virtue of authority vested in Him by His Father.

But it may be imagined that Caiaphas was perfectly willing to concede that Jehovah had appeared in human form upon the earth, but was not inclined to believe that He had ever manifested human passions and emotions, as Jesus had done when He denounced on several occasions the hypocrisy of the Pharisees; and, above all, when He overthrew the tables in the Temple, and, applying a lash to their backs, drove out the money-changers.[334] Let us imagine that the high priest demanded of the prisoner proof from the ancient Scriptures that Jehovah was possessed of ordinary human attributes; and particularly that He was at times disposed to fight. Jesus might have produced the following passages to show that Jehovah, His Father, had manifested in times past the ordinary human passions and emotions of repentance, grief, jealousy, anger, graciousness, love, and hate:

Ex. xv. 3, 6: The Lord is a man of war.... Thy right hand, O Lord, is become glorious in power: thy right hand, O Lord, hath dashed in pieces the enemy.

Gen. vi. 6: And it *repented* the Lord that he had made man on the earth, and it grieved him at his heart.

Deut. vi. 15: For the Lord thy God is a *jealous* God among you, lest the anger of the Lord thy God be kindled against thee, and destroy thee from off the face of the earth.

Psa. cxi. 4: He hath made his wonderful works to be remembered: the Lord is *gracious* and full of *compassion*.

I Kings x. 9: Because the Lord *loved* Israel forever, therefore made he thee king, to do judgment and justice.

Prov. vi. 16: These six things doth the Lord *hate*: yea, seven are an abomination unto him.

And as a final step in the examination let us imagine that Caiaphas and his colleagues had stated to Jesus that they were satisfied, from the authorities cited, that Jehovah had, in ancient days, appeared upon the earth in human form and had exhibited human attributes; that Jehovah had begotten a Son who was equal in power and majesty with Himself; that this Son had been begotten of a woman and possessed, therefore, human form and attributes; that this Jehovah had sent an angel messenger to the earth with a commission to pardon sins. Let us imagine further that the judges had demanded of the prisoner that He present and prove His credentials as the divine ambassador of God from heaven to men on earth; that He conform His personal claims to heavenly Messiahship to ancient prophecy by producing evidence before them in court. What facts, we may ask, could Jesus have shown to establish His claims to Messiahship and to Sonship of the Father?

To attempt to originate a defense for Jesus would be unnecessary, if not actually impertinent and sacrilegious. We are fully justified, however, in assuming that if called upon to prove His claims to Messiahship He would have made the same reply to the Sanhedrin that He had already made to the Jews out of court who asked Him: "What sign shewest thou, then, that we may see, and believe thee? what dost thou work?"[335] "How long dost thou make us to doubt? If thou be the Christ, tell us plainly. Jesus answered them,

I told you, and ye believed not: *the works that I do in my Father's name, they bear witness of me."*[336] Again, He would have doubtless made the same reply to Caiaphas that He did to the embassy from John the Baptist who came to inquire if He was really the Messiah. "Jesus answered and said unto them, Go and shew John again those things which ye do hear and see: The blind receive their sight, and the lame walk, the lepers are cleansed, and the deaf hear, the dead are raised up, and the poor have the gospel preached to them."[337]

Under a fair trial, in daylight, with full freedom of defense to the accused, abundant evidence could have been secured of the miraculous powers of Jesus and of the truthfulness of His pretensions to a divine origin. Testimony could have been introduced that would have been not only competent but entirely satisfactory. The New Testament narratives tell us of about forty miracles that Jesus performed during His life. The closing verse of St. John intimates that He performed many that were never reported. The circumstances surrounding the working of these wonders were such as to make them peculiarly competent as evidence and to carry conviction of their genuineness, when they were once introduced.

In the first place, miracles were entirely capable of being proved by testimony. If those persons who had known Lazarus intimately during his lifetime saw him dead on one day, and on the fourth day afterwards saw him alive and walking the streets, the senses would be perfectly competent to decide and the fact that a miracle had been performed would be conclusively proved. And it may be added that a dozen witnesses who were entirely competent to testify could have been summoned to the defense of Jesus in the matter of raising Lazarus from the dead.

Again, we must remember that the miracles of Jesus were performed in the most public manner, in the street, on the highway, in far-away Galilee, and at the very gates of Jerusalem. Both His friends and enemies, men and women, were witnesses of their performance. The number and publicity of these wonder-working performances rendered it possible for the Sanhedrin to call before them hundreds and thousands of competent witnesses who had seen and felt the manifestation of the divine power of the prisoner in their presence.

Again, the miracles of Jesus were such as to render them subject to the test of the senses, when submitted to examination. If Caiaphas and his fellow-judges had decided that there was fraud in the matter of the alleged raising of Lazarus from the dead, because the brother of Martha and Mary was not really dead, but simply swooned or slept; if they had decided that the man sick of the palsy was not cured by miracle, but by faith; nevertheless, they could not have charged fraud and faith cure in the matter of the stilling of the tempest or the feeding of the five thousand or the walking on the sea. They would have been forced to conclude that the witnesses had lied or that miracles had been wrought. In the case of the feeding of the five thousand, the witnesses would have been too numerous to brand with falsehood.

But, we may ask, was the performance of miracles by Jesus, if believed by the Sanhedrin, sufficient evidence of the divine origin of Jesus? This question we are not prepared to answer positively, either yes or no. We can only venture the personal opinion that the act of raising a person indisputably dead, to life again, would be an astounding miracle, an achievement that could be wrought by the hand of a God alone. The trouble with the question is that men like Elijah raised the dead.[338] It is true that there is no pretension that Elijah was divine or that he wrought the miracle by virtue of any peculiar power within himself. The Scriptures plainly state that he asked God to raise the dead to life through him. The same is true of the raising of Lazarus by Jesus.[339] But Christ seems to have raised the daughter of Jairus[340] and the son of the widow of Nain[341] from the dead by virtue of the strength of His own divinity; for there is no suggestion that the power of God was either previously invoked or subsequently acknowledged.

As to the weight which the testimony of the miracles of Jesus should have had with Caiaphas and the other members of the court, we have a valuable indication in the opinion expressed by Nicodemus, who was himself a member of the Sanhedrin, when he said to Jesus: "We know that thou art a teacher come from God: for no man can do these miracles that thou doest, except God be with him."[342] If Nicodemus, "a ruler of the Jews" and one of the leading members of their highest tribunal, believed that Jesus was divine because of the wonders that He had wrought, why should not a knowledge of these miracles by the other members of the Sanhedrin have produced the same impression? Nicodemus, it is true, was a friend of Jesus, but he was not a disciple. And the very timidity with which he expressed his friendship, having come at night to pay his compliments to the Master, demonstrates the deep impression that the miraculous powers of the Christ had made upon him.

But the judges of Jesus were not limited to the evidence of miracles as a proof of the divinity of the prisoner in their midst. They should have weighed "in the sincerity of their conscience" the fact that Jesus was born in Bethlehem in fulfillment of the prophecy contained in Micah v. 2; that He was sprung from the House of David in conformity with the teachings in Jeremiah xxiii. 5, 6; that John the Baptist was His forerunner like unto Elijah, who had come to prepare the way according to the prophecy in Malachi iii. 1; that He had begun to preach in Galilee, as foretold in Isaiah ix. 1, 2; that the scepter had departed from Judah and the lawgiver from between his feet, as prophesied in Genesis xlix. 10, which fact it was believed would herald the approach of the Messiah; that He had made His public entry into Jerusalem riding upon an ass, as foretold in Zechariah ix. 9; and that He had been betrayed into their hands by one of His own friends, in fulfillment of prophecies contained in Psalms xli. 9 and Zechariah xi. 12, 13.

This cumulative evidence, this collective proof, must have carried overwhelming conviction to the minds and the hearts of fair and impartial judges. More than one Nicodemus would have arisen to plead the cause of Jesus if this testimony had been adduced before a free-minded, open-hearted, disinterested tribunal. More than one Joseph of Arimathea would have refused assent in a hostile verdict against a prisoner in whose favor the record of fact was so pronounced.

In determining the weight that this evidence should have had in affecting the decision of the judges we must not forget that a Jewish prisoner was not required to prove his innocence. It was incumbent upon the Commonwealth of Israel to establish guilt beyond all doubt. We should also remember that the peculiar tendency of the Hebrew system of criminal procedure was in the direction of complete protection to the accused. Not reasonable doubt merely, but all doubt was resolved in his favor. It was a maxim of the Hebrew law that "the Sanhedrin was to save, not to destroy life." Pretext after pretext was sought to acquit. "The primary object of the Hebrew judicial system," says Benny, "was to render the conviction of an innocent person impossible. All the ingenuity of the Jewish legists was directed to the attainment of this end." If this generous and merciful tendency of Hebrew law had been duly observed, would not the production of the evidence above noted have resulted in the acquittal of Jesus?

But, at this point, let us return to the consideration of the real meaning of the objection urged in Point XII. The irregularity therein alleged is that the Sanhedrin paid no attention whatever to the defense of Jesus. And herein was the real error. The members of that court might have rejected as false the claims of the Nazarene to Messiahship. They might have denounced as fraudulent his pretensions to miraculous powers. They could not for this reason have been charged with judicial unfairness, if they had first heard his defense and had then "weighed it in the sincerity of their conscience." Infallibility of judgment cannot be demanded of judicial officers.

In closing the discussion of errors committed at the night trial in the palace of Caiaphas, the reader should be reminded that the twelve Points above mentioned are not exhaustive of the irregularities. Others might be mentioned. It seems that Jesus, being the accused, should not have been put under oath.[343] On the days on which capital verdicts were pronounced Hebrew judges were required to mourn and fast.[344] But there was evidently no mourning and fasting by Caiaphas and his colleagues at the time of the condemnation of Jesus. Again, there is no evidence that Antecedent Warning was properly administered. Still other errors might be noted, if a legal presumption in favor of the correctness of the record did not prevent. The irregularities which we have heretofore discussed, it is believed, exhaust all the material errors committed at the first session of the Sanhedrin. At least, no others are revealed by the Gospel records.

The Morning Session of the Sanhedrin.—About three hours after the close of the night session in the palace of Caiaphas, that is about six o'clock in the morning, the Sanhedrin reconvened in a second session. In the interval between these sittings Jesus was brutalized by His keepers. Exactly what the priests were doing we do not know. They were probably busily engaged in perfecting plans for the destruction of the prisoner in their charge.

The daylight meeting is thus reported in Matthew xxvii. 1: "When the morning was come, all the chief priests and elders of the people took counsel against Jesus to put him to death." In Mark xv. 1 the same session is thus recorded: "And straightway in the morning the chief priests held a consultation with the elders and scribes and the whole council, and bound Jesus, and carried him away, and delivered him to Pilate."

The exact nature of this morning sitting, whether a regular trial or an informal gathering, is not certainly known. Meyer, Ellicott, and Lichtenstein maintain that this second session was nothing more than a prolongation of the night trial, perhaps with a brief recess, and that its special object was to convene for consultation concerning the carrying out of the sentence which had already been pronounced against Jesus.[345] But this view is entirely exceptional. It is maintained by the greater number of reputable authorities that the second sitting was in the nature of a second trial. The solution of the difficulty seems to turn upon the account given by St. Luke, for St. John records the details of neither the night nor the morning session. St. Luke describes a regular trial, but it is not positively known whether his account refers to the night or to the morning meeting. If his report refers to the same trial as that described in Matthew xxvi. 57-68 and in Mark xiv. 53-65, then we have only the brief notices in Matthew xxvii. 1 and in Mark xv. 1 concerning the morning session, which indicate only a very brief and informal meeting of the Sanhedrin at daybreak. On the other hand, if the report of St. Luke refers to the daylight meeting of the Sanhedrin referred to by St. Matthew and St. Mark then we have received from the third Evangelist a description of a regular trial at the second session of the Sanhedrin. Andrews has thus expressed himself very cogently concerning this matter:

Our decision as to a second and distinct session of the Sanhedrin will mainly depend upon the place we give to the account in Luke xxii. 66-71. Is this examination of Jesus identical with that first session of Matthew xxvi. 57-68, and of Mark xiv. 53-65? Against this identity are some strong objections: First, The mention of time by Luke: "As soon as it was day." This corresponds well to the time of the morning session of Matthew and Mark, but not to the time when Jesus was first led before the Sanhedrin, which must have been two or three hours before day. Second, The place of the meeting: "They led Him into their council," ἀνήγαγον αὐτὸν εἰς τὸ συνέδριον ἑαυτῶν. This is rendered by some: "They led Him up into their council chamber," or the place where they usually held their sessions. Whether this council chamber was the room Gazith at the east corner of the court of the temple, is not certain. Lightfoot (on Matthew xxvi. 3) conjectures that the Sanhedrin was driven from this its accustomed seat half a year or thereabout before the death of Christ. But if this were so, still the "Tabernæ," where it established its sessions, were shops near the gate Shusan, and so connected with the temple. They went up to that room where they usually met. Third, The dissimilarity of the proceedings, as stated by Luke, which shows that this was no formal trial. There is here no mention of witnesses—no charges brought to be proved against Him. He is simply asked to tell them if He is the Christ ("If thou art the Christ, tell us," R. V.); and this seems plainly to point to the result of the former session. Then, having confessed Himself to be the Christ, the Son of God, He was condemned to death for blasphemy. It was only necessary now that He repeat His confession, and hence this question is put directly to Him: "Art thou the Christ? tell us." His reply, "If I tell you, ye will not believe; and if I also ask you, ye will not answer me, nor let me go," points backward to his former confession. To His reply they only answer by asking, "Art thou then the Son of God?" The renewed avowal that He is the Son of God, heard by them all from His own lips, opens the way for His immediate delivery into Pilate's hands. Fourth, The position which Luke gives (xxii. 63-65) to the insults and abuse heaped upon Jesus. There can be no doubt that they are the same mentioned by Matthew and Mark as occurring immediately after the sentence had been first pronounced.

From all this it is a probable, though not a certain conclusion, that Luke (xxii. 66-71) refers to the same meeting of the Sanhedrin mentioned by Matthew (xxvii. 1) and Mark (xv. 1), and relates, in part, what then took place. (Alford thinks that Luke has confused things and relates as happening at the second session what really happened at the first.) This meeting was, then, a morning session convened to ratify formally what had been done before with haste and informality. The circumstances under which its members had been earlier convened, at the palace of Caiaphas, sufficiently show that the legal forms, which they were so scrupulous in observing, had not been complied with.[346]

If then the second session of the Sanhedrin was in the nature of a regular trial, what were the facts of the proceedings? St. Luke says: "And as soon as it was day, the elders of the people and the chief priests and the scribes came together, and led him into their council, saying, Art thou the Christ? tell us. And he said unto them, If I tell you, ye will not believe: And if I also ask you, ye will not answer me, nor let me go. Hereafter shall the Son of man sit on the right hand of the power of God. Then said they all, Art thou then the Son of God? And he said unto them, Ye say that I am. And they said, What need we any further witness? for we ourselves have heard of his own mouth."[347]

The reader will readily perceive the source of the difficulty which we have just discussed. This report of St. Luke points both ways, toward both the night and morning sessions. "*And as soon as it was day*" clearly indicates a daybreak meeting, but the remainder of the account bears a most striking resemblance to the reports of the night trial given by St. Matthew and St. Mark. This seeming discrepancy is very easily reconciled, however, when we reflect that the second trial required by Hebrew law to be held in every case where a verdict of guilt had been pronounced, was virtually a repetition of the first trial. Benny tells us that the second trial was a critical examination of the trial of the first day, in which the questions and answers originally asked and made were carefully reviewed and reëxamined.[348] Is it very strange, then, that at the morning trial described by St. Luke substantially the same questions are asked and answers given as are found in the reports of the night trial by St. Matthew and St. Mark?

We may now ask: What was the purpose of this second trial? Why did not the first trial suffice? According to the most reliable authorities, the answer to this question is to be found in that provision of the Hebrew law which required two trials instead of one, in every case where the prisoner had been found guilty at the first trial. Not only were there to be two trials, but they were to be held on different days. The morning session of the Sanhedrin was intended, therefore, to give a semblance of legality and regularity to this requirement of Hebrew law. But we shall see how completely the Sanhedrin failed in this design. "What legitimacy," says Keim, "might be lacking in the proceedings of the nocturnal sitting of the Sanhedrin, was to be completely made up by the morning sitting, without prejudice to the authority and the— in the main point—decisive action of the former.... There nevertheless was no lack of illegality. The most striking instance of this was the fact that though they wished to bring about an extension of the procedure over two days they had in fact only two sittings, and not two separate days. But contempt of the legal ordinances was much more seriously shown by the absence of any investigation into the circumstances of the case at the second sitting, although *both law and tradition demanded such an investigation.*"[349]

If "both law and tradition demanded such an investigation," that is, if the second trial of the case on the second day of the proceedings was required to be formal and in the nature of an action *de novo*; if the second trial was required by law to be characterized by all the formality, solemnity, and legality of the first trial; what errors, we may ask, are disclosed by the reports of St. Luke, St. Matthew, and St. Mark in the proceedings against Jesus conducted by the Sanhedrin at the morning session? To be brief, reply may be made that the irregularities were virtually the same as those that occurred at the night trial. The same precipitancy that was forbidden by Hebrew law is apparent. This haste prevented, of course, that careful deliberation and painstaking investigation of the case which the Mosaic Code as well as the rules of the Mishna imperatively demanded. It is true that the second trial was not conducted at night. But the Passover Feast was still in progress, and no court could legally sit at such a time. The Sanhedrin at the second session seems to have been still sitting in the palace of Caiaphas instead of the Hall of Hewn Stones, the legal meeting place of the court. This we learn from a passage in St. John.[350] Again, no witnesses seem to have been summoned, and the accused was convicted upon his uncorroborated confession.

And finally, the verdict at the second trial, as was the case in that of the first, seems to have been unanimous, and therefore illegal. This unanimity is indicated by the combined reports of St. Matthew, St. Mark, and St. Luke. St. Matthew says: "When the morning was come, *all* the chief priests and elders of the people took counsel against Jesus to put Him to death." St. Mark says: "And straightway in the morning, the chief priests held a consultation with the elders and scribes and the *whole council*, and bound Jesus, and carried him away, and delivered him to Pilate." These accounts of the first two Evangelists very clearly state that the full Sanhedrin was present at the morning trial. Then St. Luke very explicitly explains the nature and manner of the verdict: "Then said they *all*, Art thou then the Son of God? And he said unto them, Ye say that I am. And they said, What need we any further witness? for we ourselves have heard of his own mouth."

It may be objected that no formal verdict was pronounced at the second trial. Such a verdict would have been expressed in these words: "Thou, Jesus, art guilty."[351] While such words are not expressly reported by the Evangelists, the account of St. Luke taken in connection with the report of St. Mark of the night trial, which the morning session was intended to confirm, clearly indicates that such a verdict must have been pronounced. A reasonable inference from the whole context of the synoptic writers in describing both trials certainly justifies such a conclusion.

The question again arises: If the full Sanhedrin was present at the morning session and if all the members condemned Jesus, either with or without a formal verdict, is it not true that both Nicodemus and Joseph of Arimathea, who were doubtless members of the court, were arrayed against the Christ? If they were hostile in their attitude toward Him, either openly or by acquiescence at the morning session, does this fact not help to support the contention made under Point IX that they voted against Him at the night trial? We are well aware that there is much opposition to this view, but we are, nevertheless, compelled to agree rather reluctantly with Keim that "it is a pure supposition that members of the council who were secret friends of Jesus—whose existence, moreover, cannot be established—either raised an opposition in one of the sessions, or abstained from voting, or were not present."[352] The plain language of the Scriptures indicates: (1) That both Nicodemus[353] and Joseph of Arimathea[354] were members of the Great Sanhedrin; (2) that they were both present at both trials;[355] and (3) that they both either voted against Him or tacitly acquiesced in the judgments pronounced against Him.[356] We have already discussed under Point IX the passage in Luke xxiii. 51 referring to the fact that Joseph of Arimathea "had not consented to the counsel and deed of them," which seems to furnish refutation of the contention which we have made, as far as such contention relates to Joseph of Arimathea. Suffice it to note the opinion of Keim that "the passage in itself can be held to refer to absence or to dissent in voting."[357]

"And the whole multitude of them arose, and led him unto Pilate."

The reader may ask: Why did the Jews lead Jesus away to Pilate? When they had condemned Him to death on the charge of blasphemy, why did they themselves not put Him to death? Why did they invoke Roman interference in the matter? Why did they not stone Jesus to death, as Hebrew law required in the case of culprits convicted of blasphemy? Stephen was stoned to death for blasphemy.[358] What was the difference between his case and that of Jesus? Why was Jesus crucified instead of being put to death by stoning?

The stoning of Stephen as a blasphemer by the Jews has been explained as an irregular outbreak of fanatical priests, a sort of mob violence. It has also been contended that the case of Stephen was one of the rare instances in which Roman procurators permitted the Jews to execute the death sentence. In any event it was an exceptional proceeding. At the time of the crucifixion of Jesus and of the martyrdom of Stephen the Jews had lost the right of enforcing the death penalty. Judea was a subject province of the Roman empire. The Jews were permitted by the Romans to try capital cases. If an acquittal was the result, the Romans did not interfere. If a verdict of guilty was found, the Jews were compelled to lead the prisoner away to the Roman governor, who reviewed or retried the case as he saw fit. Accordingly, having condemned Him to death themselves, the Jews were compelled to lead Jesus away to the palace of Herod on the hill of Zion in which Pilate was stopping on the occasion of the Paschal Feast, to see what he had to say about the matter, whether he would reverse or affirm the sentence which they had pronounced.

The Roman trial of Jesus will be treated in the second volume of this work.

END OF VOL. I

FOOTNOTES:

[1] "Testimony of the Evangelists," pp. 7-11.

[2] "Testimony of the Evangelists," pp. 25, 26.

[3] I "Starkie on Evidence," pp. 480-545.

[4] John x. 30: "I and my Father are one."

[5] Matt. ix. 9.

[6] Col. iv. 14: "Luke, the beloved physician."

[7] Matt. xxvi. 70-72.

[8] Matt. xxvi. 46-50.

[9] Matt. xxvi. 56.

[10] Matt. xiv. 28-31.

[11] Mark x. 35-42; Matt. xx. 20-25.

[12] Matt. xi. 2, 3.

[13] Mark iii. 21.

[14] Luke iv. 28, 29.

[15] Mark xiv. 51, 52.

[16] "Intro. Vie de Jesus."

[17] Luke i. 2, 3.

[18] "Die synoptischen Evangelien," pp. 412-14.

[19] Marcus Dods, "The Bible, Its Origin and Nature," p. 184.

[20] An opposite doctrine seems to be taught in Luke xi. 11, 12; xxiv. 48, 49.

[21] "Evidences of Christianity," p. 319.

[22] Matt. xiv. 12-20; Mark vi. 34-43; Luke ix. 12-17; John vi. 5-13.

[23] Luke xxii. 64.

[24] Luke xxii. 51.

[25] Campbell's "Philosophy of Rhetoric," c. v. b. 1, Part III, p. 125.

[26] "Intro. Vie de Jesus," p. 62.

[27] D. L. Moody, "Sermon on the Resurrection of Jesus."

[28] See also I "Starkie on Evidence," pp. 496-99.

[29] "Ant.," XVIII. 3, I.

[30] See authorities cited in "The Brief."

[31] "De iis qui sero puniuntur," p. 554.

[32] P. 1080, edit. 45.

[33] P. 1247, edit. 24, Huds.

[34] P. 1327, edit. 43.

[35] "Productique omnes, virgisque cæsi, ac securi percussi," Lib. XI. c. 5.

[36] Domit. Cap. X. "Patremfamilias—canibus objecit, cum hoc *titulo*, Impie locutus, parmularius."

[37] Book LIV.

[38] "Aur. Vict. Ces.," Cap. XLI. "Eo pius, ut etiam vetus veterrimumque supplicium, patibulum, et cruribus suffringendis, primus removerit." Also see Paley's "Evidences of Christianity," pp. 266-68.

[39] Luke xxii. 44.

[40] Tissot, "Traité des Nerfs," pp. 279, 280.

[41] Joannes Schenck à Grafenberg, "Observ. Medic.," Lib. III. p. 458.

[42] Voltaire, "Œuvres complètes," vol. xviii. pp. 531, 532.

[43] De Mezeray, "Histoire de France," vol. iii. p. 306.

[44] John xix. 34.

[45] John xix. 35.

[46] John xviii. 6.

[47] "Encyc. Brit.," vol. xv. p. 550.

[48] Mendelsohn, "Criminal Jurisprudence of the Ancient Hebrews," p. 191.

[49] Mendelsohn, p. 189, n. 1.

[50] "Jewish Encyc.," vol. xii. p. 1.

[51] Emanuel Deutsch, "The Talmud," p. 26.

[52] Farrar, "Hist. of Interpretation."

[53] Emanuel Deutsch, "The Talmud," p. 47.

[54] "Encyc. Brit.," vol. xxiii. p. 35.

[55] Emanuel Deutsch, "The Talmud," p. 58.

[56] Emanuel Deutsch, "The Talmud," p. 27.

[57] Emanuel Deutsch, "The Talmud," p. 27.

[58] Deut. xvi. 18.

[59] "Ant.," XIII. 10, 6.

[60] Horace.

[61] Emanuel Deutsch, "The Talmud," p. 12.

[62] "Jewish Encyc.," vol. xii. p. 22.

[63] Emanuel Deutsch, "Talmud," p. 12.

[64] Maimon., "H. Sanh." xv. 10-13.

[65] Mendelsohn, "Criminal Jurisprudence of the Ancient Hebrews," pp. 45-50.

[66] Mendelsohn, "Criminal Jurisprudence of the Ancient Hebrews," pp. 45-50.

[67] Mendelsohn, p. 43.

[68] Mendelsohn, pp. 39, 40.

[69] Mendelsohn, pp. 39, 40.

[70] Maimonides ("Yad"), "Sanhedrin" xix.

[71] Dr. Smith's "Hist. of Greece," p. 557.

[72] "Jewish Encyc.," vol. ii. p. 257.

[73] Ex. ii. 12-16.

[74] "Sanh." 52b; Maim., "H. Sanh." xv. 4.

[75] "H. Sanh." xv. 5.

[76] Benny, "Crim. Code of the Jews," p. 90.

[77] Mendelsohn, p. 159.

[78] Chap. I. 10; X. i, 2.

[79] Matt. xxvi. 59.

[80] "Ant.," XIV. Chap. V. 4; "Wars of the Jews," I. VIII. 5; "Talmud," "Sanhedrin."

[81] "Post Bibl. Hist.," vol. i. p. 106.

[82] Matt. xvi. 21.

[83] "Commentary on the Law," vol. ccclxvi. recto.

[84] "Sanhedrin" 32.

[85] Benny.

[86] Jose b. Halafta, l. c.

[87] R. Johanan, "Sanhedrin" 19a.

[88] Benny.

[89] Benny.

[90] "Sanhedrin" 17a; "Menahoth" 65a.

[91] Sifre, Num. 92 (ed. Friedmann, p. 25b).

[92] Yalkut, "Exodus," Sec. 167.

[93] Sotah 22b.

[94] "Const. of the Sanhedrin," Chap. I.

[95] Benny, "The Criminal Code of the Jews," p. 71.

[96] Saalschütz, "Das Mosaische Recht," p. 58; Deut. xx. 5, 6.

[97] Luke ii. 46-51.

[98] Jer. xxxvii., xxxviii.

[99] "Jesus of Nazara," vol. vi. p. 45.

[100] "The Life and Words of Christ," vol. ii. p. 517.

[101] "Archæol." 87.

[102] Acts xxiv. 1, 2.

[103] I Kings iii. 16-28.

[104] Mendelsohn, "Criminal Jurisprudence of the Ancient Hebrews," pp. 102, 103.

[105] Mendelsohn, pp. 96-98.

[106] "Sanhedrin," Chap. I. fol. 19.

[107] Mendelsohn, p. 97.

[108] Mishna, "Sanhedrin," Chap. IV. 1.

[109] Mendelsohn, p. 98.

[110] "Sanhedrin," 8b, 41a, *et al.*

[111] Mendelsohn, p. 101.

[112] Schürer, "The Jewish People in the Time of Jesus Christ," 2d Div., 1.

[113] "Sanhedrin," IV. 4.

[114] "Sanhedrin," IV. 1.

[115] "Sanhedrin," 17a, p. 176.

[116] "Sanhedrin," Chap. I. 5.

[117] Benny.

[118] Benny.

[119] Benny.

[120] Mendelsohn, p. 140, n. 327.

[121] Montaigne, "Essays," III. C. XIII.

[122] "Un homme ne jugera jamais seul; cela n'appartient qu'a Dieu."

"Ne sis judex unus; non est enim unicus judex, nisi unus."—Salvador, "Institutions de Moïse," L. IV. Chap. II. p. 357.

[123] "But let not the testimony of women be admitted, on account of the levity and boldness of their sex."—Josephus, "Ant.," IV. 8, 15.

[124] "Nor let servants be admitted to give testimony, on account of the ignobility of their souls."—"Ant.," IV. 8, 15.

[125] "Ant.," IV. 8, 15.

[126] Maimonides, I. C. XI. 6, based on "Sanh." 26b.

[127] Mendelsohn, p. 118.

[128] "Talmud," B. B. 43a.

[129] Deut. xvii. 6.

[130] Num. xxxv. 30.

[131] "Hist. Nat.," Lib. VIII. Cap. XXII.

[132] L. 20, Dig. De quæstionibus, xlviii. 18.

[133] Blackstone, iv. 357.

[134] Con. U. S., Art. III, Sec. 3.

[135] "Les lois qui font périr un homme sur la déposition d'un seul témoin, sont fatales à la liberté. La raison en exige deux; parce qu'un témoin qui affirme, et un accusé qui nie, font un partage; et il faut un tiers pour le vider.

Les Grecs and les Romains exigeaient une voix de plus pour condamner. Nos lois françaises en demandent deux. Les Grecs prétendaient que leur usage avait été établi par les dieux; mais c'est le notre."—"De L'Esprit Des Lois," L. XII. C. III.

[136] Mishna, "Sanhedrin," C. V. 2.

[137] Maimonides, "Sanhedrin," Chap. XX.

[138] "Jewish Encyc.," vol. v. p. 277.

[139] "Criminal Jurisprudence of the Ancient Hebrews," p. 29.

[140] Philo Judæus, "De Decalogo," III.

[141] Prov. xi. 10; Mishna, "Sanhedrin," IV. 5.

[142] Apocrypha.

[143] Benny.

[144] Mishna, "Sanhedrin," Chap. V. 1.

[145] Benny.

[146] Deut. xix. 18-21.

[147] Apocrypha.

[148] Maimonides, Mishna, "Sanhedrin," Chap. IV. 2.

[149] Münsterberg, "On the Witness Stand," "Untrue Confessions," pp. 137-171.

[150] Rosadi.

[151] Rabbi Wise, "Martyrdom of Jesus."

[152] "Yad," Edut, xvii. 1.

[153] "Jewish Encyc.," vol. v. p. 279.

[154] Num. xxxv. 30.

[155] Mishna, "Sanhedrin" V. 3, 4.

[156] Matt. xxvi. 60.

[157] Mark xiv. 56.

[158] Lev. xxii. 28.

[159] Deut. xvii. 5; "Sanhedrin" VII. 4.

[160] Num. vi. 2-4.

[161] "Jewish Encyc.," vol. vi. p. 260.

[162] "Einleitung in der Gesetzgebung," p. 4.

[163] "Jewish Encyc.," vol. vi. p. 260; Benny, "Criminal Code of the Jews," p. 97; Saalschütz, "Das Mosaische Recht," n. 560.

[164] Mishna, treatise Makhoth.

[165] Mishna, "Capita Patrum," I. 1.

[166] Salvador, "Institutions de Moïse."

[167] Mishna, "Sanhedrin," IV. 1.

[168] "Jesus Before the Sanhedrin," p. 109.

[169] "Talmud," Jerus., Sanh., C. I. fol. 19.

[170] Mishna, "Tamid," C. III.

[171] Geikie, vol. ii. p. 517.

[172] Lyman Abbott, "Jesus of Nazareth," pp. 446, 447.

[173] "Jewish Encyc.," vol. v. pp. 279, 280.

[174] Benny.

[175] Mendelsohn, p. 144.

[176] Josephus, "Ant.," XIV. 9, 4.

[177] Schürer, 2d div., vol. i. p. 175.

[178] Schürer, 2d div., vol. i. p. 184.

[179] "Life and Times of Jesus the Messiah," vol. ii. p. 556.

[180] "Jesus of Nazara," vol. vi. p. 37.

[181] "The Talmud," p. 32.

[182] "Ant.," xv. 6, 2.

[183] "History of the Jews," vol. ii. p. 163.

[184] "Tribus, pseudo-propheta, sacerdos magnus, non nisi a septuaginta et unius judicum consessu judicantur."—"Mishna, De Synedriis," i. 5.

[185] "Among the offenses of which it took cognizance were false claims to prophetic inspiration and blasphemy."—Andrews, "The Life of Our Lord," p. 510.

[186] "Gesch. d. Judenth." vol. i. pp. 402-409.

[187] "Life and Times of Jesus the Messiah," vol. ii. p. 553.

[188] "Vie de Jesus," pp. 303, 304.

[189] "Trial of Jesus Christ," p. 81.

[190] Matt. xxvi. 60, 61.

[191] Mark xiv. 57, 58.

[192] Matt. xxvi. 64-66.

[193] Mark xiv. 56.

[194] John ii. 20.

[195] John ii. 19.

[196] John ii. 21.

[197] "The Martyrdom of Jesus," pp. 75-77.

[198] Deut. xiii. 1-5.

[199] I Kings xxi. 10.

[200] Isa. lii, 5; Ezek. xxxv. 12.

[201] Luke xxii. 65; Acts xiii. 45; xviii. 6.

[202] Revelation xiii. 1-6.

[203] "Blackstone," vol. ii. pp. 75-84.

[204] Greenidge, "Legal Procedure of Cicero's Time," pp. 427, 507, 518.

[205] Deut. iv. 15, 16; Deut. xiii.

[206] Gen. xli. 16.

[207] Num. xx. 10-12.

[208] Num. xx. 20-24.

[209] Greenleaf, "Testimony of the Evangelists," p. 555.

[210] Matt. v. 17.

[211] John xi. 41.

[212] Matt. ix. 20-22; Mark v. 25-34; Luke viii. 43-48.

[213] Matt. viii. 24-26; Mark iv. 37-39; Luke viii. 23-25.

[214] Matt. viii. 28-32; Mark v. 1-13; Luke viii. 26-33.

[215] Matt. ix. 18-26; Mark v. 22-42; Luke viii. 41-55.

[216] Luke vii. 12-15.

[217] Matt. ix. 2, 3.

[218] Luke v. 21.

[219] John v. 18.

[220] John x. 30-33.

[221] John vi. 41.

[222] John viii. 58.

[223] "Testimony of the Evangelists," p. 562.

[224] Edersheim, "Life and Times of Jesus the Messiah," vol. ii. p. 629.

[225] John xiii.-xvii.

[226] Matt. xi. 3.

[227] Luke xxiv. 39-43; John xx. 24-28.

[228] John xiii. 33.

[229] John xviii. 9.

[230] "Jesus Devant Caïphe et Pilate."

[231] Acts iv. 3.

[232] "Life and Times of Jesus the Messiah," vol. ii. p. 494.

[233] See Cooley's "Blackstone," vol. ii. p. 330, n. 6; also Greenleaf, "On Evidence," vol. i. pp. 531-35 (10th edition).

[234] "Vie de Jesus," p. 303.

[235] John xviii. 13.

[236] Matt. xxvi. 57.

[237] Mark xiv. 53.

[238] Luke xxii. 54.

[239] John xviii. 19.

[240] Luke iii. 2; Acts iv. 6.

[241] "Life and Times of Jesus the Messiah," vol. i. p. 264.

[242] "The Life of Our Lord," p. 142.

[243] Luke iii. 2.

[244] Plummer, St. Luke, in "International Critical Commentary," pp. 84, 515.

[245] Josephus, "Ant.," XVIII. chap. ii. 2.

[246] John xviii. 19-23.

[247] Mark xiv. 58-61.

[248] Matt. xxvi. 60-63.

[249] Matt. xxvi. 63.

[250] Mark xiv. 59.

[251] Acts vi. 14.

[252] "Jewish Encyc.," vol. i. p. 163.

[253] Fiske, "Manual of Classical Literature," iii. Sec. 108; Smith, "Dictionary of Greek and Roman Antiquities," 89a.

[254] See discussion of Point I.

[255] Luke xxii. 66.

[256] Luke xxii. 2.

[257] Mark xiv. 2.

[258] Mark xiv. i; Matt. xxvi. 4 (Consilium fecerunt ut Jesum dolo tenerent et occiderent).

[259] Maimonides, "Sanhedrin" II.

[260] John xviii. 28; Luke xxii. 1; Mark xiv. 1; Matt. xxvi. 2.

[261] Mishna, "Capita Patrum," I, 1.

[262] Mishna, "Treatise Makhoth."

[263] See Part II, Chap. V.

[264] Edmund Stapfer, "Life of Jesus."

[265] Matt. xxvi. 57-66.

[266] Mark xiv. 55-64.

[267] Matt. xxvii. 1.

[268] Mark xv. 1.

[269] Luke xxii. 66-71.

[270] "Martyrdom of Jesus," p. 74.

[271] "Criminal Jurisprudence of the Ancient Hebrews," p. 133, n. 311.

[272] See Part II, Chap. IV.

[273] Mark xiv. 56-65.

[274] Mark xiv. 62.

[275] Matt. xii. 14-16; Mark iii. 7; ix. 29, 30.

[276] Luke xiii. 31, 32.

[277] Matt. xxii. 15.

[278] John iv. 26.

[279] Mark i. 34.

[280] John x. 24.

[281] Matt. xvi. 20.

[282] Blackstone.

[283] Mendelsohn, p. 143.

[284] Mark xiv. 63, 64.

[285] "Martyrdom of Jesus," p. 74.

[286] "The Trial of Jesus," p. 200.

[287] Matt. xxvi. 59; Mark xiv. 55.

[288] Matt. xxvii. 1.

[289] Mark xv. 1.

[290] John iii. 1; vii. 50.

[291] Luke xxiii. 51.

[292] John vii. 51.

[293] John vii. 50; xix. 39.

[294] Luke xxiii. 51.

[295] Mendelsohn, p. 98.

[296] Deut. xvii. 7, 8.

[297] "It is important to notice that every time the necessities of the case required the Sanhedrin returned to the Hall Gazith, or of Hewn Stones, as in the case of Jesus and others."—"Thosephthoth, or Additions to the Talmud," Bab., "Sanhedrin," C. IV. fol. 37, recto.

[298] Edersheim, "Life and Times of Jesus the Messiah," vol. ii. p. 556, n. 1.

[299] John xviii. 28.

[300] MM. Lémann, "Jesus Before the Sanhedrin," p. 140.

[301] Mark xiv. 63, 64.

[302] Edersheim, "Life and Times of Jesus the Messiah," vol. ii. p. 561.

[303] Rabbi Wise, "Martyrdom of Jesus," p. 74.

[304] Benny, "Criminal Code of the Jews," p. 81.

[305] Matt. xxvi. 65.

[306] See Part II, Qualifications of Judges.

[307] "Talmud, Pesachim, or the Passover," fol. 57, verso; see also "Jesus Before the Sanhedrin," pp. 54, 55.

[308] Benny, "Criminal Code of the Jews," pp. 28-41.

[309] Matt. xxi. 31.

[310] Matt. xxiii. 14, 15.

[311] "Life and Times of Jesus the Messiah," vol. i. pp. 93, 94.

[312] Matt. xxiii. 27, 29-33.

[313] "Vie de Jesus," p. 267.

[314] John xi. 49, 50.

[315] John xi. 53.

[316] Luke xxii. 1-3.

[317] Matt. xxvi. 3-5.

[318] Benny, "Criminal Code of the Jews," p. 56.

[319] Geikie, "The Life and Words of Christ," vol. ii. p. 517.

[320] Deut. xix. 18-21.

[321] Mark xiv. 55.

[322] Mishna, Treatise "Makhoth."

[323]

"Afresh the mighty line of years unroll'd,The Virgin now, now Saturn's sway returns;Now the blest globe a heaven-sprung Child adorns,Whose genial power shall whelm earth's iron race,And plant once more the golden in its place."

—Virgil, Eclogue IV.

[324] Gen. xlix. 8-10.

[325] "Sanhedrin," fol. 97, verso.

[326] "Martyrdom of Jesus," p. 76.

[327] John xi. 48-50.

[328] I Sam. xv. 29.

[329] Hosea xi. 9.

[330] Mark vii. 9-13.

[331] "Jewish Encyc.," vol. i. p. 583.

[332] Hodge, "Systematic Theology," vol. i. p. 485.

[333] Steenstra, "The Being of God as Unity and Trinity," pp. 192, 193.

[334] John ii. 15.

[335] John vi. 30.

[336] John x. 24, 25.

[337] Matt. xi. 4, 5.

[338] I Kings xvii. 17-22.

[339] John xi. 41.

[340] Matt. ix. 18-26; Mark v. 22-42; Luke viii. 41-55.

[341] Luke vii. 12-15.

[342] John iii. 2.

[343] See Friedlieb, Archæol., 87; Dupin, 75; Keim, vol. iii. 327.

[344] Bab. Sanh. f. 63, 1: "Cum synedrium quemquam moti adjudicavit, ne quidquam degustent illi isto die."

[345] Andrews, "The Life of Our Lord," p. 522.

[346] "The Life of Our Lord," pp. 523, 524.

[347] Luke xxii. 66-71.

[348] See Part II, Chap. V.; also Benny, "Crim. Code of the Jews," pp. 81-83.

[349] Keim, "Jesus of Nazara," vol. vi. pp. 63, 64.

[350] John xviii. 28.

[351] "Thou, Reuben, art guilty! Thou, Simon, art acquitted, art not guilty!" were stereotyped forms of verdicts under Hebrew criminal procedure. Sanh. in Friedl., p. 89.

[352] Keim, "Jesus of Nazara," vol. vi. p. 74.

[353] John iii. 1; vii. 50.

[354] Luke xxiii. 50, 51.

[355] Matt. xxvi. 59; Mark xiv. 55; Matt. xxvii. 1; Mark xv. 1.

[356] Mark xiv. 63, 64; Luke xxii. 70, 71.

[357] Keim, "Jesus of Nazara," vol. vi. p. 74, n. 2.

[358] Acts vi. 11; vii. 59.